CRICKET AND ENGLAND THROUGH FIVE MATCHES

CLASS, WAR, RACE & EMPIRE 1900-1939

Ross English

The material in this book originally appeared as a podcast of the same name and can be found at cricketstuff.blog or via iTunes

To Leonard English

Cricket and England Through Five Matches: Class, War, Race & Empire 1900-1939

Copyright © 2018

by Ross English.

All Rights Reserved.

ISBN: 9781981088270

Index

Preface   i

1. Class
Gentlemen v. Players, Lord's 1900   1

2. War
Middlesex v. Kent, Lord's 1914   34

3. Recovery
England v. South Africa, Edgbaston 1924 79

4. Race & Empire
West Indies v. MCC, Georgetown, Guiana 1930 127

5. War, once more
Sussex v. Yorkshire, Hove 1939   193

Bibliography   234

Index   240

PREFACE

This started as an idea, became a podcast and, now, this book.

The idea came from a love of old cricket scorecards. The way the rows of names and scores and modes of dismissal can come alive; painting a picture of triumph and disaster, of last-ball finishes or one-sided thrashings. Yet, stripped of context, they can only take us so far. We can read:

Bradman b. Hollies 0
or
Gatting b. Warne 4

and not see, on the page alone, the end and beginning of cricketing eras.

Even with some knowledge of the sporting stories behind the figures, much can be lost without a painting of the wider social, historical and political context. The West Indies' or India's first Test victories over England, the first match back for South Africa in 1991, or the last before an outbreak of war all gain importance for reasons that stretch far beyond cricket.

That is where this project started. To visit some matches from years gone by and place them in their context. What became clear was that the cricketing stories did not simply benefit from a little historical background, the matches themselves informed the history. The way that cricket was influenced by, reflected and resisted the changes taking place in early twentieth century England added colour to the picture.

This became a series of podcasts hosted on my occasional blog cricketstuff.blog (and available via iTunes). The material in this book is

– with some minor editing – the same as that contained within those podcasts. Treat them as a free audio book, if you will.

It must be pointed out that this is a book about cricket and *England* and, as such, is Anglo-centric. There is a wider story to be told – and we make some headway in chapter 4 – but that is for another project.

I must thank the many members of the Association of Cricket Statisticians and Historians for their helpful comments along the way. Thanks to Stephen Chalke and David Jeater for their assistance with chapter 5. Special appreciation must go to the staff at the Lord's library and at the British Library's newsroom for their help and patience. Finally, to my family who indulge such hair-brained schemes such as these. Any errors contained within are, of course, my own.

Ross English
April 2018

1. CLASS

Gentlemen versus Players
Lord's, 16-18 July 1900

As the nineteenth century gave way to the twentieth, Britain stood on the cusp of great change. Literally and figuratively, Victorian Britain was coming to an end. In July of 1900, Queen Victoria had entered what would be the last six months of her 63-year reign. Her British Empire would continue to expand over the next two decades but, by the time it began its inevitable decline, events at home would have moved on a pace: the advent of universal male suffrage, votes for many (though not yet all) women, the rise of the mass trade union movement, the last Liberal Government and the first of the Labour Party, the assertion of the power of the people's House of Commons over the aristocratic House of Lords. It was as if the very foundations of the British class system were under attack.

The whole concept of the separation of society into classes and the question of how to maintain those divisions was of great salience during the Victorian era. It had become a highly significant political and social issue because, for many, the class system seemed under threat. From the end of the eighteenth century, social tides appeared to be shifting. The French Revolution served as a warning signal to the British elite, a portent of the danger that their own lower and middle-classes might pose to the existing hierarchy. This perceived menace looked to be very real during the early nineteenth century, with agitation from the lower-classes highlighted by incidents including the 'Peterloo' massacre of 1819 and the rise of reforming movements such as the Anti-Corn Law League and The Chartists. Whether this threat was real was not the point; many in the political and social elite thought it was and believed that the British class system needed to be actively defended both at home and in the colonies.

The resulting defence of hierarchy took two main forms. The first was political reform (including the Great Reform Acts of 1832, 1867 and 1884) designed to placate the lower-classes by bringing their grievances within the system. The second was a strengthening of the formal and informal norms of class. During the mid to late-nineteenth century, the language of class and hierarchy became ubiquitous and many institutions, from the armed forces to education, were strictly organised on class lines. Increasingly the Victorian people viewed society in terms of class structures and those at the top felt a great duty to protect them.

Nowhere were these norms exemplified better than in cricket. It is true that the cricket field was of note during the nineteenth century in providing a sporting arena where labourer could compete with Lord, miner with medic, blacksmith with businessman. Any suggestion, however, that the mixing of the classes on the field of play blurred the boundaries of status was far from the mark. Because of, rather than despite, the cross-class interaction on the field, care was taken that norms of social stratification were preserved once stumps had been drawn. In first-class cricket, especially, the class boundaries were formally and clearly enforced, no more so than in the classification of cricketers as either amateur or professional or, in cricketing parlance, as Gentlemen and Players.

There was an irony in that while cricket and society sort to divide the population into distinct classes – Lords and Commoners, Officers and Enlisted Men, Gentlemen and Players – the reality of class was far more complicated. Where did the class boundaries lie? It was not always wealth; as the nineteenth century drew to a close, class and riches had often gone their separate ways with many established families struggling to maintain their way of life while middle-class businesses flourished. Was it education? What impact did one's parents' background have when the children of factory owners could rub shoulders with trainee aristocrats in Britain's public schools? There was a general perception of a three-tier system with working, middle and upper-classes, however the reality was that social standing varied widely depending on context. It was a complex social structure attempting to appear simple. Ultimately, a person's place in this class system rested on perception. "The only sure way of knowing you were a Gentleman", argued David Cannadine, "was to be treated as such."

In that observation lay the essence of the amateur-professional divide in cricket. Amateurism was not the preserve of the independently wealthy or landed gentry. Many amateurs needed to earn their keep in other jobs. The distinction was more one of class and the perceptions of class.

At a basic level, the difference between the two cricketing classes was one of payment: professionals were paid to play the game whereas the amateurs were not. Those many amateurs who needed to work to sustain themselves financially were, of course, limited to those in professions that would allow them to regularly turn out for their county or other side. For a manual labourer this would not be an option and so professionalism was the only route for the talented working-class cricketer. However, the perception of what differentiated an amateur and a professional ran much deeper than simply the ability of a man to pay his own way. The Gentlemen were viewed as the embodiment of the spirit of the game, playing for the love of the sport rather than for recompense. In some quarters, there was hostility towards the idea of professionalism in sport; cricket was leisure, not labour, to be played for its own noble ends and not to earn a living. The suspicion was that professionals were mercenaries without the unpaid loyalty to their side that the amateurs possessed (and as such rules were introduced in 1873 to restrict the movement of players between counties).

As befitted their higher status, the amateurs enjoyed privileges denied their professional colleagues; they changed in better rooms, drank in different bars, ate superior food at lunch and travelled in more comfortable style. The scorecard also served as a reminder of the class distinction: amateurs were listed with title and initials preceding their surnames; professionals were afforded no title, often their initials followed their surname and, occasionally, were referred to by last name alone. Of course, only an amateur was normally allowed to captain a county or international team.

Although a good county professional could earn more than twice what he would as a labourer, a cricket career was no route to riches and, everywhere one looked, the professional was reminded of his secondary status. Even on the field of play the class distinction was expected to be upheld; the amateurs were viewed as the artists of the game whereas the professionals were the workmen and were often expected to fit that mould (on one occasion the talented Sussex professional Joe Vine hit three flowing boundaries in an over. According to Vine, his captain, the amateur C B Fry, marched down the wicket to sharply remind him that Vine's job was to stay there and leave that sort of batting to him).

The relationship between the cricketing classes and the extent to which formalities were to be observed also could fluctuate – within acceptable boundaries, of course – depending on context. The Middlesex professional Harry Lee told of a time he was hauled in front of Lord Harris, treasurer of the MCC and a stickler for the laws of the game, to answer for a perceived indiscretion in a recent match against Kent. Harry answered the charge in a diplomatic manner, something which seemed just to irk Harris further. Lee was saved by the intervention of the Middlesex President Alexander Webbe who said it was a very good answer and exclaimed, "I see exactly what you mean, Harry." In Lee's telling of the story:

> "Lord Harris's eyebrows rose as dangerously as a
> short bumper on a fast wicket.
> "Harry?" he said "*Harry?*"

"Why, yes," said Mr Webbe. "Harry is one of *our* men."

"Very well", said Lord Harris, who seemed to feel that discipline had been strained to its limits. "Very well, *Lee*. That will do."

According to Lee, even Harris's "on-parade" attitude to professionals would soften somewhat when it concerned cricketers from his own county of Kent.

As with much in the class system by this time, appearances mattered more than reality. It was not uncommon for amateurs to make a living from the game without facing the ignominy of turning professional. For the most talented amateurs, salaried administrative posts could be conjured within their cricket club, expenses (which only they were permitted to claim) could be inflated, products could be endorsed and advertised, all which allowed them to secure an income from the game while not, officially, being paid to play. Such 'shamateurism', as it became known, was an open secret and accusations of professionalism were levelled at some of the game's biggest amateur names.

Lord's, Monday 16 July 1900
Day one

Buried on page 13 of that morning *Times* was a notice alerting readers to the commencement of the latest instalment of the clearest exhibition, indeed celebration, of the cricketing class system: the prestigious, Gentlemen versus Players contest. A series of fixtures that had, by the late nineteenth century, established itself, alongside the North versus South match, as one of the most important of the season. Especially so in years, such as 1900, where a lack of a touring international team meant there were no Test matches for the paying public to attend.

Three matches were scheduled for 1900. The first had been held at The Oval in early July and had seen the Players run out winners by 37 runs; the final match was to be played at Scarborough at the end of August (it would result in a comfortable innings victory for the professionals). The second fixture, however, described by *Wisden* as "certainly the most remarkable game of the whole season", is of the greatest interest. Held at Lord's, the home of cricket, over three sweltering days (the temperature gauge in London would peak at 92° Fahrenheit), it produced a notable finish, exhibited the skills of some of the finest players of their generation and was significant for the absence of cricket's greatest figure.

* *

William Gilbert Grace, cricket's first superstar, dominated the Victorian game in a way that (perhaps Bradman aside) is hard to find comparison in the modern world. He personified the sport, and nothing was more closely associated with him as the Gentlemen versus Players fixture.

The contest between the leading amateurs and professionals of the day originated in 1806 but did not become an annual fixture until 1819. In its early days the match struggled for credibility. Aware that they were outclassed by the fitter and generally more skilful professionals, the Gentlemen sometimes took extraordinary measures to avoid defeat. Early Gentlemen teams would feature 'given men' - two of the best players from the professional ranks co-opted to strengthen the amateur side; several matches saw the size of the Gentlemen's ranks inflated as they were allowed to field extra men (once, in 1868, as many as 20); in 1821 the amateur side took the unusual step of simply giving up on the second day of play rather than plough on to certain defeat; and, most bizarrely, in 1832, the Gentlemen reduced the size of their wicket while, in 1837, they required the Players to increase their's by defending four stumps.

Results had swung in favour of both teams during the 1820s but, in the next decade, despite the machinations of the amateurs, the professionals gained full control. Between 1830 and 1841 the Gentlemen managed only two drawn matches and a one victory. The emergence of some strong amateur players (Alfred Mynn and Nicholas Felix, particularly) saw parity return for the 1840s but in the next decade the professionals re-established their dominance and took 22 of the 24 games played between 1850 and 1864.

W G Grace's selection for the Gentlemen in 1865 was crucial in turning the fortunes their way. While his first experience in their ranks was a heavy 118 run defeat at The Oval, the next, at Lord's, saw an eight-wicket victory for the amateur side (largely thanks to the wicket-taking abilities of his brother E M Grace). While no one-man team, the importance of W G to the resurgence of the Gentlemen cannot be overstated. Over the following (incredible) 41 years he played in the fixture 85 times, captaining the Gentlemen on at least 41 occasions,[1] scored 6,008 runs at an average of 42.6, including 15 centuries, two double centuries, and took 271 wickets. A truly remarkable run that included some equally remarkable performances.

* *

On the morning of July 16th, however, Grace was conspicuous by his absence. While he had missed the occasional match before and would participate in the fixture sporadically over the following six years, his omission marked the second step into the twilight of his long and distinguished career (the first, his retirement from Test cricket the year

---

[1] A few of the scorecards which include Grace do not indicate who captained the Gentlemen.

before). It was the first time in thirty-five years than he had not been selected for the Gentlemen when available, he had not missed the Lord's fixture in that time and 'The Champion' would never play for the amateurs at the home of cricket again. If Britain was witnessing the final days of one of its greatest monarchs, the game of cricket was doing the same.

The crowd that gathered at Lord's on that morning appeared slightly down on previous years, but an estimated 10,000 people still crammed into the newly constructed Mound Stand and surrounds (the Pavilion was, of course, reserved for members only). Expectations of a Players' win were high; the dominance of the Gentlemen in the late 1860s and throughout the 1870s a distant memory. While both sides had tasted victory in the years since, the Players had been the more successful team and, in July of 1900, were widely considered to have the stronger side. Indeed, the depth of talent within the professional ranks was such that 22 different men represented the Players that summer with no noticeable change in the strength of the team.

The Gentlemen, while fielding some highly able cricketers, were missing some obvious names. Along with the absent Grace, the team-sheet was lacking the talents of men such as K S Ranjitsinhji and Archie MacLaren, two outstanding batsmen. However, despite these omissions, and the expectation that the Players would ultimately prevail, hopes of an entertaining contest were raised by the prospect of some highly-rated cricketers in the amateur ranks, particularly, C B Fry and, debutant, 'Tip' Foster.

As the crowd continued to file in, the two captains met for the toss; the Players, represented by the popular "Guv'nor" Bobby Abel, the Gentlemen by the Australian-born Sammy Woods. Woods won the toss and elected to bat. Both Abel and Woods were talented and well-liked cricketers with plenty of first-class experience under their belts. Their careers – Abel for Surrey and England, Woods for Somerset, Australia and England – crossed on many occasions but their different experiences in the world of cricket reflected the gulf between the sporting lives of amateur and professional.

* *

In 1881, at the age of 23, Rotherhithe-born Robert 'Bobby' Abel left his job as a warehouseman to make his first-class debut for Surrey, having lied about his age to be accepted as a young Surrey Colt earlier that year. His batting career got off to a slow start, with single digit averages in his first two seasons with the County, but his timing was fortuitous as, at the end of Bobby's second season, Surrey began to rethink its approach to developing professionals. As a result, the county expanded its fixture list to give the professionals more chance to gain playing experience, rather than expecting them to regularly drop in and out of sides to accommodate the whims of their amateur colleagues.

Bobby appeared to benefit from the increased match time and soon established himself as a firm crowd favourite at The Oval. Being the local lad helped his popularity and his small stature (measuring 5' 5") lent him an air of a David fearlessly battling the bowling Golliaths of the county circuit. An opening batsman who played skilfully to the off and leg-side (albeit with a slightly crossed bat), he passed 1,000 runs for a season for the first time in 1886 and again in 1888, 1889, 1891 and 1892. It was relatively late in his career that Abel had his greatest success; passing 2,000 runs in every season from 1895 to 1902. It was no surprise that he had been invited to captain the Players in 1900 as, although 42 years old, he was only just reaching the peak of his powers. In that 1900 season he would set a new English record by hitting 12 first-class centuries. The following year Abel would pass 3,000 runs. C B Fry was impressed enough by the Surrey opener to include him in his 1899 text *Giants of the Game*, hailing an Abel who "gathers runs like blackberries everywhere he goes."

Abel made his England debut in 1888 at Lord's in a match that most of England would rather forget. Their opponents, Australia, won the toss and made the best of a bad pitch by posting 116 in their first innings. Neither side would come close to that total again and England, having collapsed to 53 all out in their first, failed to chase a modest target in their second, succumbing with the score on 62. For Abel, scores of three and eight made his debut an unhappy one, though he would fare much better in the next Test. Someone leaving with much happier memories of that match was another debutant, wearing Australian colours for the first time, S M J Woods.

Sammy Woods was a genial man from New South Wales, as large as Abel was small but just as popular. W G Grace described him as "a giant in size, in strength, and in pluck." He was also an all-round sportsman, excelling at a range of activities including football, hockey, boxing, golf and, particularly, rugby for which he was capped by England thirteen times (five as captain). Cricket, though, was his main pursuit and he found a welcome home at Somerset, whom he would captain with distinction for thirteen seasons from 1894. Initially a fearsome fast bowler (he was named by *Wisden* as one of their 'Six Great Bowlers of the Year' in 1889) he earned the respect of his team by putting in the hard overs that amateur captains would often leave to the professionals. By the time of the Lord's match of 1900, however, his deliveries had lost much of their speed and potency. Such was his ability though, as his bowling declined (and he was still capable enough in that regard), his batsmanship improved and, when he was appointed (for the first time) captain of The Gentlemen for this fixture, he was considered a genuine all-rounder.

Sammy Woods was present at Bobby Abel's greatest moment as a cricketer. In 1899, while facing a Somerset team led by Woods at The Oval, Abel batted for eight and a half hours, carrying his bat for an individual score of 357. At the time it was the second highest score ever made in first-class cricket (it remains the sixth highest made in England

and the fifth highest by an Englishman) and, as a reward, The Oval crowd collected £33 for their hero; the Surrey board were less generous, awarding 'talent money' of £5.

There, in how each was paid, lay the heart of the difference between the experience of these two rival captains (and, later, friends); for both made their living from cricket but in very different ways. Bobby, as a professional, would have been paid per match (with a little extra for a win), earn a small summer wage as a 'ground bowler' (practice fodder for the amateur batsmen), occasional 'talent money', collections at the ground and, for the longer serving, a benefit game. For the professional, an injury or run of poor form could be a financial disaster and, for most, all payment ceased at the end of the cricket season (although Abel was one of a fortunate few that Surrey, from 1892, offered winter employment to, which allowed him to stop returning to the warehouse at the end of each season). We do not know exactly how much money Abel collected from cricket a year, but it is estimated that by the end of the nineteenth century a good county pro with international recognition could earn over £200.

Woods also earned that amount a year from cricket, except as an amateur. No warehouseman he, Woods had come to England at the age of 16 to be educated at Brighton College and, then, Cambridge. Needing work to sustain him, Woods attempted a career in banking but possessed neither the aptitude nor enthusiasm for it. Once installed as Somerset's captain, there was some fear at the county that financial considerations would mean a return to Australia for their new leader. The solution was found in the offer of the position of joint-secretary with an annual salary of £200.

Such was the sham of amateurism in some cases, for Woods was no full or even part-time administrator. He was, in effect, being paid so he could play cricket. This, though, was not to mean that the Somerset captain and Abel were on a financial par. While their income may have been similar, Abel was expected to pay for all travel and accommodation out of his own pocket (which could consume over half of his income) whereas Woods, as an amateur, could claim those on expenses. One was also on a salary, which meant that any periods of injury were covered; the other was paid on a per-match basis and Abel was fortunate when the Surrey board offered him half-pay for any occasional period of absence. Of course, amateurism also brought with it many other perks and comforts.

* *

So, it was the well-treated amateurs who were to open at Lord's and, accordingly, the Gentlemen's openers, C B Fry and A O Jones strode to the wicket, the latter sporting one of the finest moustaches in the game.

Nottinghamshire's Arthur Jones made his England debut in the previous summer and had acquitted himself well with three wickets and respectable lower-order batting. There was to be no heroics on this morning, however, as a disappointing game for Jones began with him edging the bowling of Albert Trott; sharply taken in the slip, for nine.

The score stood at 26-1 as Charles Burgess Fry awaited his next partner.

* *

If Grace was English cricket's first superstar, then C B Fry possesses a good case to be counted as its second. A dashing all-round athlete – he briefly held the world long jump record while at Oxford and played at full-back for Southampton Football Club in an FA Cup final – Fry captured the public imagination with attacking batsmanship and an outstanding run of scoring in the county game.

There was certain poignancy in that it was Fry who took centre stage as Grace was preparing to depart, given that, according to Fry (though, Grace's biographer Richard Tomlinson has doubts as to the veracity of the story), he had unwittingly been the man who called time on W G's Test career. Grace had liked what he had seen of C B and ensured his appointment to the newly established England selection committee after only his first home Test match. In Fry's version of events, he arrived at the meeting to choose the side for that summer's second international only to find the rest of the panel already in place. Before the new selector could sit down, Grace - his captain in the previous game - demanded he answer a question with a straight yes or no: should Archie MacLaren play in the next match? MacLaren was a talented batsman who would improve most sides and so Fry had no hesitation in answering in the affirmative. It was only after he sat down that C B realised he had cast the deciding vote to include MacLaren at the expense of Grace himself, bringing the curtain down on The Doctor's international career. Grace took the decision well and certainly bore Fry no ill will.

The greatest feats of Fry's career (including six centuries in successive first-class innings in 1901 and seven centuries in successive innings a decade later) were soon to come but, by 1900, he had already established himself as one of England's foremost batting talents. In the 1898 first-class season he scored in excess of 1,700 runs, reached over 2,300 runs the following year and was well on the way to nearly equalling that total in 1900 (he would score over 3,000 in 1901). Indeed, the day after the Gentlemen's match finished at Lord's, Fry would travel to Hove to play for Sussex against Surrey, score 125 in the first innings and 229 in the second (the first of his sixteen first-class double hundreds).

* *

On this morning however, Fry struggled to find his familiar fluency with the bat. *The Times'* correspondent reported that he played with "unusual caution" and that his cricket was not up to his usual "standard of excellence." Despite this, Fry posted the Gentlemen's second highest score of the innings - a respectable 63 - and, with the incoming batsman Charlie Townsend, constructed the highest partnership of the day; putting on 73 runs for the second wicket. With the score on 99, Townsend was run out for 30 (reports do not tell us if either Fry or Townsend were at fault) and R E Foster joined Fry at the crease.

* *

Reginald Erskine Foster, better known as 'Tip', was another supreme all-round athlete. He is the only man to have captained England at both cricket and football but was destined to remain one of English cricket's greatest untapped talents. Foster had a solid defence and could play all around the wicket but was particularly known for his brilliant off-side play, possessing a flowing cover-drive and precise late-cut.

He was also an excellent slip fieldsman; "one of the finest short slips in the country" according to Digby Jephson, a team-mate of Foster's in the Gentlemen XI. Tip was making his first appearance in this prestigious fixture and was doing so as the captain of Oxford University. He had made his first-class debut with Oxford in 1897 but it was not until two years later that he truly flowered as a cricketer and showed the sort of form that earned him his place in the Gentlemen's side. In 1899 he scored hundreds in both innings playing for Worcestershire in their inaugural first-class season (uniquely, his brother Wilfrid matched the feat in the same game) and, just a couple of weeks before his appearance for the Gentlemen at Lord's, had set a record for the highest score in the Oxford-Cambridge Varsity match, notching 171.

For his performances in 1900 he was named one of *Wisden*'s Five Cricketers of the Season, scoring close to 2000 runs (which side of that mark depends on whose statistics you choose) at an average of over 50. "We can recall no instance of an Oxford or Cambridge batsman making such an extraordinary advance in his last year at the University" noted the cricketing tome, "many fine batmen have done their best before leaving the Universities, but Mr Foster – assuming he can spare time to keep up the game – is very likely only at the beginning of his real career."

Foster's most extraordinary feat came in December of 1903. Representing England against the Australians in Sydney, he scored an unprecedented 287 runs. It was his first innings for his country and set a number of long standing records: his score was the highest ever in a Test match (a record that stood until 1930), the highest score by an Englishman against Australia (only surpassed by Len Hutton's 364 in 1938), the highest score by any player in a Test match at the SCG (eventually overtaken by Michael Clarke in 2012), the highest by a non-Australian in Australia (beaten by Ross Taylor for New Zealand in 2015) and it remains the highest score by a debutant in Test matches.

Sadly, for the game of cricket, the caveat that *Wisden* had earlier noted regarding the progression of Foster's career was to be all too real and opportunities to view his skills were severely limited. Foster was a businessman and, whether by necessity or desire, it was that part of his life that took precedence and greatly curtailed the time he could devote to sport. Despite his abundant talent, he only made eight appearances for England and, with 1901 his only full county season, could only register 139 first-class appearances in an all too truncated career. His light shone brightly yet briefly, and Tip Foster died, in London, age 36, due to complications from diabetes.

* *

On this hot July morning, however, his cricketing prowess was on full display and, after settling in during an opening half-hour in which he remained scoreless, Foster set about the Players' attack with gusto. He took a liking to the off-breaks of Walter Mead, using exceptional wrist speed to work him to the leg-side boundary. C B Fry would later observe that Foster was quicker with his bat than any other cricketer except his prolific Sussex colleague Ranjitsinhji, which was high praise indeed.

While Foster made light of the opposition attack, his team-mates failed to do the same. After Fry was bowled by Wilfred Rhodes with score on 127, there came somewhat of a procession of departing batsmen. Jack Mason was bowled for two, Surrey's Digby Jephson trapped in front for nine and "The Croucher" Gilbert Jessop fell for 18, caught by wicket-keeper Dick Lilley running in front of the wicket. Soon after Foster completed his half-century. With captain Woods come and gone, and only three men yet to bat, it began to look as though Foster would be denied a deserved hundred on debut. His hopes of a ton were raised when the Yorkshire all-rounder Ernest Smith joined him to put on 57 for the eighth wicket in 40 minutes. However, when Smith departed, undone by an excellent catch by Rhodes at mid-off, and the Essex quick Charles Kortright played-on shortly after, Foster was still short of three figures. Tip clearly had little faith in the staying power of the Gentlemen's number eleven, wicket-keeper Henry Martyn, and began to hit out. He reached his hundred in the nick of time as, two runs later, Martyn fell to the left arm bowling of John Gunn, finishing the innings.

The Gentlemen had made 297; 102 of which had come from the bat of Foster. The Players had bowled and fielded well, with only the brilliance of Foster and the tenacity of Fry posing them a problem. The total was respectable but, as *The Manchester Guardian* noted, "considering the number of dangerous run-getters in their team, it cannot be said that they did anything out of the common." Albert Trott had picked up two wickets for 43 runs ("but the figures give no idea of the excellence of his work"), John Gunn three for 61, but it was Wilfred Rhodes who had done most of the damage with a skilful display of bowling, posting a return of four for 93, including the valuable wicket of Fry.

* *

Yorkshire's Wilfred Rhodes remains one of English cricket's greatest all-rounders and, until the arrival of the incomparable Garfield Sobers, possibly the best to play the game anywhere. Raw statistics never do the great cricketers justice but, in the case of Rhodes, they are worth reciting: during a first-class career spanning 32 years he made 1,110 appearances (still a record), scored 39,969 runs with a high score of 267, took 4,204 wickets (another record that remains unbeaten) including 287 five-fers and 68 ten wicket-match hauls. He achieved the first-class double of 1,000 runs and 100 wickets in 16 seasons. In Tests he represented England 58 times taking 127 wickets and scoring 2,325 runs. By bowing out from the international arena at the age of 52 (see chapter 4), he remains the oldest person to have played Test cricket and is the only person who bowled at both titans of the game, W G Grace and Don Bradman.

Rhodes began his career as a bowler and his selection for the Players in the July of 1900 was clearly as just that: batting at number ten in both innings. And what a bowler he was. Rhythmic, unerringly accurate, thoughtful left arm spin; it was said that once Rhodes had got you out in a match he would inevitably do so twice, as he would have worked out how. The great cricket writer Neville Cardus, said of Rhodes: "flight was his secret, flight and the curving line....Every ball a decoy, a spy sent out to get the lie of the land; some balls simple, some complex, some easy, some difficult; and one of them – ah which? – the master ball." Bradman, who faced Rhodes late in the Yorkshireman's career, recalled "the economy of his action. The great accuracy and cunning of his bowling." Middlesex batsman Patsy Hendren was more direct. Rhodes, he said, was "as full of tricks as a whole zoo of monkeys." In the second Ashes Test of the 1903/4 tour, as Rhodes was on his way to taking 15 wickets, the great Australian batsman, Victor Trumper, was heard to remark, "please Wilfred, give me a minute's rest." His batting developed later but, when it did, he became a true all-rounder, moving up the order to open the batting for England. In the Melbourne Test of 1912, he and his opening partner, Jack Hobbs, put on a record stand of 323, setting up an innings victory for the English. Rhodes even managed to outscore his illustrious partner, posting 179 to Hobbs' 178.

It is a pity, that for all of Rhodes' undoubted brilliance, he was, in his time, respected and admired, rather than celebrated in the way that Grace or Fry were. There is undoubtedly a class element to this - amateurs such as they were seen as the dashing care-free young men of the game whereas the professionals were there to labour. In line with this mind-set, batting exploits were celebrated (and occasionally financially rewarded) much more than any feat performed by the bowlers, who were often treated as the team's workmen. Rhodes was also not the most outgoing character, was publicly viewed as rather dour and unsmiling, and this perception also contributed to him not receiving the sort of widespread affection afforded some of his peers.

* *

His performance at Lord's, though, was certainly appreciated and had helped make batting difficult for anyone other than Foster. Indeed, the Players could have been justified in feeling that, given their quality in the field, they had allowed the Gentlemen a few too many runs. The professionals would need to bat well to reach parity.

Things stared smoothly for the Players, with their diminutive captain Abel and the veteran Albert Ward (a Yorkshireman who plied his trade for Lancashire) putting on a partnership of 48 runs before Ward edged one to the slips off the bowling of Jack Mason. Only thirteen more runs were added before the Players found themselves two wickets down when Tom Hayward failed to keep out one of Gilbert Jessop's quick deliveries and departed for eight. Jessop had found his rhythm and aggression and threatened to have more Players back in the pavilion before the close of play. Some dogged resistance by Abel and his new partner, the similarly height-restricted Willie Quaife, saw them through the remaining overs. When the umpires finally called time, the Players had reached 66-2, leaving the game evenly balanced.

Tuesday 17 July 1900
Day two

If the Players' plan was to bat deep into the day before releasing Rhodes, Trott and Gunn at the opposition batsmen, they quickly found that the Gentlemen's own bowling trio of Mason, Jessop and Kortright had other ideas. The resuming batsmen barely had time to adjust to the morning heat before they were back in the changing room; Abel added a solitary run to his overnight score before being accounted for by a yorker from the speedy Jessop and Quaife fared little better in departing to the same bowler for nine. Matters were not about to improve for the professionals and Abel's 30 was to be their highest score. Jack Brown, Herbert Carpenter and Dick Lilley all reached double figures (though not much more) and the rest perished while still in single digits. The Players had been skittled for 136, some 161 runs behind the Gentlemen.

That the Players had failed to cope with the either the bowling or the conditions shed even greater light on the brilliance of Tip Foster's innings the day before. It also said much about the difference in the bowling attacks employed by the two teams. The Gentlemen's success in the field during the first innings had rested on a group of quick bowlers; Mason was classed as fast-medium, Jessop genuinely quick and Charles Kortright was hailed by many as the fastest bowler the game had ever produced. Woods, himself no slouch in his day, said Kortright was "the fastest, but not the best, I ever saw" and, fellow quick, Ernest Jones, when asked who was the most rapid, responded

"Kortright of Essex, and I'm next." These pacemen found they could extract more from the pitch, and consequently cause the batsmen far greater problems, than the Players' attack which, while skilful, was based on medium-pace and spin.

While *The Times* conveyed the impression that the Gentlemen had been helped somewhat by the pitch during the second day, most observers and participants argued that the surface was more than playable. *Wisden* reported that there had been, "nothing the matter with [it]." The correspondent from the *Daily News* also absolved the surface from much of the blame and reported the Players' batsmen concurred that it was "almost perfect." Bowler Gilbert Jessop described the wicket as "plumb"; and well he might, as the track clearly had given *some* assistance to him and the other Gentlemen quicks. Both Bobby Abel and Willie Quaife had been hit by the bowling of Jessop late on the first evening, Abel several times – one delivery was said to have nearly taken away the peak of his cap – and was still hobbling when he resumed the next morning. Abel received little sympathy from the assembled crowd, many of whom reportedly "looked on the affair as a huge joke."

Possibly to protect their fast bowlers from the heat of the day, perhaps because Sammy Woods was keen for his Gentlemen to push home or even showcase their advantage with the undoubted batting talents at their disposal, the follow-on was not enforced and the amateurs were to bat again. As they took the field for a second time, things were not looking good for the professionals.

The Gentlemen, buoyed by their commanding lead, approached their second innings with attacking intent. Runs came quickly but risks were evident as a couple of wickets fell before 50 runs were on the board; Jones was castled by Rhodes for five and Charlie Townsend succumbed to the same fate for a quick-fire 22. Still at 43-2, the lead stood in excess of 200 and the Gentlemen saw no need to slow down. However, as with the previous day's play, C B Fry was uncharacteristically restrained, seeming to struggle to find his usual freedom. He instead took the role of anchor to another outstanding knock by Reginald Erskine Foster.

Foster took a little time to settle into his innings but, once set, laid into the Players' bowling with brio, scoring 136 out of a partnership of 195 with Fry in an hour and 40 minutes; the first time in the history of the fixture that any batsman had scored a century in both innings. He joined W G Grace as the only people to have achieved this feat in three separate matches; no others, at this point, had managed it more than once. Once he reached his ton, Tip Foster cut loose, flashing his blade at almost every ball. When he was finally caught at long-on, he left the field to a thunderous ovation. If his first innings had been excellent, came the reports from Lord's, the second had been brilliant. Foster departed with the lead a tick under 400 and still seven batsmen yet to come. It was a near fatal blow to any hopes the Players may have had at the start of the morning's play. The mood of the professionals would not have been improved by the knowledge that John Gunn had missed a catchable chance off the centurion when he was on 40.

Still, the Players' attack persevered and, with the Gentlemen under instruction from their captain to continue their daring batsmanship (or in the words of the correspondent from *The Manchester Guardian,* their "indiscriminate hitting"), wickets started to fall. Fry unfortunately hit his own stumps (b. Ward) having made 72, Trott picked up the wicket of Mason for 27 and bowled Jessop for, a six-ball, 18 (Woods had told the big hitting Jessop that he had "five minutes"). After Albert Ward dismissed Sammy Woods for a duck, the tail wagged a little but Trott finally saw off the last three men. The score sat at 339, a lead of 500. The Gentlemen had made their total in little over three hours, rattling along at a rate of more than five runs an over.

The Players' bowling attack had every right to feel a little bruised by their mauling at the hands of Foster and his fellow Gentlemen. Albert Trott, who had seen his efforts punished at a rate of almost seven runs an over, could at least take solace in the fact that he had taken most of the wickets to fall, finishing with six for 142. The haul had pushed his wickets tally for the season above 100.

* *

Albert Edwin Trott, an Australian from Melbourne who, like Sammy Woods, had the distinction of playing Test cricket for both Australia and England, is, in some ways, a curious figure in cricketing history. A highly talented round-arm bowler with good variations and a solid batsman, he was rarely given the credit or international recognition his undoubted skills deserved.

Picked by Australia for the last three Tests of their home Ashes series in 1894/5, Trott scored over 200 runs (finishing the series with an average in excess of 100) and took eight wickets at an average of 21 (in the penultimate Test, he was denied any chance to add to his wicket-taking tally by swift England collapses in both innings, leaving him unused as a bowler). Despite this more than respectable performance, Trott found himself omitted from the Australian touring party to England the following summer. In lieu of an Ashes series to keep him occupied, Trott paid for his own passage to England and found a home as a professional for Middlesex. He represented the county with distinction until 1910, racking up a career first-class record of over 10,000 runs and 1,674 wickets. His greatest year was in 1899 where, in addition to becoming the only man to ever hit the ball over the Lord's pavilion, he scored more than 1,000 runs and took 239 wickets. The previous summer he had been selected for England and played two Tests in the South African tour, claiming seventeen scalps.

While he had another productive season in 1900, it was not long before weight gain and a fondness for sharing ales with spectators while fielding, quickly reduced his effectiveness. He continued playing for his county for the rest of the decade, achieving the feat of four balls in an over plus another hat-trick in his 1907 benefit game. Unfortunately, this caused the game to be ended extremely early, denying him much of the money that would have come from spectators yet to arrive. On retiring from county cricket in 1910, Albert became an umpire but, falling into poverty and, affected by illness and depression, in 1914, he took his own life.

* *

Trott and his team-mates faced an uphill battle to save the game. Set an unlikely 501 runs to win, the more realistic route to salvation appeared to lie in batting out the remaining overs of the day and finding some way to resist throughout the next to salvage a draw.

If a Gentlemen's victory seemed highly probable at the change of innings, it looked a nailed-on certainty when the Players' lost their first wicket: Ward, caught off the bowling of Jessop for just four. Adding to the Players' difficulties was the fact that their number three in the first innings, Tom Hayward, was unable to take his place at the crease, having been so affected by the heat that he had left the field earlier in the day. Even so, Brown and Quaife batted gamely for the remaining overs and, when time was called, the Players stood at 44-1, some 456 runs behind.

Wednesday 18 July 1900
Day three

With play scheduled to run until half past six in the evening, the Players' chances of surviving against the five quick bowlers at the Gentlemen's disposal looked remote. A healthy crowd gathered in anticipation of a splendid amateur win and all looked to be following the script when, after a respectable partnership of 37, Willie Quaife was trapped LBW by Jones for 29.

81-2. 419 runs behind.

With Hayward still unavailable, skipper Bobby Abel joined Jack Brown in the middle. Brown, a short, stocky Yorkshireman, whose career and life were both cut woefully short by heart problems, was a pugnacious batsman most comfortable on the back foot. Strong against the short ball, especially around off-stump, he found the conditions and bowling now very much to his liking. The Gentlemen's quicks may have been able to exploit what life was in the wicket on the morning of day two but no strip could have possibly have stood up to such unrelenting heat and, consequently, by day three, it had been baked into a hard, flat, batsman's track (though Dick Lilley recalled that it had also worn a little and so would have given some help to the bowlers). Furthermore, the bowlers soon began to tire and started to drop the ball too short (the pacemen's cause not helped by the fact that the MCC had changed the laws at the start of the season, increasing the balls delivered in an over from five to six, adding to their already arduous workload). With Brown employing his favourite late-cut and Abel strong on the leg-side against the short ball, the Players finally began to see some success with the bat. The pair dominated the amateur's attack until, shortly after lunch, Abel, only two frustrating runs short of a century, let his eagerness get the better of him and, attempting "a big pull off a short-pitched ball from Jessop", was easily caught at forward short leg. The Players' captain had gone, yet his and Brown's efforts ensured that the balance of the game had begun to fidget, if not entirely shift.

246-3. 254 runs behind.

Tom Hayward, having finally recovered from his problems of the day before, made his way to the crease. This was an important moment in the game. Undoubtedly, the match was still the Gentlemen's to lose;

while the professionals had made a more than encouraging start, they were still a long way behind and a couple of wickets would all but see them off. However, if Hayward and Brown could continue the flood of runs, the game would remain very much alive.

Perhaps inevitably, the pair could not maintain the scoring pace of the morning but still managed to settle into a productive partnership and began to frustrate the Gentlemen's bowlers again. The pitch remained true and the batsmen's timing immaculate. Brown soon reached his century and, late in the afternoon, when he finally succumbed, caught in the slips off the bowling of Smith, he had been at the crease for just under five hours for a handsome 163, containing 29 fours.

348-4. 152 runs behind.

The impossible task now looked distinctly possible. 152 runs; more than the professionals had made in their first innings but, with batting to come, favourable conditions and a tiring bowling attack, few would have staked their reputation on the winning target not being reached. It was still no easy task and, when Herbert Carpenter was bowled by Woods for nine, the Players' changing room would have been forgiven for experiencing a strong case of the jitters.

Dick Lilley arrived looking to take the game away from the Gentlemen and to do so quickly. Relying on his confident drive, the Players' wicket-keeper made a rapid 30 before cutting a ball from Mason into his stumps. Another one gone.

448-6. 52 runs behind.

While the likes of Rhodes, Gunn and Trott were no fools with the bat (indeed, as we have seen, Trott had a proven record (as did Gunn) and Rhodes would go on to have a distinguished batting career), they had been picked for their bowling prowess and so all eyes were fixed on Hayward to see the Players home. The tension ratcheted further when, only 19 runs after Trott had joined him at the crease, Hayward was gone; caught by the wicket-keeper, standing back to Kortright, for a fine 111. Nelson had struck again.

469-7. 31 runs behind.

Now firmly into the tail, the Gentlemen must have sensed their chance to snatch victory. For the Players, the 32 runs needed for victory would have seemed a mountain. Trott and Gunn started to eat gradually into that lead, every run lessening the tension, every false stroke tightening it still. The end was almost in sight when Gunn received a thunderbolt from the arm of Kortright and departed with his stumps in a mess.

485-8. 15 runs behind.

Rhodes was the penultimate man for the Players and, while it may not have been appreciated at that stage of his career, how fortunate for his team to have a man of such natural batting ability coming in so low down the order. For all the tension of that late afternoon, on the stroke of 6:30 - the scheduled close of play - the pairing of Albert Trott and Wilfred Rhodes knocked off the remaining runs to bring the scores level.

500-8. Scores level.

This was the moment when the umpires should have called time, drawn stumps and seen the teams shake hands on a momentous draw. The Gentlemen's captain, Sammy Woods, who felt that draws were "no good except for bathing", had other ideas and convinced the umpires to allow him to take the ball for another over. While Woods may have harboured ideas of taking the remaining two wickets to claim the tie, it was unlikely, and, on the fifth ball of the extra over, Rhodes saw the Players home with little fuss.

With little fuss but amongst scenes of great excitement and some controversy. For all those lucky enough to be present at Lord's on that day knew they had witnessed something very special. The result itself - the chasing down of over 500 runs in a final innings, only the second time a team had achieved that feat - was noteworthy enough.[2] However, the match was so much more than an unlikely victory. Those spectators, over three sweltering days, had been treated to 1,274 runs scored, in often high style, off 372 overs. They had witnessed some of the finest players to grace the cricketing field of play: from the lightening quick bowling of Kortright and his colleagues; the skill and tenacity of the slower deliveries of Rhodes, Trott and Gunn; a century in each innings from the brilliant Foster who, along with Fry, hardly deserved to be on the losing team; and, finally, the winning contribution of hundreds from Brown and Hayward. It was a feast of cricket.

Not everyone was delighted with the outcome. The Gentlemen's captain, Sammy Woods, came in for criticism for his tactics. Not only had he failed to enforce the follow-on during the second day, but his insistence that his team hit out during the second innings drew disapproval, most noticeably from *Wisden*, which reasoned that the decision has allowed the Players their chance at victory. This was harsh; Woods' aggressive tactics had given the Gentlemen what should have been an unassailable lead with more than enough time left in the game to bowl the Players out again. For *Wisden*, though, "that was all very

---

[2] The only time before this match that a team had chased over 500 to win was when Cambridge University defeated the MCC at Lord's in 1896. There was some question as to whether the finish to that game had been treated in all seriousness.

well but the fact remained that there was only one possible way by which the Gentlemen could lose the match, and that their captain adopted it. It is," the report counselled, "a wholesome rule to take nothing for granted in cricket, and to throw nothing away except under stress of absolute necessity." Somewhat grudgingly, *Wisden* did concede that, "though the Gentlemen suffered a defeat to the risk of which they need not have been exposed, the public profited, the cricket on the last day being quite a marvel of sustained interest."

Others were far more supportive of Woods' approach. The *Daily News* praised Woods for "his great effort to win the game." The Players' wicket-keeper Dick Lilley saw it as a straightforward choice as "there could be no possible suggestion...at the time, that any risk was being run in adopting this course." One of Woods' Gentlemen colleagues that day, Gilbert Jessop, called the criticism "scarcely justifiable" and argued for the value of allowing the bowlers a crack at the opposition late on the second evening. Furthermore, he countered, it had been only by giving the Players a sniff of the hope of victory that had prevented them from grinding out the final day on a flat pitch for a draw; "what might so easily have resulted in a long-drawn-out match with a tame finish had been converted by 'Sam's' enterprise into a most stirring game." As for Woods, Jessop finished, "a more inspiring leader I could not wish for."

The issue of the extra over after the scheduled close of play that allowed the Players to snatch victory brought with it praise, criticism and confusion in equal measure. Plum Warner, writing about the match some years later, took the umpires to task for not drawing stumps at half past six. "The extra over", he argued, "was too magnanimous...what were the umpires about?" Dick Lilley, for whom Woods' action allowed him to emerge on the winning side, was fulsome in his praise of "that good spirit of sportsmanship so characteristic of him." The *Daily News* report, however, argued that carrying on for a result was quite normal in "matches of this sort." The correspondent for *The Times* seemed unaware of the dispute and simply assumed that play had been scheduled to continue until seven.

Woods was fully aware of the controversy caused by both his approach in the second innings and the extra over allowed. "Of course," he noted, "next day (and the day before in the pavilion) my action was very much criticized." For Woods, however, there was no issue: "Well, had I left my side to bat until time on the second day and not have given the Players a chance of getting the runs, a pretty day's play would have resulted....To win or lose a game is the game, and not to bother about first and second innings wins or the championship." It was, one must say, a traditionally *amateur* approach.

Another line of complaint concerned Woods' use of his bowling attack, with the argument that Kortright could have been asked to bowl more than the 18 overs he was given (perhaps unsurprising for a fast bowler given the heat) and that when Woods did turn to his slower alternatives he gave Charlie Townsend, a very good leg break bowler, only two overs, while giving Arthur Jones twenty-three. Warner recalled that, in his view, Woods' captaincy on that day was "not up to his usual standard." Sammy Woods would not captain the Gentlemen again.

In any case, whatever the decisions made by Woods on the final day, the abiding memory of this fixture remains the exceptional achievement of the Players. Conditions may have been favourable for batting on that last day but the difficulty of scoring over 500 runs against bowlers of the quality of Kortright, Mason, Jessop and Jephson should not be underestimated.

The Gentlemen versus Players fixtures now seems a curious anachronism (though English cricket's attachment to the British class system has hardly disappeared) and, since its stumps were drawn for the final time in 1962, gains little attention in wistful glances back through cricketing time. It did though, for a while, not only encapsulate the social distinctions so embedded in the game of cricket, it also captured the public's attention and provided some glorious moments for some wonderful players.

Gentlemen v Players
Lord's Cricket Ground, St John's Wood
16th, 17th, 18th July 1900 (3-day match)

Toss: Gentlemen

Umpires: J Phillips, J Wheeler

Gentlemen first innings

AO Jones	c Ward	b Trott	9
CB Fry	b Rhodes		68
CL Townsend	run out		30
RE Foster	not out		102
JR Mason	b Trott		2
DLA Jephson	lbw	b Rhodes	9
GL Jessop	c Lilley	b Rhodes	18
*SMJ Woods	c Lilley	b Rhodes	7
E Smith	c Rhodes	b Gunn	26
CJ Kortright	b Gunn		4
+H Martyn	c Brown	b Gunn	3
Extras	(15 b, 4 lb)		19
Total	(all out, 95.3 overs)		297

Fall of wickets:
1-26, 2-99, 3-127, 4-132, 5-177, 6-201, 7-216, 8-273, 9-277, 10-297

Bowling	Overs	Mdns	Runs	Wkts
Rhodes	30	4	93	4
Trott	27	11	66	2

Mead	21	5	58	0
Gunn	17.3	3	61	3

Players first innings

*R Abel	b Jessop		30
A Ward	c Jones	b Mason	16
TW Hayward	b Jessop		8
WG Quaife	c Foster	b Jessop	9
JT Brown	c Foster	b Mason	18
HA Carpenter	run out		14
+AFA Lilley	b Mason		10
AE Trott	c Foster	b Mason	9
JR Gunn	c Martyn	b Kortright	4
W Rhodes	not out		1
W Mead	b Kortright		4
Extras	(9 b, 4 lb)		13
Total	(all out, 52.4 overs)		136

Fall of wickets:
1-48, 2-61, 3-67, 4-79, 5-97, 6-111, 7-120, 8-125, 9-131, 10-136

Bowling	Overs	Mdns	Runs	Wkts
Kortright	12.4	4	30	2
Jephson	4	0	9	0
Mason	17	7	40	4
Jessop	14	5	28	3
Jones	5	0	16	0

Gentlemen second innings

AO Jones	b Rhodes		5
CB Fry	hit wkt	b Ward	72
CL Townsend	b Rhodes		22

RE Foster	c Brown	b Trott	136
JR Mason	c Lilley	b Trott	27
DLA Jephson	not out		18
GL Jessop	b Trott		18
*SMJ Woods	c Carpenter	b Ward	0
E Smith	c Brown	b Trott	16
CJ Kortright	c sub	b Trott	12
+H Martyn	c Quaife	b Trott	4
Extras	(5 b, 4 lb)		9
Total	(all out, 67.2 overs)		339

Fall of wickets:

1-5, 2-43, 3-238, 4-258, 5-260, 6-298, 7-302, 8-306, 9-306, 10-339

Bowling	Overs	Mdns	Runs	Wkts
Rhodes	15	2	51	2
Trott	20.2	0	142	6
Mead	14	1	57	0
Gunn	7	3	23	0
Ward	10	3	39	2
Quaife	1	0	18	0

Players second innings

A Ward	c Martyn	b Jessop	4
WG Quaife	lbw	b Jones	29
JT Brown	c Jones	b Smith	163
*R Abel	c Jones	b Jessop	98
TW Hayward	c Martyn	b Kortright	111
HA Carpenter	b Woods		9
+AFA Lilley	b Mason		30
AE Trott	not out		22
JR Gunn	b Kortright		3

| W Rhodes | not out | 7 |
| W Mead | did not bat | |

| Extras | (13 b, 8 lb, 4 nb, 1 w) | 26 |

| Total | (8 wickets, 156.5 overs) | 502 |

Fall of wickets:

1-4, 2-81, 3-246, 4-348, 5-379, 6-448, 7-469, 8-485

Bowling	Overs	Mdns	Runs	Wkts
Kortright	18	4	60	2
Jephson	14	2	46	0
Mason	34	11	92	1
Jessop	28	8	74	2
Jones	23	4	69	1
Woods	19.5	3	70	1
Smith	18	3	57	1
Townsend	2	0	8	0

2. WAR

Middlesex versus Kent
Lord's, 31 August-2 September 1914

There's a breathless hush in the Close tonight
Ten to make and the match to win –
A bumping pitch and a blinding light,
An hour to play and the last man in.
And it's not for the sake of a ribboned coat,
Or the selfish hope of a season's fame
But his Captain's hand on his shoulder smote –
Play up! Play up! And play the game!

The sand of the desert is sodden and red –
Red with the wreck of the square that broke –
The Gatling's jammed and the Colonel dead,
And the regiment blind with dust and smoke.
The river of death has brimmed his banks
And England's far and Honour a name,
But the voice of a schoolboy rallies the ranks;
Play up! Play up! And play the game!

Henry Newbolt - 1898

Lord's, Friday 28 August 1914
Day two

Colin 'Charlie' Blythe stood at the end of his run waiting for Middlesex's stand-in captain, Leslie Kidd, to settle in his crease. The home side were establishing a healthy second-innings lead and the partnership between Kidd and George Hebden, which had quickly passed fifty runs, would have begun to irritate. If Kent were to turn this around, wickets needed to fall quickly. With Kidd ready, Blythe began his approach – a shuffle of the feet, then a hop before the final approach and a side-on delivery that allowed the ball to be hidden from the batsman until the moment his left arm finally swung into view – the ball pitched, turned and, evading bat, thudded into the Middlesex man's pad. An appeal rang out and all eyes turned to the umpire, who raised his finger to send Kidd on his way. At 35 years of age and still at the peak of his cricketing powers, no one could have foreseen that it would be Charlie Blythe's last wicket in first-class cricket.

* *

Any person at Lord's enjoying the contest between Middlesex and Kent, and who had shelled out a halfpenny for a copy of that morning's *Daily Mail*, would have eventually turned the page of their newspaper and seen a photograph taken at the match the day before. This picture was not of the game itself but of spectators gathered in front of what appears to be the old Lord's Tavern. With an estimated two thousand people in attendance on the first day of the game, any photographer wanting to capture a well-populated part of the ground had plenty to choose from. He may have selected this particular grouping because – with the exception of one child whose gender is unclear – it was universally male. It may also have been because a number of those in his sights, particularly on the front row, were young. Young and male – just the ticket for this assignment. The men in this photograph, clad in suits and ties, flat caps and boaters, sit mostly with hands clasped or arms folded and stare passively; some at the camera, others straight ahead, presumably at the game. Perhaps a shout to keep still for the shot had held them in pose. There are some exceptions. A few look away, one tilts his head down so that his hat obscures all but a fine moustache. A heavily bearded man standing behind the seats near the camera appears the oldest of the group. One serious looking younger man two rows in front of him sports a black arm-band in memory, perhaps, of a recently deceased relative. In contrast, two others further along on the front row, appear to observe the cameraman with amusement.

The reason the *Daily Mail*'s photographer was more interested in the crowd than the cricket was clear. This was no celebration of Middlesex's final game of the season. It was not designed to mark the closing of the county season at Lord's. Its purpose was to shame and intimidate. Headlined 'Cricket Enthusiasts During The War' the photograph was supplemented with a brief explanation from the paper: "People are anxious to see the type of men who look on in the cricket field while the manhood of Europe is in the battlefield. This photograph is a section of the crowd at the Middlesex v. Kent match at Lord's yesterday." Ominously, it threatened, "further selections will be published." The call to arms was causing tensions at home and it seemed cricket was in the firing-line.

On 4 August 1914, Parliament formally declared war on Germany. Tensions had been building between the great powers for some time but came to a head for the British Government over the German threat to the neutrality of Belgium, towards whom Britain had treaty obligations. On 3 August, after Austro-Hungary had declared war on Serbia, leading to the mobilisation of Russian forces - which, in turn, led to states of war existing between Germany and Russia and Germany and France - the British Government sent an ultimatum to Germany demanding guarantees of Belgian security. The next day German troops entered Belgian territory and Britain entered the war.

The day after the declaration of war, Field-Marshall Lord Kitchener – born Horatio Herbert Kitchener – was appointed Secretary of State for War. Kitchener, who had made his reputation on the battlefields of Sudan and South Africa, did not accept that this war was likely to be won quickly, and accurately predicted that the existing British Expeditionary Force would be far too small for the job ahead. To remedy this, Kitchener declared that not only would the part-time Territorial forces be employed in active overseas service but a series of 'new armies' would be created and, almost immediately, a call for volunteers was issued. By 6 August, a large box ran in many national newspapers declaring "Your King and Country need you." It asked "all...young unmarried men to rally round the flag and enlist in the ranks of her army"; the initial age-range was set between 18 and 30.

The overall impression given by newspapers and newsreels of the response to the call to enlistment was one of a great early success, with nearly half a million men committing themselves to armed service between 4 August and 12 September 1914. However, these images and figures obscure two pertinent facts. The first was that in the initial two weeks following the declaration of war, enlistment was slow relative to later weeks, especially in rural areas where recruitment organisations were not so quick to establish themselves. The second was that Kitchener was aware that, even when enlistment picked up by early

September, his armies were still well short of the numbers needed to fight the necessary scale of battle that was becoming apparent.

As Kitchener continued to lead the effort to swell the ranks of his new armies, questions began to swirl around the cricketing world as to what its responsibilities were in regards those young men who played and watched the game. Should, indeed, the game continue at all when so many of those who participated could be employed in the service of their country?

Many of the men who made an early decision to forgo the county cricket field and commit themselves to the army were drawn from the ranks of the amateurs. To some extent this fitted into a familiar pattern. Most amateurs of the game were used to declaring themselves available or unavailable for selection as circumstances allowed whereas professionals, under contract with their county and reliant on wages to support their families, were expected to be at the disposal of their employers.

There was also a cultural factor which linked many of the amateurs of the game to expectations of military serve via the schools of their youth. It was quite common for a public schoolboy's career to wind its way via the Officer Corp of his or her majesty's army. Almost one hundred years before, it had been said that the Duke of Wellington claimed the Battle of Waterloo was won on "the playing fields of Eton." While the quotation is likely apocryphal, the extent to which it took hold in the popular imagination is not. The link between the training of a superior soldier and the playing of sports – particularly cricket, rugby or rowing – was evident in the folklore of the British aristocracy. In 1898, on the eve of the Boer War, Henry Newbolt made this link explicitly in his poem *Vitai Lampada*, with which we began this chapter. The language of cricket, already prevalent in wider popular use, penetrated discussion of war. Running a picture-piece on captured enemy soldiers in 1914, the *Daily Mirror* assured its readers that "the prisoners will be treated with every kindness and consideration. As a nation of sportsmen we always 'play the game' according to rules, be it war or cricket."

The call to arms fed into a late-Victorian notion of 'muscular Christianity' where, according to Keith Sandiford, "Godliness and manliness, spiritual perfection and physical power, became inextricably woven." This link between physicality and moral worth was prevalent in public schools during the nineteenth century and, accordingly, it was no coincidence that cricket had become an essential part of the public school curriculum by the 1860s. In August of 1914, then, it was a socially natural step for many – though not all – young amateur cricketers, not that long from having graced the playing-fields of Eton, Harrow, Winchester or elsewhere, to decide that the time to fulfil their duty as an Officer had arrived. For some, such as Middlesex's usual Captain Pelham Warner, the call to arms (the cause of his absence from the side in August 1914) was but a continuation of service which had begun some years before in the Territorials.

Professional cricketers were by no means immune to the call to war but they also had their duty to their county employers and, with the season drawing to a close, most saw out the remaining matches before making any such decision. In having to decide whether to leave their current employment to heed Kitchener's appeal, these men were no different to their friends and neighbours working in factories, mines and shops. On the one hand, patriotic zeal and a sense of adventure appealed to some to take up military colours immediately; on the other, for most working and middle-class men, the call to arms was an unfamiliar one, the reasons for war unclear and the proximity of the battle to them and their families, remote. There was also a financial consideration. Pay for the lowest ranks of soldiers was small compared to that which most workers received – only slightly above that of an agricultural labourer – and even many unmarried men of enlistment age had responsibilities to help support the family home.

As August wore on, the public continued to be bombarded with messages urging young menfolk to answer the call. The *Daily Mirror*, amongst many others, regularly presented features imploring its readers to enlist. On 27 August, the first day of the match at Lord's, it ran a full-page spread headed by a large picture of Lord Kitchener with the banner "Your King and Country Need You: Join The Army To-Day" and went further when it challenged that "the death of a brave man is worth more to the world and a woman than the life of a coward." On the same morning, the Middlesex and Kent players would have been greeted by the *Daily Express*'s broad headline "Britain's Greatest Need Is Men To Fight Her Battles" and a lead article which not only called on men to do their duty but advised its female readers to "make patriotism a test of their affection." Similar calls for women to shame their men into serving ran across the popular press.

The sporting community was an obvious target for recruitment efforts, given the assumed prevalence of young, fit men in their ranks, and sporting authorities were keen to show that they were playing an active role in the war effort. The Football Association called on all its clubs to place grounds at the disposal of local military units between matches and, on game day, to allow well-known figures to appeal to the crowd for eligible men to enlist at recruitment centres set-up nearby. Proposals were put forward in the press for special 'footballer units' to be created to encourage players to enlist. Other sports were equally as keen to show their spirit; boxing benefits for the Prince of Wales' War Relief fund - established to help the families of serving men and those suffering from "industrial distress" - were held and venues such as London's Premierland boasted of the numbers of boxers who had enlisted after appeals at their tournaments.

Often, appeals to sportsmen and spectators were made with an accusatory tone. In early September, *The Sportsman* ran a cartoon depicting a short, flat-capped, smoking, football fan holding onto a muscular footballer who, in turn, looks indecisively as he is beckoned by a departing soldier. The caption ran 'The Idle, The Idol and The Ideal'. Letters and comment in the press often berated those who did not offer their service. One missive to *The Sportsman* on 29 August branded bachelor amateur cricketers who had not signed up as "fools or cowards". We have already mentioned the ominous *Daily Mail* photograph from Lord's. This idea of leisure as the hiding place of the reluctant serviceman extended beyond sport to other forms of entertainment, prompting one theatre-lover to express his dismay at such attitudes to the *Daily Mirror*, proclaiming that "the closing of all places of entertainment would spell absolute destitution to tens of thousands of the theatrical profession, both men and women and the children dependent upon them."

Cricketers were by no means immune from public pressure. On 17 August, five Middlesex professionals playing in a match against Nottinghamshire received a letter from an irate member of the public. Scrawled in red ink across all angles of the page, the angry communication accused the men of rank cowardice and "funk" for not having gone to the service of their country.

While *The Sportsman* was happy to give space to those with grievances towards sporting participants and spectators, *The Sporting Life* was keener to launch the case for the defence. Stressing the paper's support for recruitment efforts among the sportsmen of Britain, it nevertheless decried the "crank and the panic-monger", the "purveyors of cheap sneers" and their "senseless outcry against sport"; asking why it was so wrong for the men who would, through age or injury, be remaining at home to enjoy an hour or two of recreation in the spirit of "keeping on".

Although soon after the declaration of war the MCC had claimed that "no good purpose can be served at the moment by cancelling matches", the cricketing authorities made it clear that they were doing their best to encourage all cricketers of enlisting age to do their duty. Lord Alverstone, President of Surrey County Cricket Club, wrote from his "sick bed" to "earnestly appeal to all amateurs and professionals to show that they are not behindhand in patriotism and love of their country." Hampshire's J C Moberly and Russell Bencraft, (President and Chairman of the Committee, respectively), wrote to several newspapers defending their players. While they insisted it was right the season should continue in the interests of their professionals ("a most deserving class"), they pointed out that "ten amateurs who have played for Hampshire this season are either at the front or have volunteered and been accepted for service; that all the professionals have volunteered for home service" thus proving that, amongst their men, "there has been no lack of loyalty towards the pressing needs of the Empire." The leading cricketers of the day also wanted to show their loyalty towards the war effort. A long list of notables – including W G Grace, Jack Hobbs, Frank Woolley, Gilbert Jessop, Johnny Douglas and others – put their names behind an appeal to the "cricket loving public" for donations to the Prince of Wales' National Relief Fund.

Yet, despite the efforts of the sporting community to demonstrate their commitment to the war effort, the image of young men enjoying sport rather than marching to battle was too much for some and calls for the cessation of sporting contest continued to be heard. The continuation of the county cricket season roused none other than W G Grace from his retirement for one last salvo. On 27 August 1914 *The Sportsman* published a letter from The Champion where he noted that, while many cricketers had already heeded the call to arms, there were others than did not "seem to realise" that they will have to serve. "I think", he proclaimed, "the time has arrived when the county cricket season should be closed, for it is not fitting...that able bodied men should play day after day and pleasure-seekers look on", before concluding that he, "should like to see all first-class cricketers of suitable age, etc., set a good example and come to the help of their country without delay in its hour of need."

The response to this clarion call, in the pages of *The Sportsman* at least, was not universally in agreement. Two days later 'The Wanderer" used his column to take issue with Grace's view, asserting that there was a contradiction in that "on one hand we are enjoined to carry on the business and work of the country as far as possible; on the other, that watching a match is a form of relieving the mind from the tension of the war that ought to be tabooed." Pointing out that many of Grace's pleasure-seekers were themselves in military uniform, he asked "where is the harm?"

On 31 August, regular columnist "An Old County Player" joined the debate, arguing that one could not blame the professional players as, while the counties continued to agree to matches, they "had no option but to go on serving their employers" and that "there is not a single first-class cricketer today unready to do something serviceable" but thought it unfair that "they all ought to join the Army." He contended that eight out of ten professional cricketers would, in any event, likely fall out of the qualification for Army service. Qualified amateurs, he conceded, should go.

W G Grace was obviously stung by some of the criticisms sent his way and another communique from the Grand Old Man of Cricket appeared in the pages of *The Sportsman* on 2 September. His previous letter, he said somewhat grumpily, had been misunderstood by "a few people, some of whom think more of the County Championship than of their countries dire need." Grace seemed to backtrack somewhat from his previous position when he claimed he had no problem with games being played and watched by those who were unfit or too old for military service but exclaimed that it was "a disgrace at such times for any able-bodied man of suitable age and good health to be wasting his time in playing or watching games."

He had not been the first notable figure from within the game to come to this conclusion. Middlesex's captain Pelham Warner had cabled his County Committee on 6 August suggesting the cancellation of all remaining fixtures. His proposal was quickly rebuffed on the grounds that the committee "dislike[d] the idea of their employees having to suffer." Pressure continued to be placed on counties throughout England, prompting Lord Harris to initiate a public response from the Kent Committee arguing that they were simply responding to the Government's request that the people "should endeavour as far as possible to live our normal lives." The Committee were clearly not as one, however, as after an exchange of letters with Lord Harris over the issue, the Hon. Major J S R Tufton resigned.

As pressure grew on the counties and players began to respond to Lord Kitchener's appeals, a premature end to the season began to take on an air of inevitability even to some who urged it toward completion. The question started to become one of when, rather than if. Would the curtain fall if Surrey secured the title at Sussex in their match scheduled to begin on 3 September? Would Yorkshire's fixtures at the Scarborough Carnival, planned for the same week, survive, leaving only Surrey's final fixture and a first-class match between an MCC South African touring side and Lord Londesborough's XI unplayed? In the end, the close came suddenly. On 2 September, at Hove, when Herbert Wilson and George Hirst, the captains of Sussex and Yorkshire, shook hands on a drawn game, it was to be the last county cricketing action for over four years.

In early September, the Rugby Union authorities had come to the same conclusion and declared that "it was no time for Rugby football; that young and active sportsmen should play the game by serving their country in a military capacity." Their clubs were instructed to cancel all international and county matches and, rather optimistically, said that those fixtures should stand in the next season. They also urged all rugby players to immediately enlist and announced that they were approaching the War Office about the possibility of a Rugby Footballers Corps.

Such a sacrificial attitude was not shared across all sports. After meeting to consider the matter, the Football Association urged eligible players to enlist but decided that a suspension of the season would be "mischievous rather than good." The Management Committee of the Football League concurred, declaring that their competition should continue in order to "help the nation bear its sorrow, relieve the oppression of continuous strain and save the people at home from panic and depression." The 1914-15 football season was played out in full – Everton finishing as champions – though, once completed, the Football League would follow the lead of rugby and cricket and not return until 1919. Local football associations took their own decisions and many made a much earlier choice to suspend competition. That horse-racing continued to entertain the public was in no little part due to royal intervention. None other than George V made it clear that he wished the sport of kings to continue. Compromises were necessary as many prominent racecourses were commandeered by the War Office but racing would keep going throughout the duration of the conflict.

Cricket was not to be completely moribund for the duration, however. The leagues were not in unanimous agreement with the counties over the need to put away bat and ball for the duration of the war. Several, including the important Lancashire League, not only saw their season to a full conclusion but would continue to schedule matches the next year and thereafter.

Thursday 27 August 1914
Day one

The coin fell Middlesex's way yet their skipper, Leslie Kidd, did not respond immediately. He was no novice at captaincy having been asked on several occasions to assume the role when Middlesex's usual leader – Pelham Warner – was absent but this may have been his trickiest call yet. The previous two days had seen considerable rain in London and, with showers having passed overhead that morning, the pitch would have been damp at best. It was also very humid and that combination promised assistance for the bowlers in swing, turn and break. However, while the clouds overhead might help the ball move in the air, the most pressing issue was when they would lift. If the sun were to make its way through and turn the damp pitch 'sticky', the three-pronged Kent attack of Blythe, Woolley and Freeman could be unplayable. The cloud-cover looked set in for the immediate future, however, and so, after quite some hesitation, Kidd decided to trust his batsmen and make use of the freshly rolled surface before a change in overhead conditions could work any mischief. A shake of the hands with Kent's captain Lionel Troughton and the Middlesex skipper headed back to the Lord's Pavilion to tell his openers to pad-up.

Though late in the season, this match still had meaning in terms of the destination of the County Championship. Kent, the reigning champions from 1913, were out of the running but Middlesex's championship ambitions were still alive. Surrey, sitting in first place, were the clear favourites but, with three games outstanding, if they were to stumble, Middlesex had the opportunity to take the title. That is, if they first could defeat this very good Kent team at Lord's.

Middlesex's Frank Tarrant and Harry Lee strode to the middle to begin the home side's innings and to find out what life the damp pitch was going to offer their opponents. The situation was far from ideal; taking your guard on a wet-one in overcast, humid conditions was challenging enough but do to so against the reigning County Champions whose opening bowlers already had over 280 scalps that season between them and included the leading wicket-taker in first-class cricket, was akin to staring down the barrel.

* *

With August centuries under each of their belts, the Middlesex openers were no slouches, although they were a contrast in levels of experience. Originally a bowler, Australian Frank Tarrant had begun his first-class career in 1899 with his native Victoria but struggled to make much of an impact. It would only be when he tried his luck in England, first for the MCC and then, after qualification for the county in 1905, as a professional with Middlesex that his all-round talent began to show. Tarrant's batting came on in leaps and bounds. He soon became a fixture at the top of the order and, frequently, an opening bowler as well. By 1914, he had scored just shy of 15,000 first-class runs, including 27 centuries. His career finished in 1933, by which time he had racked nearly 18,000 runs and over 1,500 wickets, as well as the double of 1,000 runs and 100 wickets in a season eight times. Despite this and being named one of *Wisden*'s Cricketers of the Year in 1908, Tarrant remained uncapped in international cricket.

His partner, Harry Lee, would go on to international recognition – albeit a single England cap ("by accident" according to his memoirs) – but, in 1914, he was a relative novice in County Cricket. He had joined the Lord's ground-staff in 1906 and made his Middlesex debut in 1911 but opportunities in the side had been limited and, when they came, he usually found himself batting very low down the order. Consequently, Lee found it difficult to make any sort of impact on the Middlesex Committeemen; his few notable performances coming more with his off-breaks and slow-medium pace deliveries than with the bat. By the end of the 1913 season he had managed only 12 appearances, accrued just 106 total runs and taken 9 wickets. 1914 had got off to a similarly unpromising start, notching just two County Championship appearances and two University games before August, when Lord Kitchener's call to the recruiting offices affected so many Middlesex amateurs that all available hands were needed to produce a competitive XI. With Frank Tarrant's regular partner William Robertson one of those missing, the job of opening the innings was offered to Lee. After a couple of respectable scores against Yorkshire and Lancashire, Harry made his first big 'un; at Lord's, against Nottinghamshire, scoring 139 second innings runs and sharing a stand of 183 with the brilliant Patsy Hendren.

The dark clouds that had gathered over Europe would see his new career as an opener rudely interrupted but, after spending the later war-years coaching and playing in India at the invitation of his opening partner Frank Tarrant, Harry returned to Middlesex colours and remained a loyal servant of the County right up until 1934. While more expansive colleagues such as Hearne or Hendren would take the headlines, Lee scored his runs in a grittier style. Gritty, patient, but effective and, by the time his Middlesex days ended, he had contributed over 20,000 first-class runs for the county, including 38 centuries, and passed 1,000 runs in a season thirteen times.

* *

Harry Lee, reasonably new to the openers berth, would have watched carefully as Tarrant faced up to Woolley for the first over; keen to see what dangers the damp pitch held. It soon became clear that, while not a 'sticky' wicket, it was slow and offered turn, with the odd-ball leaping awkwardly. Still, a vigilant Frank Tarrant saw off the first six balls with little alarm, leaving Lee to face Blythe from the other end.

Settled into his familiar low, crouched stance, his body almost bent to almost 90 degrees, Lee waited for Blythe to work his magic. The first few deliveries navigated, he went after one; it took the edge of his bat and, with no mistake from wicketkeeper Fred Huish, the umpire's finger was up. History does not preserve whether the ball spat from the surface, bounced excessively or if Harry had just misread the line. Whatever the truth, he was on his way for a duck, leaving the distinct impression that his captain's decision to bat may have been hasty.

If there was a middle order for a tricky situation, however, it was Middlesex's. With J W Hearne and Patsy Hendren due in at three and four, the home team had two players who would go on to imprint their names on their county's record books.

* *

J W Hearne (known as 'Young Jack' to distinguish him from the other Hearne – J T – in the Middlesex squad) was one of those players who, while prolific for his county, was never able to reach his full potential at international level. A classy, intelligent all-rounder and fine fielder, Jack joined the Lord's ground-staff at the tender age of 15 and only three years later made his county debut. With the bat he played classically straight but was able to cut, drive through the covers or play though the on-side with ease. Despite being quite thin as a young man he was capable of generating remarkable power in his shots, though, as he aged, Jack would become a much more patient batsman, relying on his exceptional ability to thread the ball though any field to accumulate runs. His career first-class record is nothing short of astonishing, passing one thousand runs for the season 19 times and in four of those years pushing on past the two thousand mark. With 96 first-class centuries – eleven of them doubles – under his belt, Young Jack Hearne sits in third place on the list of Middlesex's all-time run scorers; only bettered by his good friend Patsy Hendren and the much later batting talents of Mike Gatting.

With the ball J W Hearne was a genuine wicket-taking front-line bowler in his younger years and a steady-enough (though often more expensive) part of the Middlesex attack by the end of his career. Coming in off only a few paces, Young Jack would deliver his leg breaks and googlies with such a whip of the arms that they would come down at almost medium-pace. He took over 100 wickets in a season five times; on each occasion completing the double with 1,000 runs and, in three of those years, the outstanding feat of 2,000 runs and 100 wickets. Jack would end his first-class career with 1,839 wickets at an average of 24.

It is frustrating, then, that Jack never truly managed to display his skills at international level. He won his first cap in 1911 on England's tour of Australia and, although his bowling struggled on flat Australian wickets, started promisingly with the bat; 76 and 46 his first match and a match-winning 114 in the next. Unfortunately, that was to remain the peak of Jack's international career and he would only pass fifty once more in England colours. In and out of the side until his final appearance in 1926, Jack Hearne's international figures pale in comparison with his county exploits: 24 Tests with a batting average of 26 and 30 wickets at a shade under 49.

* *

Walking to the wicket on this sultry morning, Young Jack Hearne would have no doubt been aware that he was only thirteen runs shy of achieving a two thousand run-hundred wicket double for the season. To reach even that small number, however, he would need to be at his most watchful against Woolley and Blythe. With two master craftsman bowlers operating on a difficult pitch Hearne, at first, looked somewhat shaky. Tarrant appeared settled in comparison. Camped on the back foot, the batsmen watched the ball warily, trying to meet it with the full face of the bat. Only when the bowler erred slightly would the ball be worked into the leg-side for the occasional run. Scoring was slow but soon Hearne called Tarrant through for Jack's thirteenth run and the season landmark was passed. That was nearly as good as it got for Jack Hearne as, having only scored six more runs, he played at a ball from Woolley and mistimed the shot straight to Arthur Fielder at mid-off. Fortune was on the Middlesex man's side that morning and Fielder made a complete hash of what should have been a straightforward chance. The reprieve seemed to have a restorative effect on the batsman. From that moment, Hearne appeared to grow in confidence and, while runs would never flow freely, he found more balls to place to leg and keep the scoreboard ticking.

The problems would be at the other end. While Hearne was finding his rhythm, Frank Tarrant remained cautious, allowing his partner to make most of the runs. Then, almost an hour into play, with the score on 44, Blythe – now bowling in tandem with Tich Freeman – snuck one past the bat of the Australian and sent him on his way LBW for 16.

If anything would settle the nerves of Middlesex supporters if would have been the arrival of the considerable talent of Patsy Hendren at the wicket. Hendren, short but strong, and destined to become a mammoth of the game, gave the impression of being able to score runs for fun; his scoring prowess would rank him alongside Hobbs in the pantheon of the English game. On this morning however, his normal superb timing eluded him and Hendren struggled to get either of the bowlers away. At the other end, Hearne pushed on – hitting Freeman for a couple of threes – but Hendren could not settle against these bowlers on this pitch. Sensing the Middlesex man's discomfort, particularly to Blythe, Captain Kidd brought the field in close and, with Hendren on only five, the pressure almost paid off. The batsman's patience tested, Hendren tried to take advantage of the close field and use his power to crunch a delivery past point. He got hold of it but placed the shot far too near to the close-in fielder, Edward "Punter" Humphreys, who went one handed to the powerful low cut and spilled it. A tough chance but the second one to go that morning and seldom did people give Patsy Hendren two bites of the cherry without regretting it. Fortunately for Kent, the reprieve did not last long this time. The dropped chance seemed to embolden Hendren and, despite the trickiness of the pitch and quality of the bowling, he decided that attack was the way forward and promptly lifted Blythe to long-off where George Whitehead took a well-judged catch. The powerhouse Hendren gone for five, Middlesex had lost three wickets for 67 runs; 46 of them from the bat of Hearne.

It appeared that Jack Hearne was playing a different game from his county colleagues. He was watchful but never let himself get tied down; using a combination of good footwork and expert placement to keep notching ones, twos and threes, often off good length balls. Boundaries were not to be in great supply that day. His growing confidence on what should have been a bowler's morning clearly started to affect the Kent attack who began to release the pressure by serving Hearne with hittable balls.

It was not so at the other end as Jack Hearne's batting partners struggled to get a measure of the bowling or the pitch. This was no collapse; every partnership got started, but when it had edged itself into double figures, perhaps into the twenties, a wicket would fall and another Middlesex man was heading back to the pavilion. The contrast between Hearne and his colleagues was stark, standing out like "a Dreadnought surrounded by fishing boats" according to *The Sporting Life*.

Soon after Hendren's departure, Jack Hearne reached his fifty. With the dependable Nigel Haig now at the crease, Middlesex carefully pushed on for half an hour before, at close to twenty-past one, Haig was trapped in front by Freeman and departed for 13; the score six shy of three figures. The Middlesex hundred would be passed shortly and, when lunch was taken at half-past one, the total stood at 101 for 4. Hearne on 65. Given the conditions and the bowling, the home side would have felt pleased with how they stood at lunch. A "capital score", judged the correspondent for *The Sportsman*.

That the home team had managed to eke out their century in the morning session was brought into sharp focus as dark clouds spread across St John's Wood and light rain fell during luncheon. From a batsman's point of view, the last thing this Lord's pitch needed was another sprinkling of water to give it more zip.

The second session continued in the same vein as the first – small, promising, partnerships followed by the fall of a wicket, with Young

Jack Hearne unmoved. Left-hander Henry Weston looked to be positive, finding a rare boundary early on, but came perhaps too eager and was skilfully stumped ("a beautiful act" – *The Sportsman*) by Fred Huish off Blythe. Captain Leslie Kidd joined Hearne to add another 23 runs to the score before he had his stumps rearranged by a delicious full-length Woolley delivery. The 150 was posted on the scoreboard before the pitch did for George Hebden, who steered a spitting ball from Woolley into the hands of Lionel Troughton at a close point. It was very nearly two-in-two but, once again, the Kent fielding let them down and Tich Freeman dropped a straight-forward chance from Stanley Saville at mid-off.

* *

Whichever way you look at it, Frank Edward Woolley was one of the most versatile cricketers to grace the game. He stands 28th on the list of all-time wicket-takers: 2,066 wickets, taken at an average of a shade under twenty. Able to bowl left-arm medium or slow, he took a wicket, on average, every 45.9 balls (a better strike-rate than, say, Locke, Laker or Underwood). While used sparingly with the ball in his later years, he still managed one hundred-wicket seasons eight times.

As a fielder his record is without peer. 1,018 first-class catches taken (mostly at slip). No outfielder in the history of the game comes close. Add wicketkeepers to the list and Woolley still stands tenth. A moment to savour that: in the history of first-class cricket all but nine wicketkeepers have failed to take more catches than the non-wicketkeeping Woolley.

But it is with the bat that Frank Woolley will be remembered best. In a career that spanned thirty-two (war interrupted) years and 978 matches he scored 58,959 runs at an average of 40.77 including 145 centuries and a high score of 305 not out. Only Hobbs can boast a better career runs aggregate. Woolley passed 1,000 runs in a season an extraordinary 28 times. In fact, only once – in his debut year of 1906 – did a domestic season go by without Frank Woolley notching a thousand runs. Two-thousand run seasons came twelve times and, in 1928, 3,352 first-class runs were accumulated from Woolley's bat. In 64 Test Matches he scored over 3,000 runs and took 83 wickets.

A Tonbridge boy, he was spotted at the age of twelve by his later teammate Colin Blythe who, discovering the child watching his net-practice was a left-hander, invited Woolley into the nets. Seven years later Frank would make his full Kent debut. It was an inauspicious start. Woolley dropped a couple of simple catches and registered a first-innings duck, bowled by Lancashire's (Yorkshire-born) Willis Cuttell. He made amends in the second innings with a brisk 64 and had earlier picked up a wicket, catching Albert Hornby off his own bowling; though neither contribution could prevent a comprehensive Lancashire victory. It did not take long for Woolley's all-round talent to shine and he picked up his first five wicket haul in his second match and registered a maiden century in his fourth. Kent and Woolley would never look back.

Standing over six feet tall, Woolley used his long reach and good foot movement to great effect. Playing with the straightest of bats, he was not afraid to attack anything he saw as hittable or, as Lord Hawke put it, Woolley was "the most consistent exponent of the idea that the ball is there to be hit, and not patted, or played with the pads." He could score all around the field but his cover drives and cuts were the shots that seemed to stick most of his contemporaries' minds. For Pelham Warner, Woolley was simply "one of the greatest cricketers the game has ever produced."

* *

Whether the remaining batsmen simply did not fancy their chances on this pitch or instructions had come from the captain, the Middlesex men arrived at the crease looking to hit out in the fading light brought by increasingly ominous rainclouds. Stanley Saville – the 24 year-old right-hander who was known more for his international hockey exploits than his occasional appearances for Middlesex – bludgeoned Blythe for one boundary before skying another which was safely pouched by Woolley moving in from cover. Both Joe Murrell and the other Hearne – J T – helped push the score towards and then over the two-hundred mark before both were relieved of their duties by Freeman. Middlesex were all out for a decent 205.

Young Jack Hearne finished undefeated. It had taken him three hours and twenty-five minutes to reach his century and he stood on 110 not out at the close of the innings. It was a remarkable innings in that, on an unpredictable pitch which had troubled all other batsmen, he had given only two chances – the drop on 19 and a difficult caught and bowled on 95. It had been a patient one too, with only three fours and nine threes by his name in the scorebook.

The Kent bowling had not been perfect – there were too many loose deliveries – but drizzling rain had meant the ball was often difficult to grip and they had come across a man in impeccable nick. Hearne had scored over half of the runs accrued by his team and no other batsman had managed more than Frank Tarrant's sixteen. Blythe had been the pick of the attack, taking 5 for 77 off 33 overs and had shared the bulk of the work with Woolley (2 for 77 off 24). Freeman took the other three wickets, though he had been the more expensive, conceding 42 from 11.5 overs.

* *

Colin 'Charlie' Blythe, born in 1879 in Deptford to Walter (an engineer) and Elizabeth, became one of English cricket's premier spin bowlers. Spotted by Captain Walter McCanlis – then coaching young players at Kent – in the nets at Blackheath in July of 1897, Blythe was invited to the Tonbridge Nursery to try out his skills. The Nursery was an impressive innovation by the Kent Committee; a centre where promising youngsters from around the area could come to be assessed, trained and, if good enough, propelled to the county proper. In Charlie Blythe's case it did not take long. A year after he had taken the eye of McCanlis, Blythe bowled his first overs for Kent's second XI and, in August of 1898, was introduced to the firsts. Not many present would forget Blythe's first XI debut as, while his overall return was simply respectable, he manage to take a wicket with his very first ball. It was a decent scalp too: Yorkshire's Frank Mitchell, who would make his international debut the following season.

Blythe was a graceful, classical left-arm spin bowler. Upright in his delivery stride, he could deceive a batsman in the air with flight, loop and variation in pace as well as beat them off the pitch with his turn. He was never afraid to pitch the ball up against an aggressive batsman; tempting them to drive his fizzing deliveries into a packed off-side field. For Pelham Warner, Blythe was "the very model of what a slow left-hand bowler should be."

His first full season in 1900 saw Blythe take 114 first-class wickets. In his second, he fell seven short of the hundred-wicket mark; his form no doubt impacted by the combination of an illness suffered over the previous winter and a dry summer that robbed him of any sticky tracks on which to weave his magic. He would never again claim fewer than one hundred victims in an English summer and, in 1909, bagged over 200. By the time war closed the 1914 season, he had taken over two and a half thousand wickets at an average of 16.81, including an astonishing 218 five-wicket innings and 71 ten-wicket matches. Of all Blythe's notable performances, the one that particularly stood out was against Nottinghamshire in 1907 where he took all ten wickets in the first innings – skittling them out for 60 – and another seven in the follow-on. He finished the match with seventeen wickets for 48 runs. With

Blythe in the side, Kent were crowned County Champions in 1906, 1909, 1910 & 1913. Without him, they would not win another until 1970.

Blythe's international career was, ultimately, to be one of some frustration. Selected for Archie MacLaren's XI to tour Australia in 1901-2, Charlie had a respectable series with the ball but would need to wait until 1905 before his first taste of a home Test; an Ashes contest at Leeds. Over the next five years he would come and go from the international team. The Headingley Test was his only one of 1905 but he was selected for all the fixtures against South Africa, away and then home, in 1906 and 1907. Picked for the Ashes tour in 1907/8 he only played in the opening Test, at Sydney. While his international career lasted until 1910, appearances for country would be occasional. It was a truncated England career but a decent one. In 19 Tests he took exactly 100 wickets at an average of 18.63 with a best bowling return of 8-59; secured at Headingley against South Africa.

The reasons for his spotty England appearance record were varied and disputed. At certain points in Blythe's career – especially in the early years – his difficulty in securing a regular place was down to the fact that he operated at a time when another quality slow left-arm bowler – one Wilfred Rhodes – was also available. Blythe also suffered from health issues which appeared to be exacerbated by the pressures of international cricket. The exact nature of those issues is not clear – at times there have been mentions of epilepsy, though the evidence for that is not obvious – but whatever the condition, he found his international career disturbed. In 1909 he missed the Lord's Test against Australia after a doctor he had consulted at the wishes of the Kent committee advised against his selection. When the match went badly and the England selectors faced criticism over their decisions, they took the extraordinary decision to release Blythe's medical report to the press which outlined the "strain on [his] nervous system caused by playing in a test match [that] lasts for a week afterwards." His biographer (and relative) John Blythe Smart has also suggested that conflict between Blythe and C B Fry may have also played a part in his omission from England sides in the years before the outbreak of war.

* *

The Kent openers – Punter Humphreys and Wally Hardinge – had little reason to be optimistic that the pitch would be kinder to them than their opponents but at least the effects of the heavy roller might temporarily becalm the surface, the light was improving and they would not have to face the wiles of Charlie Blythe. Middlesex's opening bowling partnership of Tarrant and (J T) Hearne, however, were experienced adversaries and the batsmen would need to play a vigilant game. Neither bowled with express pace – though Hearne had the ability to push it through a little faster than his Australian colleague – but the combination of Tarrant's accurate left-arm slow-medium and Hearne's quicker off-breaks would be enough of a challenge on a drying pitch.

Wally Hardinge led the way, batting with his usual style: athletic, patient, with a watchful eye. Unfortunately, few of his Kent teammates seemed inclined to follow his lead. Whether an 'end of term' atmosphere had descended on the changing room or Hardinge's colleagues had decided that they were unlikely to survive too long on that pitch and so needed to make some quick runs, the modus operandi appeared to be to hit out. The result was perhaps inevitable and Hardinge had only three runs to his name by the time that two of his partners had been sent on their way; Humphreys (who had a reputation as a strong back-foot player good against the turning ball) was LBW to J T Hearne, and James Seymour found himself caught in the deep off the same bowler when he decided to try and launch the ball into the crowd. While, earlier in the day, Middlesex may have got away with a few loose strokes through errant Kentish fielding, the home team were in no mood to return the favour and every catch that went to hand stuck.

The sight of the formidable Frank Woolley striding to the crease would have given Hardinge more hope that the tumble of wickets would cease and he began to grow in confidence; watchful but ready to powerfully dismiss anything loose to the boundary. The partnership for the third wicket passed twenty, with Hardinge the dominant partner. Yet, with the score on 35, it was Woolley's patience that snapped and he belted a ball from Frank Tarrant high into the outfield where it was pouched by the large, safe hands of Patsy Hendren.

Another stylish batsman in the Kent ranks, Sam Day, did not hang around for long either; adding only a couple to the score before being trapped in front by J T Hearne. Sensing his supply of capable partners was diminishing, Hardinge became more aggressive, regularly hitting through the field to the boundary. At last, better support was found at the other end; initially from George Whitehead and, when he had been cleaned up by J T Hearne, from his captain Lionel Troughton. It was in partnership with the latter that Hardinge notched a hard-won half-century.

Comparisons between Hardinge's efforts and those of J W Hearne were obvious; the Middlesex man's play was more about placement, the Kent opener based on power, but both held steady in difficult batting conditions while wickets fell at the other end. Eventually, it was the power of Hardinge's strokes that was his undoing and, cutting a ball from Tarrant too close to Young Jack Hearne at point, he was on his way. His 58 had taken over an hour and a half, containing six fours and (thanks to overthrows) one five, and he left the field with the score on 91 for 6. None of the colleagues who had preceded him into the pavilion had managed more than six. Lionel Troughton, still out in the middle, had managed to make it into double figures but, before another run could be added to the total, he was quickly back in the hutch as well;

unwisely lifting J T Hearne into the deep, straight to the waiting hands of Nigel Haig.

When the first day's play came to an end, Kent had been batting for less than two hours and were in all sorts of trouble at 96 for 7. Huish and Blythe the not out batsmen.

Friday 28 August 1914
Day two

Next morning the players awoke to a much brighter day. The clouds had mostly lifted, the sun began to shine and the temperature promised to remain pleasant. If the drier conditions could take some of the devil out of the pitch, there was the prospect of a better day for batting. Kent were to resume the day still 109 runs behind the home side and needed unlikely heroics from Huish, Blythe, Freeman and Fielder if they were not going to concede a potentially unsurmountable deficit.

Play began at 11 in front of a growing crowd. The chance to catch a day of the last 1914 County Championship match at Lord's was being taken by good number and about 3,000 people would take their places by the end of the day. It was clear from the start that the surface had settled down somewhat and was a lick quicker than on the first day, though still one to navigate with caution while any morning dew evaporated.

Frank Tarrant and J T Hearne, who had bowled unchanged the previous evening, were to resume their duties with the ball. The Kent tail-enders had clearly decided to approach their task with a positive intent; no use hanging around waiting to be knocked over, perhaps. The predictable outcome was that runs came quickly but wickets fell that way too. A rapid eleven runs were added by the Kent numbers eight and nine before Fred Huish had his stumps rearranged by J T Hearne and – one run later – Blythe followed in an identical fashion. It fell to Frank Tarrant to finish the job and, twenty minutes into the day's play, he bowled Tich Freeman to bring Kent's innings to a close with only 116 on the board. Middlesex led by 89 and their hopes of a late challenge for the Championship remained on course.

Tarrant and J T Hearne had bowled just shy of 55 overs between them and had been an exceptional partnership. Hearne had the greater success, taking seven of the wickets to fall, conceding 65 runs. Tarrant was the more economical, picking up his three wickets at the cost of only 47. While J T Hearne could go and put his feet up for a long rest, Frank Tarrant needed to hurry back to the pavilion and get his pads on to open the innings.

Kent skipper Lionel Troughton had been alert to the slight change in the condition of the pitch and knew that, with a draw unlikely, if Kent were to turn this around, quick wickets were key. Accordingly, while his main wicket taker from the first innings, Blythe, would have the second over, Troughton threw the new ball to Arthur Fielder.

Fielder was a fast bowler in the 'modern' style who would maintain a consistent line outside off-stump, swing the ball away and hope to tempt the drive which would bring the slips into play. He had the ability to break the ball back in towards right-handed batsmen but would mostly hammer away with his out-swingers. The fact that his captain had entrusted him with the first over rather than Woolley was an indication of how conditions had begun to change. With the dampness all but gone, the pitch had regained much of its firmness and with it a yard of pace, something which Fielder, who was genuinely quick, should be able to exploit. And so, at twenty minutes to twelve and with the sun beating down on his back, Fielder tore in from the Pavilion End to try and turn the match around for the visitors.

Given that so many of their batsmen had struggled in the first innings, it was clear that if Kent were to stand any chance of getting back into the game, they would need to get on top quickly. Fielder and Blythe started well enough and, after an errant ball apiece were dispatched for fours, the bowlers began to make life difficult for the

Middlesex openers. A streaky boundary for Tarrant off Fielder seemed to awaken the Australian and he looked to go after the fast-bowler, scoring quickly enough to prompt Captain Troughton to signal to Tich Freeman to come on for a bowl.

By the half hour mark, though batting was still by no means easy, runs had come at one a minute; mostly off the bat of Frank Tarrant. As in the first innings, it would be the skilful Blythe who struck first. Harry Lee had more problems than his partner moving the score along and, with only nine to his name, Lee played back to a quicker one from the Kent spinner which sped past the bat and crashed into his stumps. 35-1.

Time for the hero of the first innings, Young Jack Hearne. The next hour or so was going to be the most crucial of the match. If Young Jack and Frank Tarrant stayed together, with Hendren in at four to add further power, the match could easily be taken completely from Kent's reach. If, however, Blythe, Freeman and Woolley could knock out the middle-order cheaply, the game would be very much alive.

Initially, it appeared that it was to be the home team that would have their way. Tarrant continued in a positive vein and Hearne took a liking to Freeman, crashing an over-pitched ball to the boundary early on and then hanging back for the cut to bring up the Middlesex fifty. A lead of 139 that, with only one wicket down, was threatening to become insurmountable.

Freeman had been put under pressure but it was the diminutive leg-break bowler who would bring the game back to life. The score had reached 64 when Tich managed to turn one past the bat of Frank Tarrant and send him on his way LBW. Out strode Patsy Hendren who took guard and promptly edged his first ball from Freeman to Woolley at second slip. 64 for 3; Freeman on a hat-trick.

* *

Alfred Percy Freeman – "Tich" due to his five feet, two inches of height – was in his debut season in first-class cricket. This was his seventh match for Kent and in the previous six he had only given hints of what was to become a magnificent spin-bowling career. Born into a cricket-connected family – his father was groundsman at Streatham; his brother John played for Essex – Tich came to Kent in 1912 at the age of 24 after a spell at Essex Club and Ground. In 1913 he took 125 wickets for Kent's second XI, prompting the county to give him his full debut the following season. War robbed the young spinner of some of his best cricketing years but, on County Cricket's return, Tich, then 31, made up for lost time. 'Only' 60 first-class wickets came in 1919 but thereafter not a season would go by, before his retirement from the county circuit in 1936, aged 48, without over one hundred wickets being in the bag.

Coming in off a short run, Tich would deliver his leg-breaks, googlies and top-spinners with remarkable accuracy. While he could turn the ball at will, it was his control of flight and variations in speed that did for many a batsman; often foxed by what had looked like a playable delivery. Such was his ability to beat a batsman in the air that 'stumped Ames' (or Hubble), 'bowled Freeman' was a regular note in Kent's scorecards; accounting for almost 13 percent of his first-class wickets. Happy to bowl for long periods without tiring, Tich was a captain's dream.

A run of consecutive English seasons with the wickets column registering in the 100s was broken in spectacular fashion during the dry summer of 1928 when Tich Freeman took 304 first-class scalps; a truly astonishing feat that had never been achieved before and probably will never be again. Every season from 1929 to 1935 saw Tich take over 200 first-class wickets and he notched up the rarest of all bowling feats – all ten wickets in an innings – an incredible three times (once each in 1929, 1930 and 1931). Add to that three hat-tricks and a final career tally of

3,776 first-class wickets at an average of 18.42 that stands above all except the great Wilfred Rhodes in history's bowling annals.

The only aspect of Tich's career that did not hit such heights was his Test career. Perhaps because he played most of his international matches on overseas tours with unfamiliar wickets, he struggled to replicate his county form when wearing England or MCC colours. Whatever the reason, 12 matches gave him 66 Test wickets at an average of 25. For a lesser bowler it may have seemed a respectable return, for Freeman it looked a curious anomaly.

Named one of the *Wisden* Cricketers of the year in 1923, Tich became an honorary life member of the MCC in 1949.

* *

It would not be three in three for Freeman this time at Lord's but Kent's tails were up and, only eight runs later, Woolley got in on the act, pinning Young Jack Hearne LBW. At 72-4, with the lead standing at 161, Kent were still in the hunt.

It was, though, Middlesex's turn to apply the pressure. Rather than dig-in until lunch to stem the fall of wickets, Nigel Haig and Henry Weston decided to counter-attack. Both batsmen went after any delivery that was pitched up, launching drive after drive, first off Freeman and Woolley and then off Blythe and Fielder. In the half-hour before lunch the pair added a valuable 51 runs, pushing the lead to over 200 by the time the break came.

While they enjoyed their Lord's luncheon, Middlesex would have been aware that their work was not yet done. It was true that Kent had only made 116 in their first innings but this had become a different surface. On day one it had been a damp spinners' pitch; now the sun had done its work, it was on its way to becoming a batsman's.

As so often happens, Lunch can bring a change in fortunes: batsmen's concentration can be interrupted; full stomachs can dull the sharpness of the eye; bowlers enjoy a brief rest for their weary bones and take time to re-think their lines of attacks. Or, perhaps, sometimes, lady luck just takes the opportunity to change sides. Whatever the forces at work, the lunch-break did the trick for Kent and it was not long before both batsmen were back in the hutch. Only five extras had been added to the score when Haig was trapped in front by Freeman and, seven runs later, Weston was comprehensively beaten by the same man, bowled while trying to hit-out. 135 for 6, a lead of 224.

A quick clean-up of the tail would have left the game in the balance; perhaps even slightly in Kent's favour on a rapidly improving surface. However, at that moment, in strode George Hebden, who was to prove a thorn in the visitors' side and tilt the odds firmly towards Middlesex. Hebden had been an occasional player for Middlesex since his debut in 1908 and it had taken until the 1914 season before he managed to post his first century; 101 in a victory against Lancashire in mid-August. He could never be described as the most classically-styled batsmen but was resourceful and could latch onto the bad ball with power and good timing. In the second innings against Kent he took a little time to settle into his innings but, once his eye was in, Hebden set about the bowling. Chiefly relying on drives and hits to square-leg he made sure the score pushed quickly upwards in tandem with, first, Leslie Kidd (LBW Blythe for 21, the partnership worth 57), then Stanley Saville (neatly stumped by Huish off Freeman for ten; 22 runs having been added) and, finally, alongside Joe Murrell. Hebden finally gave way for 58, edging behind a ball from Arthur Fielder that had leapt off the surface. His efforts had seen the score rise to 240-9, giving the home side a now formidable lead of 329.

If the match had begun to slip away from Kent via the bat of Hebden, things were to get even worse with the arrival of 'Old' Jack Hearne at the crease. Even at his peak at the end of the late-nineteenth century he could make no great claim to prowess with the bat – a career first-class average of 11.98 being testament to that – and now, with Jack at the age of 47, the Kent openers would have thought their time to pad-up would soon be on them. Jack, though, was not about to go anywhere. He equally had no intention of scoring any runs and took to steadfastly blocking every delivery that came his way. The tactic proved extremely effective and, by the time Joe Murrell was bowled by Frank Woolley, the pair had added another 36 runs to the total. J T Hearne's contribution? A deceptively valuable nought.

Kent had every reason to be disappointed. At 135 for 6 they had been truly in the hunt but, even with the talents of Blythe, Woolley, Freeman and Fielder at their disposal, had been unable to kill off the innings. Freeman emerged with the pick of the figures – having taken 5 for 87 – but forceful batting from Hebden and Murrell, stubborn resistance from J T Hearne and some lacklustre Kent fielding had allowed the Middlesex tail to help set a formidable total of 366 for Kent to chase for victory.

Formidable, yet not totally impossible. It was true that, if Kent were to pull off a handsome victory, it would mean making by far the largest score of the game. However, the pitch would be in a more batsmen friendly condition at the start of their innings than at any time previously in the match. It would also mean setting a Lord's County Championship record. On only three previous occasions had teams chased down over three hundred runs to win a county match on the ground – Middlesex in 1900, Somerset in 1902 and Yorkshire in 1910 – and, with Yorkshire's 331 standing as the highest chase, no county had ever made over 350 in a successful run chase. If Kent looked for historical encouragement, they would have found it in representative matches at Lord's where a winning score in excess of 400 had been posted four times. Even so, the odds were firmly with the home side and Kent would need a strong performance from their top-order batsmen to get even close.

Leslie Kidd may have only been Middlesex's acting captain but he had some wiles about him and, as Troughton had done when Kent were in the field for the second time, he decided to respond to the change in conditions and make a switch in his opening bowling partnership. With the pitch now offering far less off the surface, Kidd decided to try and beat the batsmen in the air and turned to Nigel Haig's fast-medium swingers; Frank Tarrant to come in from the other end.

It was an inspired choice and the 26-year-old Etonian amateur caused Kent problems from the start. In the first over, Wally Hardinge nudged a single, leaving 'Punter' Humphreys to face Haig. The contest did not last long as, before either the over was finished or Humphreys had troubled the scorer, he was making the long walk to the pavilion having edged Haig to the safe hands of Patsy Hendren at slip.

1 for 1

Things were not going to get any better for Kent soon. Haig's tail was up and, six runs and a bye later, he had another scalp: Hardinge. Kent's top scorer last time around was bowled by a ball that kept low, for four.

8 for 2

Kent's formidable task was starting to look an impossibility. Yet, if there was a chink of light, it was in the form of Frank Woolley making his way to the wicket. If there was any way out of this muddle for the visiting team, they would need every ounce of Woolley's talent.

They would also need others to give him support and that was where the immediate problem lay. Before Woolley could even open his account, James Seymour was gone, brilliantly stumped by Huish off Tarrant. He was still scoreless when Sam Day came and went; caught Hendren, bowled Haig for one. Woolley and George Whitehead managed to put on four runs between them but could manage no more before the latter was on his way as Haig's fourth victim, this time caught behind. Only half an hour had been played of Kent's second innings and the score stood at 13 for 5. The victory target of 366 a pinprick in the distance.

It was time for the captain to stop the rot and, in Lionel Troughton, Woolley finally found the support he needed to truly show what he was made of. The Kent left-hander quickly made the game look very easy with effortless sweeps to square-leg and flashing drives to both on and off sides. Troughton knew that his job was simply to hold up an end and let Woolley score the runs. After half an hour of the Woolley-Troughton partnership, Kidd rotated his bowlers; firstly bringing on J W Hearne for Haig and, shortly after, J T Hearne for Tarrant. Within fifteen minutes, the change had done the trick. It was 'Old' Jack – J T – Hearne who made the breakthrough and, taking the crucial wicket: Woolley, bowled for 40.[3] With the score on 67-6 and Woolley gone, the game was as good as over. For the last four batsmen to muster the remaining 299 runs was beyond hope.

Any Kent supporters at Lord's could, though, have expected slightly more fight than the debacle which unfurled before them. Before J T Hearne's first over was finished, another batsman was on his way: Fred Huish LBW for a duck. J W Hearne began the next over and soon got in on the fun, trapping Troughton in front before he could add further to the 12 runs he had put on with Woolley. It was nearly two in two when Tich Freeman immediately offered a chance to mid-off but it was not taken. It did not matter as, the very next ball, Hearne snuck one past bat and pad and onto the stumps. Nine wickets down and the match was all but finished as Kent's number eleven, Arthur Fielder, was not going to make people stay around for too long. Receiving his first ball, Fielder attempted to launch J W Hearne out of the ground and made contact only with fresh air; Joe Murrell completed a straight-forward stumping.

---

[3] Reports differ on whether Woolley was clean bowled by Hearne or if he played-on.

One hour and twenty-five minutes after Humphreys and Hardinge had begun the innings, Kent were all out for a pitiful 67; having not manage to add a single run after Woolley was dismissed at six down. The sudden nature of the late-order collapse was illustrated by the two Hearnes' second innings returns: J T took 2 for 3 off 2 overs (giving him nine wickets in the match); J W finished with 3 wickets for 6 runs.

Handshakes were exchanged and, while Kent were still due a trip to Bournemouth to face Hampshire in their last fixture of 1914, Middlesex were finished for the season. They cannot have known that the next time their county caps would be pulled on for a competitive fixture would be over four and a half years hence. As for the present, they had done their bit to ensure their Championship ambitions remained alive and could only now watch and hope that Surrey would stumble in their final three matches. They didn't. In the first, against Gloucestershire, Surrey won by an innings thanks to centuries from Hobbs and Knight, and when the final two fixtures were cancelled, Surrey claimed the title. The season closed, the cricketers of 1914 went their various ways, most to service in some form.[4]

* *

Not all of those who represented Middlesex or Kent in this their final meeting for five years went into the armed services. Fred Huish and J T Hearne were too old to enlist and so were not required to serve. Hearne, despite being over fifty by the time of the cessation of hostilities, would return to first-class cricket after the war. The Australian, Frank Tarrant, had perhaps the most unusual of journey during the war years, when he took up an offer to play cricket in India

---

[4] Service records for the 1914-18 war can be patchy - largely due to damage inflicted in the Second World War – so the occupation of some of cricketers during this period is not known.

under the Maharaja of Cooch-Behar. Tarrant played for many years after the War for the Europeans and Palatia in Indian cricket, where he once achieved the outstanding feat of taking all ten wickets in an innings and scoring a century in the same match. He remained in the game as an umpire after retiring from playing.

Tich Freeman, well within the age limit for overseas service but under the required height, volunteered for Home Service as a Special Constable. James Seymour, with a family (and a motor business to run), joined him. Arthur Fielder, who at 37 was on the cusp of the upper age limit for the regular army, also volunteered at home as an Auxiliary Policeman with the Kent Constabulary.

The Kent committee were keen to see their men take up arms and those professionals of serviceable age who were still in civilian clothes by early 1915 received a letter which asked why that was the case. It also offered to make up any shortfall in their wages caused by joining the services. Among those in receipt of this missive were Frank Woolley, Wally Hardinge and Punter Humphreys. Each had their reasons for not having taken up arms – Woolley had recently married; Hardinge and Humphreys both had family members reliant on their support – but the pressure from their county worked and all three volunteered. Woolley was initially rejected on medical grounds (compacted toes) but was eventually accepted into the Royal Naval Air Service where he helped rescue downed airman from a base at Felixstowe in Kent before being transferred to North Queensferry, Scotland. Wally Hardinge also spent most of the war on home shores, again with the RNAS. Punter Humphreys took a different route and signed up to the Royal Navy with whom he served in the Dover Patrol.

Pressure to enlist from within their county was not a preserve of Kent. Middlesex's Harry Lee recounted the circumstances that led to his call to arms. When war was announced and the drift of cricketers exchanging whites for military uniforms began, Lee was unmoved, viewing the war as nothing to do with him. Lee's only interest was his burgeoning cricketing career. It was the grand figure of Pelham Warner that began his change of heart. As county colleagues their paths inevitably crossed at Lord's where Warner cast a paternal eye over the junior professional. "Well, young Lee," began the county captain, "You look as though you'd make a fine soldier." Harry indicated that he didn't entirely agree with this assessment. "Aren't you going to join up?" enquired a surprised Warner. Harry said he was not thinking of it, prompting his captain to leave with a parting, concerned "hmmm". Standing nearby, listening to this exchange, was Harry's friend, the Middlesex wicketkeeper Joe Murrell, who upbraided him for answering back to Warner in that way. When Harry asked why, Murrell explained, "Well, you know, everyone'll be joining up, and you won't get much of a show around Lord's if you don't." Harry Lee signed up the next day.

Middlesex's Patsy Hendren was fortunate to avoid facing the guns on the front line despite signing up before Christmas of 1914 and being placed in the 1st Sportsman's Battalion of the Royal Fusilier's (otherwise known as the 23rd (Service) Battalion). A form of 'pal's' battalion, Patsy was grouped with other sportsmen including the lightweight boxing champion of England Jerry Delaney and fellow England cricketer Andrew Sandham. The unit saw action during the Battle of the Somme (Delaney lost his life there) but Patsy did not travel with them. Instead, after initial training, he was transferred to the reserve depot at Leamington Spa, where he saw out the remainder of the war. His brother, John, was not so lucky and lost his life in the Battle of Delville Wood; the same action that had killed Delaney.

At least three of the Middlesex eleven from their last fixture of 1914 faced action and yet managed to return home physically intact. Young Jack Hearne served with the London Regiment, Stanley Saville fought with the 2nd Essex Regiment and Nigel Haig earned the Military Cross for his service with the Royal Field Artillery.

Others were not so fortunate as to return in good physical shape. Kent's Captain, Lionel Troughton, rose quickly through the ranks of the

Royal Fusiliers to Lieutenant-Colonel where he led with great courage. In charge of a company in the Battle of Somme, Troughton led from the front in the face of intense enemy fire. For his gallantry he was awarded the Military Cross. In November of 1917, however, Troughton was captured by German Forces and saw out the remainder of the conflict in a prisoner-of-war camp. Eventually repatriated, he was discharged in 1919 on grounds of his physical condition.

Amateur George Hebden was quick to sign up for duty following the close of the season and was already in France by the end of 1914. Serving in the Royal Flying Corps he was injured in action but recovered sufficiently to play one final match for Middlesex in the 1919 season.

War appeared to have taken the life of one of Middlesex's opening batsmen. Less than a month after scoring his maiden century at Lord's, Harry Lee found himself facing an even greater challenge when he signed up for military service with the 13th (County of London) Battalion "The Kensingtons". By February of 1915 he was in France, by March had seen action and, in May, his Battalion took heavy casualties during the Battle of Aubers Ridge. Harry was among them. Shot in the leg, he lay injured in no-man's land for three days before being captured by the Germans. The news that reached England was that he was missing, presumed dead and a memorial service was held in his honour. Thankfully, while hurt, Harry was alive. He recovered slowly and was returned to England in October of the same year (after exaggerating the extent of his injury to the German authorities). On his return home, Lee was greeted with the news that the damage to his leg was such that he would be granted an honourable discharge from the army and that it was unlikely he would ever play cricket again. Once again, Harry defied the odds and, with treatment paid for by Middlesex and a spell playing and coaching alongside his old friend Frank Tarrant in India, he returned to county colours.

All of those who were wounded in action made sufficient recovery to play first-class cricket again, but for six of those men who took the field in 1914 for the home of cricket's final county match of the season, it would be for the last time. In the cases of Frank Tarrant, Fred Huish and Arthur Fielder their careers, interrupted by war, came to a peaceful end; Tarrant was enjoying his cricket in India, Huish and Fielder were aged over 40.

The occasional Middlesex amateur Henry Weston also made his last county appearance in the game at Lord's. His fate, though, is somewhat unclear. There have been suggestions that he lost his life while serving in the war but the evidence to support this remains elusive.

For two of the Kent side which succumbed to Middlesex at Lord's, their fate is well known. George Whitehead, having served in the College Engineer Corps while at Clifton, soon applied to the Royal Military Academy and passed the entrance examination with flying colours. The early months of 1915 were spent in training but, by September, Lieutenant George Whitehead found himself in action at the Battle of Loos with the Royal Field Artillery. Although he saw a great deal of action on the front, George avoided physical injury until appendicitis brought him down and he spent most of 1917 at home. By 1918 he returned to active service but this time as a pilot with the Royal Flying Corps, to whom he had applied during his convalescence. There was a tragic irony in that George saw the transfer from trenches to the air as one that would bring greater safety. "The danger of spills", he wrote, "is almost always due to over confidence and carelessness which is a very good reason why I shouldn't come to grief....Can you ever remember me trying to hit just because I had made fifty, or because I had hit a couple of fours unless there was no need for my side to make runs? Well, I don't see myself doing unnecessary stunts."

His last day began as one of celebration. On the morning of 17 October 1918, George Whitehead and fellow Lieutenant Reginald Griffiths flew low over Lauwe in Belgium. They were on patrol, looking for German artillery. As they passed over the town, George raised himself up in the cockpit and waved a flag to the people below who greeted them with great cheers. They made several passes over Lauwe, much to the delight of the local population. Still flying low, they headed towards the nearby railway station when their plane was peppered by bullets from a German machine-gun. Both men were hit and, by the time their crashed plane was reached by Belgian services, Lieutenants Griffiths and Whitehead were dead. Both were buried in the Military Cemetery the next day.

Kent and England's Colin Blythe was one of the first to answer the call of duty, along with his friends and fellow Kent Nursery graduates David Jennings, Henry Preston and Claude Woolley (brother of Frank and who played for Gloucestershire and Northamptonshire). Joined by David's brother Thomas (who would go on to play for Surrey), they were photographed as they enlisted together for the Kent Fortress Engineers. For most of the first three years of war Colin Blythe was stationed close to home at Gillingham. In September of 1917, however, both Blythe and Claude Woolley found themselves on the way to Belgium, having been transferred to the King's Own Yorkshire Light Infantry, where they would be put to work laying and maintaining railway lines through Ypres. On November 8, during the Third Battle of Ypres a shell landed close to their unit while they were carrying out work on the line between Wieltje and Gravenstafel. Woolley was injured; Blythe was dead.

Whitehead and Blythe were far from alone, of course. As far as can be told, 245 men with Test or first-class cricketing experience lost their lives in the conflict. Many more returned injured, both physically and mentally. Cricket would resume once more, albeit after an extended hiatus. For many of the young men of the cricketing field up and down the country - in counties, in towns, in villages - however, that late summer of 1914 would be their last.

County Championship, 1914
Middlesex v Kent
Lord's, London
27,28 August 1914 (3-day match)

Result: Middlesex won by 298 runs

Toss: Middlesex

Umpires: RG Barlow, CE Richardson

Middlesex 1st innings

F A Tarrant	lbw	b Blythe	16
H W Lee	c Huish	b Blythe	0
J W Hearne	not out		110
E H Hendren	c Whitehead	b Blythe	5
N E Haig	lbw	b Freeman	13
H Weston	st Huish	b Blythe	13
*E L Kidd	b Woolley		10
G L Hebden	c Troughton	b Woolley	6
S H Saville	c Woolley	b Blythe	8
+H R Murrell	b Freeman		12
J T Hearne	c&b Freeman		12
Extras			0
Total	(all out, 80.5 overs)		205

FoW: 1-0, 2-49, 3-67, 4-94, 5-118, 6-141, 7-153, 8-164, 9-185, 10-205.

Bowling	Overs	Mdns	Runs	Wkts
Blythe	33	9	77	5
Woolley	34	7	77	2
Freeman	11.5	2	42	3
Humphreys	2	0	9	0

Kent 1st innings

E Humphreys	lbw	b JT Hearne	6

H T W Hardinge	c J W Hearne	b Tarrant	58
J Seymour	c Haig	b J T Hearne	4
F E Woolley	c Hendren	b Tarrant	5
S H Day	lbw	b J T Hearne	2
G W E Whitehead	b J T Hearne		4
*L H W Troughton	c Haig	b J T Hearne	10
+F H Huish	b J T Hearne		9
C Blythe	b J T Hearne		5
A P Freeman	b Tarrant		3
A Fielder	not out		6
Extras	(b1, lb 3)		4
Total	(all out, 54.4 overs)		116

FoW: 1-7, 2-13, 3-35, 4-37, 5-63, 6-91, 7-91, 8-107, 9-108, 10-116.

Bowling	Overs	Mdns	Runs	Wkts
Tarrant 27.4	9	47	3	
JT Hearne	27	8	65	7

Middlesex 2nd innings

FA Tarrant	lbw	b Freeman	40
HW Lee	b Blythe		9
JW Hearne	lbw	b Woolley	19
EH Hendren	c Woolley	b Freeman	0
NE Haig	lbw	b Freeman	35
H Weston	b Freeman		18
*EL Kidd	lbw	b Blythe	21
GL Hebden	c Huish	b Fielder	58
SH Saville	st Huish	b Freeman	10
+HR Murrell	b Woolley		47
JT Hearne	not out		0

Extras   (b15, lb2, nb2)   19

Total   (allout,80.2overs)   276

FoW:1-35,2-64,3-64,4-72,5-128,6-135,7-192,8-214,9-240,10-276.

Bowling	Overs	Mdns	Runs	Wkts
Blythe	17	4	48	2
Woolley	15.2	4	56	2
Freeman	28	5	87	5
Humphreys	2	0	7	0
Hardinge	3	0	7	0
Fielder	15	4	52	1

Kent 2ndinnings (target: 366runs)

E Humphreys	c Hendren	b Haig	0
HTW Hardinge	b Haig		4
J Seymour	st Murrell	b Tarrant	2
FE Woolley	b JT Hearne		40
SH Day	c Hendren	b Haig	1
GWE Whitehead	c Murrell	b Haig	2
*LHW Troughton	lbw	b JW Hearne	12
+FH Huish	lbw	b JT Hearne	0
C Blythe	not out		0
AP Freeman	b JW Hearne		0
A Fielder	st Murrell	b JW Hearne	0
Extras	(b 6)		6
Total	(all out, 26.4overs)		67

FoW:1-1,2-8,3-8,4-9,5-13,6-67,7-67,8-67,9-67,10-67.

Bowling	Overs	Mdns	Runs	Wkts
Tarrant 11	0	32	1	
JT Hearne	2	1	3	2

Haig	10	2	20	4
JW Hearne	3.4	1	6	3

3. RECOVERY

England versus South Africa
Edgbaston, 14-17 June 1924

The signing of the Armistice on 11 November 1918 signalled not just the end of war and the human toll which accompanied it but the start of fresh challenges for the nations on both sides of the conflict as to how to adjust to the new, peaceful, yet inevitably changed world. Along with all other pre-war institutions, the questions posed to English cricket as to how to re-emerge from its self-imposed slumber, would mirror and be challenged by the post-war era into which it emerged.

It is tempting to try and provide a concise line of narrative for the period between the two great wars of the twentieth century. To construct an unbroken picture of recovery or of slump or of class turmoil. The reality, as with most of history, is more fragmented, confusing and contradictory. The 1914-18 War was characterised by tales of great human misery both at the front and at home, yet by many indicators it was also a prosperous time with near full employment, rising income levels (towards the later years of the conflict) and greater opportunities for women in the workforce.

In the immediate aftermath of the end of hostilities, the UK as a whole looked to be making a welcome and speedy recovery. With wages continuing to rise and unemployment remaining low, the years 1919 and 1920 saw middle and lower-class Britons enjoy better housing, affordable luxuries and more leisure time than ever before. Yet the image of a country gaily barrelling into the 'Roaring Twenties' belies the reality of individuals, families, communities and the nation still adjusting to the incredible loss of life and physical and mental injury bestowed by war, together with questions of how cope with the challenges of the immediate future.

Perhaps inevitably, the financial boom was to be short lived and, by 1921, with demobilisation complete, the economy struggled to cope with increased demands on employment, food and housing. From March 1915 to the end of the war, UK unemployment never rose higher than 1.2 percent; following a brief spike in late 1919, the figure was still under three percent during the summer of 1920. In May of 1921 it had risen to 23.4 per cent. While that figure would again fall – at least until the effects of the Great Depression began to be felt in the early 1930s – unemployment levels would remain between nine and fifteen percent for the rest of the decade; much higher than the norms of the 1880s, 1890s and 1900s.

The economic turmoil of the immediate post-war years was hastening and coinciding with great social and political changes. In Westminster, the Labour Party grew from a small insurgent parliamentary group to minority government in 1923 to, in 1929, the largest party in the House of Commons. Trade Unionism in the United Kingdom continued its pre-war development with increased membership, recognition and agitation, culminating in the General Strike of 1926. Women's role in society and the political arena was also in flux, not least due to the opening of previously closed avenues of employment during the years of conflict and by the extension of the parliamentary franchise to women over the age of 30 in 1918 (equal terms would be won ten years later). While no revolution was taking place, British society was changing. Cricket was to be buffered by those same winds and, like society, it also struggled to know how to adapt.

Only six months and five days following the signing of the Armistice to end the First World War, the County Championship resumed; Lord's and The Oval witnessing the first overs in the tournament for nearly five years as Middlesex took on Nottinghamshire and Surrey hosted Somerset. The decision to resume the competition so soon was far from universally welcomed; Sidney Pardon, the editor of *Wisden*, argued that the counties should be allowed a year to "make such arrangements as seemed best fitted to their own needs, while the game was being gradually brought back to its old footing."

For the game truly to be restored to its "old footing" was no doubt an impossible dream given the events which had occurred since stumps were last drawn at Hove in 1914. As the war lengthened year on year, questions had been raised as to whether the game of cricket would ever regain its stature when peace arrived. Lord Harris had been the loudest voice to reassure those who cared that, when the war ended, the game would re-establish itself in the heart of the English people. When peace finally came, the most immediate difficulty for the counties was finding enough players of sufficient quality to sustain a credible championship. Only 226 of the 489 men who had played first-class cricket in 1914 were to do the same in 1919 (180 out of 377 in the County Championship), a loss of over a half of all cricketers. Replacing those who had died, been injured, retired or were simply no longer playing at the required standard proved no easy task.

The war had not only robbed first-class cricket of many good men who would have still been in their prime and called time on others through age, it also disrupted many of the proving grounds for young cricketers. The decision to halt all first-class cricket meant that no longer could promising youngsters take their first steps in county, representative or university sides. Some league cricket, notably the Lancashire and Bradford leagues, did continue but, for the majority of men, opportunities to test their mettle in decent standard cricket was limited to (and dependent on selection for) intra-military matches and the occasional exhibition game.

In particular, first-class amateur cricket was hit hard. Young upper-class men, who formed a significant part of the amateur cricketing ranks, were disproportionately likely to be casualties of war. These were the army's junior officers; first over the top to lead their men into battle.

It is estimated that Eton alone lost more than a thousand former pupils; some 20 percent of the Etonians who donned military uniform. For those that did not make their way to the front, the suspension of university cricket ended a common route into the first-class game. Public school matches continued throughout the conflict but very few men in the history of the game had developed sufficiently by school leaving age to make the step straight into first-class cricket. Furthermore, the economic realities of the post-war period made it difficult for many amateurs to devote sufficient time to the game. This impact on the amateur cricketer would take a little time to dawn on the counties as, initially, in the rush to repopulate sides that had not operated in nearly five years and with demobilisation still ongoing, necessity led to amateurs filling many of the places. In the first match for each county in the 1914 season, amateurs made up 29 percent of the cricketers on display, the equivalent figure for 1919 was 44 percent.

That first season back, with many notable names missing, the 15 counties (Worcestershire chose not to participate) faced a challenge to consistently fill their XIs with players of a pre-war standard. No county was excluded from the problem but, numerically at least, Hampshire fared the worst, finding itself able, in 1919, to call on the services of only eight of the 23 men who had worn their colours in the truncated season of 1914. The 22 others who were called into Hampshire's service on the Championship's resumption were a mismatch of recalled county veterans and debutants with only school or local club experience. For example, selected for the county in August of 1919 were 48-year-old Ledger Hill, capped by both Hampshire and England and 28-year-old Lionel Isherwood, who had no notable previous cricketing experience. Both were to make only one appearance that season; indeed 17 of the 31 players appearing for Hampshire in the 1919 season would play in fewer than five matches.

As the 1919 season drew to a close, the overwhelming feeling was one of relief. First-class cricket, despite all the challenges it faced, had returned and for that alone the season was rightly viewed as a success. *Wisden*, in its 1920 edition, heralded, "The season of 1919 proved, beyond all question or dispute, that cricket had lost nothing of its attraction for the public." However, any expectation of an immediate recovery of the game's health to pre-war standards was to prove misplaced. The patient was, indeed, alive but would need some time to get back on his feet. The question of how that was to happen often split those who wanted to see the game to adapt to wider changes in society and those who saw cricket's survival in a return to a strict orthodox rooted in an imagined halcyon past.

Of particular concern for the long-term prospects of the county game was the decline in attendance. At first all seemed well in this aspect. In the immediate post-war period, despite entrance prices being inflated by the imposition of an entertainment tax, attendances swelled. Exact figures of match attendances are hard to find but in 1921 – a year in which a home Ashes series helped draw crowds – Yorkshire reported 284,677 paying spectators at their home matches. Inevitably, however, the end of the post-war boom had its effect and, while numbers fluctuated year-on-year, by 1929 that figure had fallen to just over 135,000 and would only again pass 200,000 three times between 1927 and 1939. Counties such as Yorkshire, Lancashire and Surrey, relatively well-off both financially and in terms of the crowds they could attract, were in a better position to ride any short-term storm than those such as Northamptonshire, who saw its annual income from gate receipts dip below the £2,000 mark at least seven times in the inter-war period. These figures did not reflect well when compared to other forms of mass entertainment, particularly football.

They often did not compare favourably to some of the attendances at league cricket either. In 1921, 1922 and the entire decade of the 1930s, spectator numbers for the Lancashire League topped those reported by Lancashire County Cricket Club and dwarfed those from some of the smaller counties. This trend, added to the ability of some of the bigger league clubs to offer good terms to their professional players, provoked a brief period of hostility from the MCC towards the leagues, who were looked on by some as having become a rival and thus a threat to the vitality of the first-class game. Pardon, in the 1920 *Wisden*, wrote of the "menace of the Lancashire and Yorkshire Leagues" who "constantly" offered professionals better terms than did the counties for far less work. Similar rumblings in the MCC concerning league teams enticing the better professionals away from the counties led the Advisory Committee to recommend that no player should be chosen for any representative match or overseas tour unless they made themselves available to their county whenever they were selected. In 1921 Lord Hawke went one step further by publicly castigating clubs in the Lancashire League for poaching county professionals.

Concerns over the success of the leagues were not simply a case of pounds, shillings and pence. There were also fears for the traditional spirit of the game and it cannot be a coincidence that they came to light at a time when society was changing around it. Once cricket had resumed after the armistice, its leaders were concerned to try and ensure the game not only survived but maintained its pre-war character, traditions and class distinctions. As such, the popular and often populist league cricket was frowned upon as a salutary example of the game where "bad strokes were cheered just as lustily as good strokes." This theme of a decline in the 'correct' technique on behalf of players was echoed in many quarters. Archie Maclaren, in his 1924 book *Cricket Old and New*, warned budding cricketers of the perils lurking in innovation and passionately bemoaned the methods of many modern batsmen, who, "in their eagerness to experiment…are getting away from those immutable first principles which men like W. G. Grace and F. S. Jackson – both innovators in their day – never for a moment departed from." Maclaren's warnings were embraced by *The Observer*, which asked, "If all is well with English cricket, why is Rhodes now, on his own confession, an industrious shadow of his former self, still one of the most successful bowlers playing? How is it that Quaife, a man over fifty, could say that he found run getting last season easier than ever before."

Neville Cardus in the *Manchester Guardian* was particularly concerned with the loss of the attacking play that had become associated with the pre-war 'golden' era of the game. He wrote of the inter-war period,

> "In these twenty seasons I saw...a change in cricket. It is not fanciful, I think, to say that a national game is influenced by the spirit and atmosphere of the period. In 1920 cricket retained much of the gusto and free personal gesture of the years before the war of 1914-1918. Then, as disillusion increased and the nation's life contracted and the catchword "safety first" became familiar and a sense of insecurity gathered, cricket itself lost confidence and character."

Equally as alarming for the great and the good of English cricket were the forces of social change, which, for many of the fearful gentry, had reached its zenith in revolution in Russia but was exemplified by the rise in the trade union movement and Labour party in Britain. Emancipation of working men and women, and the associated threat to the British class structure, was of no small matter to a sport which had so embraced and embodied social distinction. Thus, in this post-war period, talk of Bolshevism abound. Lord Harris, when on a mission during this period to ensure that counties only engaged the services of those players who met the MCC's strict qualification regulations, argued that "Bolshevism is rampant and seeks to abolish all rules and this year cricket has not escaped its attack." This made the ongoing debates about allowing professionals to captain county or international sides all the more apposite. The pretence of the purely amateur captaincy was maintained throughout the period even though cracks were glaringly obvious; by 1933, 13 counties had used professionals as captain when no amateur was available, at Yorkshire Wilfred Rhodes was widely known to be the de facto leader, if never officially captain, and even England was led by Jack Hobbs in 1926, albeit temporarily when Arthur Carr was taken unwell.

Concerns over the game's prospects led to a great deal of soul searching as to what, if anything, the cricketing authorities could do to maintain standards and keep the public's attention. The MCC had already shown itself willing to tinker with match regulations in response to post-war circumstance. The 1919 County Championship had been played as a series of two-day matches, with play extended until half past seven each evening. This change had not been welcomed in all quarters (most noticeably by *Wisden* editor Pardon, once again) and, with the counties experiencing the financial impact of the loss of a third day's cricket each time, together with the predictable rise in the number of drawn matches (from 49 out of 182 played in 1913 to 55 out of 124 in 1919), the experiment was abandoned and three-day fixtures returned in 1920.

Suggestions to improve the appeal of the game came from many observers and were a common topic of debate in cricketing circles. Proposed innovations included restricting the number of professionals in a team to three or four to encourage attacking 'amateur' play, shortening the boundary, penalising batting sides for every maiden bowled and even banning left-handed batsmen. While all of those were dismissed out of hand, some that took root in this time were later adopted. The eight-ball over used in Australia was proposed as a means of packing more play into a day and, supported by notable figures such as Pelham Warner, was eventually implemented in English cricket in 1939 (though the change was abandoned after the Second World War). Modifications to the leg-before-wicket rule to encourage a more even contest between bat and ball (and thus increase the chance of a result in three days) by allowing dismissals from balls which pitched outside off-stump were discussed and eventually, in 1935, implemented. Also, in an attempt to increase the likelihood of a result, the MCC Advisory Committee discussed lengthening the number of days Test matches were allowed to run. That the committee voted to maintain the three-day Test – with only the representative from Lancashire dissenting – prompted Archie Maclaren to write a stinging rebuke in the *Manchester Guardian* accusing Yorkshire and, by implication, Lord Hawke, President of the County, of placing undue pressure on the rest of the committee and stifling proper debate. Hawke had been prominent in opposing any proposal that Tests be allowed to play to a finish, saying the idea was "absurd" and would "change the whole spirit of English cricket."

During the early 1920s, the one aspect of the game that cast a long shadow over English cricket and provided a constant reminder of the difficulties that faced the sport, was the disappointing performance of the national team. Test match cricket had lay dormant since March 1914 and the Ashes uncontested for almost a decade when the England team, under the banner of the MCC, took sail for Australia in late 1920. If county teams were still in a process of recovery, managing the end days of many of their established players while searching for new talent, it was inevitable that this would impact on the national side, and so it proved.

With the domestic game still so unsound, the MCC had been understandably reluctant to resume international competition and had turned down an Australian invitation to send a touring side the previous winter. However, apparently bowled over by the level of Australian enthusiasm, the MCC relented when the invitation was reissued the following year. With not a huge wealth of obvious new top-class talent to choose from – particularly in the bowling department – it was a side of largely familiar names who took the field at Sydney in late December 1920 for the first Test.

Led by the veteran amateur J W H T Douglas, the XI in that first Test featured only four debutants and the remaining seven players boasted an average age of 36 and a total of 137 test matches under their collective belt. They faced a younger Australian side with extremes of experience; seven debutants played, while the other four men shared 96 Test caps between them.

It was, in the words of *Wisden*, a "disaster". The five Test matches were horribly one-sided affairs and the Australians ran out winners by 377 runs, an innings and 91 runs, 119 runs, 8 wickets and 9 wickets, respectively. In particular, England's bowling attack was found wanting, allowing the Australians to score 589 more runs than England over the course of the series while taking 17 fewer wickets. A glance at the Test series bowling figures makes for grim reading, even on the true Australian pitches. Excepting Rockley Wilson who played only one Test (finishing with match figures of 3-36) the series averages of England's front-line bowlers were 34, 41, 58, 59, 61 and 66. The batting, which promised to be England's stronger suit, fired in fits and starts. From the ten innings played, only one team score of over 400 and two in excess of 300 were posted. If Jack Hobbs' exploits were ignored, the individual returns looked mediocre; a century apiece from Makepeace and Russell and four players emerging with Test averages over 30 (but under 40). If batsmen returned boasting higher tour figures it was only through scores against state and local sides.

Hobbs, as so often the case, was a class apart. While not near his best return in terms of centuries and fifties (two and one, respectively), he ended the tour with a Test average in excess of 50 and a runs aggregate of over 500; some 150 more than his nearest team-mate.

* *

John Berry Hobbs, 'The Master', born in Cambridge in 1882, was destined to become not just one of the great batsmen but easily the most dominant English cricketer since W G had bestrode the game. Having a father who made his living from cricket – John snr was on the staff at Fenner's and, later, groundsman and umpire at Jesus College – the bat and ball was a part of Jack's life from an early age. It also gave him an early, solid grounding in the 'correct' techniques of batsmanship and, particularly, the importance of a straight bat; a principle drilled into young Jack by his father.

Such strong foundations allowed Hobbs to develop a batting game that was not only pleasing to the eye but would eventually give him mastery of all types of bowling on all kinds of wicket. Appreciation of his skills came quickly and from the very best. Making his first-class debut for Surrey against the Gentlemen of England in 1905, the opposing captain was reported to have stroked his beard and commented, "he's goin' to be a good'un." That captain was W G Grace.

The interlude in Hobbs' career brought by war – he served in the Royal Flying Corps – changed him as a player. Before 1914, he was a dynamic batsman; quick to the ball, playing with attacking intent, using his wrists to dispatch deliveries to all parts of the ground. For John Arlott, he typified "the 'modern' school, quick footed, forward or back, dealing with late swing, leg theory or the googly by fresh methods, involving, in particular, sophisticated on-side techniques." When Jack returned to the field of play in 1919, now a veteran of 36 years of age and soon plagued by serious injury and illness, his daring spirit had been somewhat tempered. In its place, was a classical, graceful mastery of his game. For some, while he remained the foremost practitioner of the art of batting, something had been lost. According to his England colleague Frank Woolley, "There were two Jacks, the Pre- and the Post-War Jack. The real one was the Pre-War." Even Hobbs himself once commented that he would wish to be remembered for the way he batted pre-war. Such laments, however, should only be viewed as comment on the style of his batsmanship because, in terms of his prowess, skill and run-getting, neither age nor injury would dull Jack Hobbs' dominance.

So prolific was the run scoring during Hobbs' first-class career, it becomes hard to find parallel in the English game; only once in his career - during his Surrey debut season of 1905 - did he have a serious run of bad form. Of course, some years brought better returns than others but, following his 1905 average of 25, Hobbs would never let it dip below 30 again and, during a career spanning 26 (war-interrupted) seasons, he would post a home-season average above 50 sixteen times (and over 60 eight times). His standout year was 1925 in which he scored over 3,000 runs, including 16 centuries, finishing with an average of 70.32. Or it might be 1926 where, in seven fewer innings than the previous season, he racked up 2,949 runs at an average of over 77 with a high score of 316 not out. Or it might be 1928 with its season ending average of 82, including twelve centuries and ten 50s from just 38 innings. Or it might be.....

When The Master put away his pads for the last time in 1934 he could reflect on a first-class career that had produced 61,760 runs at an average of 50.70 and brought the watching public a phenomenal 199 centuries; 100 of them struck after the age of forty.[5] His career total remains unbeaten today. During his illustrious career, *The Cricketer* was moved to comment that, "since Test matches were inaugurated England has possessed many good men to open the innings, but never a better than Hobbs." With apologies to Messrs Sutcliffe, Hutton, Boycott, Gooch and Cook, the same could be said today. Such is his legacy that Hobbs was deservedly named as one of *Wisden's* Five Cricketers of the Twentieth Century.

* *

---

[5] Figures from Cricket Archive. Earlier accounts of Hobbs' career give slightly different figures owing to changes on which matches are considered first-class (particularly, two centuries scored in Sri Lanka in 1930 are often omitted).

Hobbs and his fellow tourists arrived home at the end of the ill-fated winter Ashes series in 1921 knowing that it was only a matter of weeks before they had a chance of revenge on the old enemy. The Australians remained the toughest of all opponents but, on home pitches with English conditions, a better contest was expected. By the time the England players trudged from the field at the close of the first Test, defeated by 10 wickets, those hopes were well and truly dashed.

The first blow suffered by England occurred three weeks before the two sides met. Australia were taking on a strong L G Robinson XI, which featured some of the men who were expected to represent the full England side later in the summer. Jack Hobbs was proving to be the main obstacle in the way of the tourist once again. Mid-way through the second morning, Hobbs, not out on 85, looked to be marching to yet another century when, taking off for a run, a reoccurrence of an old thigh injury pulled him up sharply. His batting partner, Vallance Jupp said he could hear the muscle snap. It was a cruel blow to Hobbs and to any slim hopes England had of reclaiming the famous urn.

Without their leading run scorer, it was perhaps predictable that the first Test ended in a comfortable tourist victory; England failing to reach 150 in either innings. It was also a Hobbs-less side that succumbed in a similar fashion in the second Test, losing by eight wickets. Only a pair of scores in the 90s by Kent's Frank Woolley gave home supporters any reason to cheer.

The third Test, at Leeds, offered a glimmer of promise with a fit-again Hobbs returning to the starting line-up. That promise turned to disaster on the first afternoon when the returning Master became ill and was under the surgeon's knife for an emergency appendectomy before he had faced a ball. Hobbs was out for the rest of the series and England slumped to a 219 run defeat.

To few people's surprise, the Ashes returned to Australia that summer. What was most disappointing was that the contest − if one could call it that – had been so one-sided and the result decided in the bare minimum of matches. Sidney Pardon, in his *Wisden* Editor's notes, concluded there had "never been a season so disheartening as that of 1921. England was not merely beaten, but overwhelmed....At Lord's the contrast was humiliating."

The Ashes gone, the final two Tests were at least not to repeat the embarrassment of the first three. With some help from the weather, both finished in draws and even saw three English centuries: one from Phil Mead and two from opener "Jack" Russell. If these last two results saved some face, they did little to compensate for a sobering nine months for English cricket. Much like Hobbs, English cricket was clearly still in recovery.

There would, at least, be some time for both Hobbs and England to attempt their, inevitably linked, returns. England did not play Test cricket again until late December 1921 when an MCC party travelled to South Africa. For Hobbs, his international recuperation was to last even longer as - never the most enthusiastic tourist due to chronic sea-sickness - a combination of family ties, business commitments and lingering doubts over the effect of a long tour on a body that was still not fully recovered, led him to turn down the invitation to return to the Test arena.

Despite missing some key players, there was optimism that England could use the next winter tour as an opportunity to return to winning ways. The South Africans may have been playing in home conditions but it was widely viewed that they were the weakest of the three Test-playing nations and that the tourists would prevail. English hearts sunk, then, when the news returned from Johannesburg shortly after Christmas 1922 that the South Africans had taken the first Test by 168 runs; their captain, the talented Herbie Taylor, hitting a fine 176 in the second innings. England had still not won a Test match since the outbreak of war.

That streak would be broken in the New Year match at Newlands, Cape Town. It was a victory for England but by no means a convincing one as, chasing 173 to win, they stumbled over the line by one wicket, numbers nine and eleven at the crease. Matches three and four were draws, leaving the fate of the series resting on the final rubber at Durban; a timeless match to be played until a result was secured. On the sixth day, it finished; a 109-run victory for the MCC thanks to a century in both innings by Jack Russell. It was the first time that feat had been achieved in Test matches and was all the more remarkable given that Russell had been unwell during the second innings, forcing him to give up his openers berth for a later entrance at number six.

The series had been secured but, while the result was celebrated, few took the news as a reason for renewed optimism. As *Wisden* argued, "the trip, though in many ways highly satisfactory, did little to restore the damaged prestige of English cricket and afforded no real compensation for the crushing defeats so recently inflicted by Australia." Not many of the side returned with their reputations enhanced. On the batting front Russell had the most to feel proud of, finishing the Test series as England's top scorer with an average of 62 to add to his record-making double centuries in the final match. Phil Mead was the other player to average over 40 yet only one more – captain Frank Mann – could boast a return in excess of 30. Of the bowlers, Hampshire's Alex Kennedy dominated the figures, taking 31 of the 80 wickets to fall to a bowler, at an average of 19.

1924

English cricket entered the 1924 season with any hopes overshadowed by the reality of still how short the available talent was compared to the perpetual yardstick of the Australians. There had been no Test matches for England in the summer of 1923 and no overseas tour the following winter. What representative cricket there was –

particularly Gentlemen versus Players and an August Test Trial – left *Wisden* editor Pardon unimpressed. "One had an uneasy feeling", he complained, "that if our best men went on like that the prospect of beating Australia in the near future, either away or at home, must be remote." He did, however, concede there had been improvements both in the English county bowling stocks (Maurice Tate, Roy Kilner and Arthur Gilligan in particular) and in the standard of amateur batting.

It was unfair on the South African party that arrived in England in the spring of 1924, ahead of a Test series, that the summer matches were largely seen as prologue. An away Ashes series scheduled for winter 1924/5 loomed on the horizon and the ability of the national side to compete with the Australians was the prism through which all cricket was viewed. Anyhow, having defeated South Africa in the recent series on their own soil and with the promise of the return of Hobbs, an England victory was widely expected.

For the South Africans, the build-up to the first Test started badly and went downhill from there. A key culprit was the British weather. The South African team was young, inexperienced and, used to playing on matting wickets at home, needed all the time in the middle they could get to adjust to English conditions. In that respect, the fact that the early summer of 1924 was exceptionally wet dealt the tourists two blows. They not only faced an unfortunate amount of time sat in their changing room watching the puddles gather on the outfield but, when they did manage to cross the boundary rope, the South Africans found themselves faced with wet, then sticky, wickets in which to face bowlers who revelled in such conditions.

In their seven matches against county opposition before the first Test, the tourists finished with five draws and two defeats, including a thumping loss at the hands of Lancashire by an innings and 78 runs; potential England bowlers Cecil Parkin and Dick Tyldesley taking all twenty wickets between them. The only cheer for the luckless South Africans came in victories over Scotland and Cambridge University, and a couple of centuries from the bat of 45-year-old veteran 'Dave' Nourse. Their early experience of England was summed up by the final warm-up game against Oxford University. Fewer than 58 overs were possible and the match was abandoned before the visitors were able to bat. *The Observer* noted that since international teams began visiting these shores "no touring side can ever have undergone so disheartening an experience." The weather, though, had not finished playing tricks on the South Africans and, having served up muggy atmospheres and sticky batting tracks to adjust to, when the teams gathered in Birmingham for the first Test, the sun decided to shine and the wicket quickly dried out.

Those build-up fixtures also sent alarm bells ringing in the South African camp regarding the quality and suitability of their bowling attack to English wickets. Sid Pegler, as expected, was the tourists' main threat and took 38 wickets in the warm-ups at an average of under 15. The other leading bowlers – Claude Carter, Cec Dixon, Jimmy Blanckenberg and Buster Nupen – were certainly no disgrace (each took wickets and emerged with a respectable average) but the lack of any pace, exceptional spin or consistency of length gave the impression of an attack which lacked penetration and was "too much of a muchness."

With the start of the first Test match fast approaching, concern that their bowling attack would not be up to the task prompted the South African leadership to start looking around for alternatives. Understandably, international-level South African-qualified bowlers who could get to Birmingham in time were in short supply. One name did emerge: George Parker, a 25-year-old fast bowler from Cape Town who had been in England for four years and was plying his trade for Eccleshill in the Bradford League. With only one warm-up fixture left before the Test, Parker was summoned and pressed into action for his first-class debut against Oxford University. The decision looked vindicated as Parker bowled well on a surface that was not obviously ideal for a quick and was unlucky not to take more than his 4-34 before rain caused a premature finish (the usually keen South African catching let him down on four occasions). Three days later, Parker would make his second first-class appearance in the Test match.

For England, the choice of side looked a more settled issue; at least to the extent that the selection committee had clearly made up its mind some time in advance. Less than three weeks before the start of the South African series a Test Trial match between an England XI and 'The Rest' was organised to give the selectors an opportunity to see their options. As a spectacle, the Trial gave spectators a close finish – 'England' running out winners by three wickets – but, in terms of individual performances, it was an unremarkable game. For the England XI, only two scores in excess of fifty were posted (Percy Fender scored 81 in the first innings and Frank Woolley made 72 in the second) whereas three were conjured by batsmen for 'The Rest' (Holmes, MacBryan and Chapman notching the runs). Wickets were shared around both sides, with only 'England's' uncapped fast-medium bowler Maurice Tate catching the eye for his consistent economy. Nothing in the performances had made the selectors change their minds about their best side and ten of the eleven 'England' men were named in the Test squad announcement. Missing was the unfortunate Jack Hearne who had injured his hand whilst in the field and his place was given to Percy Chapman; a reward for his runs in the Trial. A twelfth name of Ernest Tyldesley, was added to complete the squad (despite the fact that he had not participated for either side in the Trial match; he would be twelfth man for the Test). The balance of the twelve was eight professionals and four amateurs, and from the latter group Arthur Gilligan was appointed captain.

Edgbaston, Saturday 14 June 1924
Day one

Pressure was on the England eleven who donned their whites in the Edgbaston changing rooms that dry morning. They were expected to win and win well. "Unless we can beat the South Africans very comfortably," opined *The Times*, "it will be of little use to send a team to Australia next winter."

Initial omens were not so encouraging for the English men. The weather that had denied their opponents good batting wickets in early summer had changed and the sun was beginning to beat down on the pitch. Accordingly, when Arthur Gilligan and Herbie Taylor met for the toss and the coin fell the South African's way, the England captain could have expected a morning in the field. Taylor had other ideas and, to the surprise of many in the initially small Birmingham crowd, invited England to bat or, in Frank Woolley's words, "put us in on a plumb 'un."

Taylor's decision had been prompted by his experiences of the past few weeks and, given that the Birmingham pitch had been under water only a week before, he may have thought that any 'stickiness' remaining would be present on the first morning and not thereafter. The emergency call-up of Parker had demonstrated the lack of confidence in the tourists' attack and so Taylor would have been keen to secure for his men any assistance, however small, from the conditions as he could. Alternatively, it may have simply been that he did not fancy his batsmen surviving long against the likes of Gilligan, Tate and Parkin on a wicket that might be still drying out. The decision was not universally derided; former England batsman turned journalist Archie Maclaren, for one, defended Taylor's move as "quite understandable" as, had he chosen to bat on the drying wicket, "the game...might have been virtually all over." Plum Warner, writing in *The Cricketer*, concurred, "had I won [the toss]...I should have acted as he did...[Taylor] had everything to gain and nothing to lose by putting England in."

Whatever the reasoning Taylor had for inserting England, it soon began to look like an error of judgement. The sun was quickly drying out the surface and producing a true, yet soft and slow, track that was good for batting. If the pitch was not going to give the South Africans' fragile attack any help, then the last man they needed to see strolling out to the middle, bat in hand, was Jack Hobbs.

It was a significant moment. Not only was Hobbs back, fit and firing for the first time since the Ashes tour of 1920/21 but, as he walked to the wicket, he did so in the presence of a new opening partner: Herbert Sutcliffe.

* *

Born 24 November 1894, Herbert Sutcliffe, was destined to become a Yorkshire and England legend. He was a stylish batsman whose "off-drive wore a silk hat and [whose] hook was a ready response to the aggressive intent of any bumper." Style and grit were not mutually exclusive and Herbert succeeded as much through determination as flair. On his death in 1978, *Wisden* was prompted to reminisce that Herbert "never knew a season of failure" and one would find it difficult to argue with that contention.

The demands of war meant that Sutcliffe was aged 24 before he could make his first-class debut, for his native Yorkshire, in 1919. As debut seasons go, it was impressive: 1,839 runs at an average of a shade under 45, including five centuries. It propelled him far enough into the national cricketing consciousness that, still a novice, he was named one of *Wisden*'s cricketers of the year for 1920. The following two years, however, did not see Herbert make the strides that many expected of him. His figures remained respectable but nothing more; averages in the low thirties and, in 1921, no first-class century to call his own. The 1922 season, however, started an extraordinary run of form and, from then until 1935, Herbert passed 2,000 runs every domestic season and posted more than 3,000 in 1931 and 1932; finishing the former of those two years with a first-class average of 96.96.

His importance to twentieth-century cricket was not just a matter of runs and averages but, rather, the new breed of professional he represented. Neville Cardus, writing in 1947, described Sutcliffe thus:

> "his hair resplendent with brilliantine and wore immaculate flannels and on the whole comported with an elegance which in the Yorkshire XI was unique and apocryphal.... The advent into cricket and into the Yorkshire XI of all places, of a Herbert Sutcliffe was a sign of the time; the old order was not changing, it was going; the pole was fall'n; young boys and girls level now with men; captains of cricket were henceforth called "skipper" by all self-respecting professionals, never "Sir." Our Sutcliffes and Hammonds, with their tailors obviously in Savile Row, have taken us far far beyond echo of Billy Barnes and his rough horny-handed company of paid cricketers of the 'eighties and 'nineties – savages born too soon to benefit from Mr Arnold Foster's acts of Education."

On the cricket field, Sutcliffe would become synonymous with the opening partnerships he contributed so much to; for Yorkshire, originally, Sutcliffe and Holmes and, later, Sutcliffe and Hutton. For England, starting at Edgbaston in 1924, Hobbs and Sutcliffe. Hobbs, the senior partner on that day, passed on some simple advice to his new colleague: "Play your own game." "Four words", Sutcliffe remembered, "they counted for much."

* *

At Edgbaston, the sun shone and this new English opening partnership began to make hay. The slow wicket gave the batsmen plenty of time to see the ball and the bowlers little assistance, calling into doubt not only the South African decision at the toss but also their selection policy which had included the quick debutant George Parker at the expense of players more suited to a slow wicket such as Claude Carter or Cec Dixon.

Taylor did what he could with the attack at his disposal. Parker opened with Sid Pegler and their initial overs were encouraging. Pegler, though restricted by an ankle injury, tested Hobbs with some well disguised leg breaks and Parker initially stuck to a good length, even finding a little swing. With disciplined bowling and a sluggish outfield restricting the boundaries, runs were slow to come, though equally, neither bowler truly threatened a breakthrough against solid batting technique.

Half an hour of settling in was enough for Sutcliffe and he started to milk the tiring Parker; hitting him for a couple of sumptuous leg-side boundaries. Taylor rang the changes to mixed effect. Blanckenberg, on for Parker, bowled a respectable length but it was when Nupen relieved Pegler that the fun started. Buster Nupen was a fast-medium right arm bowler who gained a reputation for being deadly on the matting wickets of his home but who could struggle on turf. Sutcliffe took an instant liking to the Johannesburger, scoring quickly with cuts and leg-glances, including an enormous six over square-leg. The captain then turned once more to speed of Parker, who unwisely decided to test the batsmen's abilities against shorter deliveries to a packed leg-side field. The ploy bothered Hobbs little and he joined in the run feast with relish. At lunch, England had reached 122 without loss; Sutcliffe on 61 to Hobbs' 57.

News of a burgeoning partnership between the Master, Hobbs, and his new partner must have spread, as the crowd had noticeably increased in size. Some estimates put the numbers at 10,000 or even 12,000, though official gate receipts had it nearer 7,000; a fairly small number for the first Test of the summer and certainly affected by the relatively expensive half-crown admission charge.[6] If the people of Birmingham were hoping to settle down to a masterclass from the opening pair, they were to be disappointed as, with only 14 more runs added to the total, Sutcliffe departed to a swinging yorker from Parker for 64; his first Test wicket.

Frank Woolley, the Kent left-hander, joined Hobbs and ensured that the rate of scoring was maintained, timing the ball perfectly from the off. Their partnership was brief, however, as, with the score on 164, Hobbs was trapped in front for 76 playing across a length delivery from Blanckenberg. Next in was Patsy Hendren who seemed content to play an anchor role to Woolley's assault on the South African attack. Aided by a now dry wicket and increasingly erratic bowling, the Kent man knocked the ball to all parts of the ground until, having made 64, he was surprised to see the umpire's finger raised after a ball from Parker clipped his thigh on the way through to the wicket keeper.

Hendren continued in his own way, accumulating runs as partners came and went. When he was finally dismissed to a smart catch at fine-leg for 74 the score had moved on to 356 for 6 and, by the close of play, to 398 for 7; all batsmen except Chapman ("shaping wildly and having his off stump taken") having made a respectable contribution to the score.

Yet not all spectators were happy with England's display. Hendren was a particular target for criticism for his cautious approach, cheered sarcastically by a section of the crowd for often seeming to have "dawdled in the midst of luscious half-volleys." *The Manchester Guardian*'s Neville Cardus, was particularly scathing, exempting only Hobbs, Sutcliffe, Woolley and Fender from his ire. The rest, he harrumphed, "did not look grand enough for the occasion." "Our

---

[6] *Wisden* states 10,000; the 12,000 figure is mentioned in several newspaper reports. The official returns reported 7,634 people having paid at the gate (not including members).

batsmen" he argued, "must carry themselves like masters and not like opportunists."

Although they fielded keenly, the weakness of the South African bowling had been exposed after lunch, with Pegler the only man seemingly able to exert any control. The novice Parker found the demands of Test cricket exhausting, maintaining line and length over an extended period impossible ("grotesquely erratic" according to Cardus) and his pace greatly diminished as the day wore on. Having bowled unchanged for more than three hours he was spent and, late into the evening session, took his jumper from the umpire and headed off the field without a word. His captain, Taylor, went to see what the matter was. "I'm simply whacked, I can't bowl another ball" replied the debutant, who didn't return that day.

Nevertheless, Parker had been the most successful of the attack, taking five of the wickets to fall. Even though at times he seemed uncertain of how to proceed. Frank Woolley recalled that at one point the South African had walked down the pitch to ask, "My field placed all right, Frank?" Understandably taken aback by the question Woolley replied: "Yes, I think it seems just right." Parker thanked him and walked back to his mark.

Monday 16 June 1924
Day two

Sunday having been a rest day, the players returned to Edgbaston on Monday morning to resume England's first innings. Given an extra day to feel the heat of the June sun, the wicket looked to have hardened some more. England's wicket keeper, George Wood, thought the pitch would give more help to the quicker bowlers, reporting before play started that it looked faster by a yard and a half.

That the remaining batsmen added only another 40 runs to the overnight score was less to do with any change in conditions and more with England's desire to move the match along. With all batsmen under instruction to hit out, Gilligan was the first to go, bowled by Pegler for 13; Wood quickly followed, also castled, this time by a Parker delivery that he was early on. Finally, the innings was wrapped up when Roy Kilner played too soon to a dipping Pegler full-toss and was caught and bowled. All out for 438, a record for England against South Africa. Parker finished with six for 152, the other wickets evenly shared between Pegler and Blanckenberg. It was time to see what life the, now dry, Edgbaston pitch could offer the home attack.

The South African innings would be opened by Captain Herbie Taylor and the free-scoring 23-year-old Bob Catterall. The young South African took strike and the innings got off the mark immediately with a no-ball from Arthur Gilligan. Returning to the top of his run, the England captain came in to bowl the first legitimate delivery of the innings and promptly knocked Catterall's leg stump out of the ground.

1 for 1

What followed was a brilliant spell of bowling from Gilligan and Maurice Tate; both bowling fast, with Gilligan regularly landing a perfect yorker. According to Tate, who had seen much of Gilligan's bowling over the past four years, he had never seen his captain bowl so well.

Fred Susskind, next to the crease, improved on his predecessor's performance by getting off the mark with a two and then keeping the strike with a single from the last ball of Gilligan's over. That was as good as it got for Susskind and, facing Tate's first ball in Test cricket, he planted an in-swinging half-volley into the hands of Roy Kilner at short-leg. A single off the sixth ball of the over from the incoming Dave Nourse meant he would be facing Gilligan's next and, six balls later, Nourse was heading back to the pavilion, LBW, for one.

6 for 3

As the carnage of the first three overs unfolded, Taylor had watched aghast from the non-striker's end, yet to face a delivery. Now joined by his vice-captain Mick Commaille, the two experienced batsmen attempted to stem the flow and began building a partnership.

Their efforts lasted precisely eight runs, seven of them scored by the skipper, before Taylor was cleaned-up by an exceptional ball from Tate, "bowled...neck and crop, spread-eagling his stumps all over the landscape." Only six runs later Jimmy Blanckenberg suffered an identical fate and was back in the hutch for four. It would be the second highest score by a South African in their first innings, only beaten by Taylor's seven.

20 for 5

Now it was Commaille's fate to watch the unfolding calamity from the relative serenity of the other end. With the score on 23, 'Nummy' Deane and 'Buster' Nupen were seen off by consecutive deliveries from Gilligan. Sid Pegler then did his best to provide the England captain with a Test hat-trick when he played around a ball that narrowly missed the stumps. Still, he would not hang around for much longer, seeing his wicket rearranged by Tate for a duck.

24 for 8

Only two questions remained: could South Africa avoid setting a new record for their lowest total in Test cricket and who, out of Gilligan and Tate, would finish with the best return? It was to be Gilligan that finished ahead in that particular duel, knocking over Tommy Ward for one and trapping George Parker in front for a duck. Commaille, having face 22 balls, remained unbeaten with a single run to his name. South

Africa had avoided the ignominy of setting a new lowest score, though only through the feat of equalling it.

30 all out

For the South Africans, it was a cricketing embarrassment. Not only had every one of their players failed to reach double digits on a pitch which had given up over 400 runs in the England innings but, with one bye, seven leg-byes and three no-balls, the eleven batsmen had mustered only 19 earned runs between them. The whole innings had taken only 48 minutes and was wrapped up before lunch. So few deliveries had been necessary to see off the South African batsmen that the ball, which would find a home in Arthur Gilligan's study, still clearly showed the maker's name.

There were some attempts at mitigation by the assembled press pack, mainly by ruminating on a change in the state of the pitch. Archie MacLaren who, in that morning's *Daily Express*, had unfortunately proclaimed, "the South Africans, I feel sure, will not be skittled out on Monday for a negligible score" was moved to argue that "the wicket was faster this morning, and the heavy roller which Taylor was bound to put on brought the "juice" to the top: the ball was certain to turn for twenty minutes, especially with the new ball." It was an assessment with which England's captain concurred. "All I did was hold the seam upright", claimed Gilligan, "and the ball moved violently off the pitch either way." Others, including Pelham Warner and the *Daily Mirror*'s correspondent, tried to give the visitors some solace in the undeniable fact that they were undercooked in terms of preparation and had, in their warm-up matches, not once experienced a pitch in character like this one.

Nothing, of course, could disguise or excuse such a total collapse but the one thing that all could agree on was the brilliance of the performances of Messrs Gilligan and Tate. Both had seemed unplayable, getting pace off the surface and causing the ball to break, often dramatically. Wicketkeeper George Wood said that he had never before seen the ball move as much as it did from Gilligan that day. Their figures, impressive as they were, did not flatter. Gilligan, despite having bowled while strapped up after having been hit earlier in the match, finished with six wickets for only seven runs; Tate with four for twelve.

It may have been Tate's international debut but his pairing with Arthur Gilligan was a familiar one on the county circuit, having been bothering batsmen up and down the land as Sussex's opening bowling partnership.

* *

Despite being only six months older and having made his first-class debut seven years later than Tate, Arthur Gilligan had quickly established himself as the senior of the two cricketers. A large part of that stemmed from the fact that, as an amateur, Gilligan was not only held in higher esteem by the cricketing establishment but was in line to be offered the captaincy of both his county and national side; positions which Tate, for all his ability, would have been highly unlikely to achieve.

As with so many talented, cricket-mad boys of his generation (and class), Gilligan was to find the well-worn path from public school to university to county cricket interrupted by war. Arthur had entered Pembroke College, Cambridge in 1914 but within a year found himself at the Western Front, serving as a Captain in the Lancashire Fusiliers. When the war came to an end he returned to Pembroke to continue his education and cricketing pursuits.

While his overall figures on the cricket field for Cambridge during the 1919 season were unremarkable, Gilligan's timing was impeccable and he put in a couple of notable performances at key moments to bring his name to the attention of county committees. An excellent attacking century while batting at number eleven against Sussex and five wickets on the last day of that year's Varsity match at Lord's turned heads on the Surrey committee and Gilligan had made his county debut by the end of the season.

Gilligan's first steps into county cricket with Surrey would prove brief and unspectacular but he would make a little more progress the next season; this time with Sussex. The invitation from Hove had been most welcome as Arthur had been a supporter of the county as a boy and, thanks to qualification via a Sussex-born grandmother, his brother Harold was already representing the team. He made his Sussex debut in 1920 and pledged his cricketing attention to the county full-time in 1921, having left Cambridge to take up a position in his father's firm. His bowling figures in those years were respectable, if expensive, and the overall view of Gilligan was of a quick, yet patchy, bowler and a dashing, if vulnerable, batsman who only really excelled in his fielding at mid-off.

Though not setting the cricketing world alight with his performances, Gilligan was a Sussex regular and an amateur, the combination of which led him to being offered the county captaincy at the start of the 1922 season. It was a pivotal point in his career that either inspired or coincided with an upturn in his results with both bat and ball; scoring close to a thousand runs and taking over one hundred wickets in that season at an impressively low average. As a captain he also drew admirers for the attractive nature of Sussex cricket under his charge, if not, perhaps, always for their results.

His assent to the England captaincy began at the end of 1922 when Gilligan was picked to tour South Africa by the MCC and instantly installed as vice-captain under Frank Mann. He may have been a debutant but he was one of the few amateurs and, with the main alternative Percy Fender having developed a habit of irritating the cricketing authorities ("incidents attached themselves to Fender like barnacles to a ship", according to his biographer Richard Streeton), the genial Gilligan's position was assured.

Throughout 1923 Gilligan continued to grow in stature as a bowler and comfortably achieved the feat of a thousand runs and a hundred wickets in the season. By the start of 1924 he was one of the best fast bowlers in England, if not the world; quick and, according to *Wisden*, while "his action may have been slightly low...he was accurate and regarded it as a cardinal sin to bowl short." His performances in 1923 led him to being named one of *Wisden*'s five bowlers of the year, though, in a rather churlish tribute it noted he was not "among [the] great fast bowlers" but, it conceded, "he is a very good one, combining with the right temperament and tireless energy just the extra bit of pace that to many batsmen is so distasteful."

When Frank Mann was deemed too old and out of form to be reappointed England captain for the 1924 home series against South Africa, Gilligan was the man for the MCC panel and, at Birmingham, he led the team for the first time. Unfortunately for Gilligan, his performance in that match was to be the peak of his career. Between the first and second Tests, representing the Gentlemen at The Oval, he was struck near his heart by a rising delivery from Frank Pearson. Unwisely, by his own admission, Gilligan continued in the game, scoring a second-innings century. The damage done, whether physical, psychological or both, was lasting and Arthur Gilligan was never the same bowler again. He continued as England captain until the end of the next Ashes tour and played for Sussex for another eight years but had lost his mojo; never, after 1924, taking more than a hundred wickets in a season or achieving them at an average of lower than twenty.

If Gilligan had been one of England's two best quicks, the other was his Sussex partner Maurice Tate, who was destined to become one of the game's greats. A well-liked and light-hearted man with unusually large feet, Maurice, known as "Chub", had been born into the world of cricket as the son of Fred Tate, a Sussex professional who had represented England. Despite such heritage, Maurice showed little aptitude for the game as a child, recalling that, according to his family, he "was an absolutely dud cricketer and even as late as the age of fifteen it was thought that [his] only chance in sport was as a soccer full-back."

Regardless of these apparent limitations, and having played little organised cricket as a youth, his father was still asked by the Sussex committee if he would send Maurice to Hove for a trial. He was fifteen, had recently left school and begun work as a fitter. In the nets, the younger Tate quickly demonstrated his severe limitations with the bat but Arthur Millward, the ex-Worcestershire professional who was coaching at Sussex, saw in Maurice a useful off-break bowler and took him on as a ground-staff bowler at a pound a week. Two years later, aged only seventeen, Maurice made his County debut away to Northants, batting at number eleven.

Maurice had received very little formal training but had clearly picked up much from watching his father as, in his approach to the wicket and bowling style, he was a chip off the old block. After one county appearance in 1912 and four in 1913, he was farmed out to Eastbourne to gain more experience. It was a good move, allowing him to work on his batting, scoring runs up the order for the local club. By the end of the 1914 season Tate had begun to establish himself in the Sussex team; even moving up to bat at number eight.

War intervened and Maurice signed up; assigned to the 2nd/6th Sussex Cyclists Battalion and then to the 6-inch howitzers Royal Artillery as a signaller. Sent to the Western Front, Tate said of his service, in characteristic style, "I didn't see a lot of fun in the War." When he returned to Sussex in 1919 he had transformed from a lithe boy to a sturdy man with wide hips and heavy shoulders. He also began to impress more with his batting skills. Making 69 runs at number eight in his first innings back, Tate found himself swiftly promoted to four. Though he would not always remain at such lofty heights, he produced some decent scores, ending the 1919 season with over a thousand first-class runs at an average of a shade over 27, including a maiden century against Lancashire at Old Trafford and four half-centuries to add to his haul of 48 wickets. It was not a spectacular return but Maurice ended the year with every right to call himself an all-rounder. His batting would continue to improve over the next couple of years, the highlight being a score of 203 against Northamptonshire at Hove in 1921.

For Tate, his breakthrough year came in 1922 and Arthur Gilligan played a large part in the leap forward. Bowling in the nets to his county captain, Maurice let a quicker one go and would have smiled at the sight of Gilligan's stumps being uprooted. Tate returned to his usual slow off-breaks next ball and found the delivery being returned with interest via his captain's bat. Bowler's pride kicked in and Maurice tried his faster ball twice more, taking the stumps both times. Gilligan could see this was more than a fluke. He immediately advised his professional to change his style of bowling, telling him, "I have never seen anything fizz off the wicket like those fast deliveries of yours." In the next match Tate took 8-32 in Kent's second innings at Tunbridge Wells.

From then on, Maurice was a fast-bowling all-rounder; perhaps not quite as quick as Gilligan through the air but with an uncanny knack of seeming to get speed off the wicket. In his first season with the new approach he took 119 wickets at 17 apiece, the next he would break the two hundred mark at an average of fewer than 14 and became, along with Gilligan, one of *Wisden*'s bowlers of the year. In fact, except for 1933 when he took 99 scalps, Maurice would take over one hundred first-class wickets in every domestic season from 1922 to 1935. He would do the double of a thousand runs and one hundred wickets nine times. By the time he ended his professional playing career in 1937, Tate had taken 2,784 first-class wickets, scored over 21,000 runs plus 39 England caps, 155 Test wickets and an international century to his name; a great return for a man who, like most of his contemporaries, had lost some of his best years to the war.

**

Because of the premature end to the South African innings Tate and Gilligan had no time to savour their impressive bowling feat, as the latter, with no hesitation, enforced the follow-on. So, only an hour after taking guard for the first innings, Herbie Taylor, accompanied by Mick Commaille, prepared to face their tormentors again.

This time, it seemed an entirely different game and, in the 35 minutes before lunch, 34 runs were added by two batsmen who appeared mostly comfortable. Given how little time had elapsed between first and second innings, it is unlikely that such an improvement in the tourists' fortunes could be pinned on a radical change in conditions. What seemed a more likely explanation was a combination of the batsmen having started to adjust to the Edgbaston pitch, a bowling attack that, while not spent, had continued unchanged for over an hour, a degree of assistance by some ragged English fielding and the raw fact that it was unlikely that the South Africans would perform so poorly again.

Following lunch, the batsman took up from where they had left; Taylor collecting runs on the leg-side and playing attacking shots either side of Hobbs at cover-point, while Commaille dug in for a more dogged approach. It was clear that the duo of Gilligan and Tate was not going to be enough on their own this time round. Fortunately for the captain, he could throw the ball to county cricket's leading wicket-taker who, after only eleven matches (and just 20 innings bowled) in the 1924 season, boasted 89 first-class wickets at an astonishing average of 8.35.

**

Cecil Parkin – 'Ciss' – was one of crickets most watchable characters. Mercurial, colourful and plain-speaking, he was capable of entertaining crowds and infuriating administrators in equal measure. In particular, he had an unfortunate habit of running afoul of the influential Lord Hawke. Their paths first crossed when Parkin joined Yorkshire as a professional; making his first-class debut in 1906, aged 20. It was to be his lone appearance for the county as, soon after his debut, a complaint was received from the MCC as to his credentials for qualification. It was noted that Ciss had been born twenty yards the 'wrong' side of the border with County Durham and, as a result, his association with Yorkshire was terminated. Lost was the irony that President of the County Cricket Club, the Lincolnshire-born Hawke, had himself managed to carve out a 30-year playing career with the county.

Ciss crossed the Pennines and found a home playing for Church in the Lancashire League. There, and in occasional minor county cricket for Durham, Parkin continued to develop his bowling skills until he was invited to fill a player shortage for Lancashire. It was his second first-class appearance, taking place some eight years after his first. It had been a long time in coming but Parkin immediately proved his worth, taking seven wickets in each innings and finishing with match figures of 14 for 99. He would play a further five matches for his new county that year and end the season with 34 wickets at an average of under 16.

Parkin's resurrected career was to be interrupted again by the outbreak of war and he would have to wait a further five years to make his eighth first-class appearance, now aged 33. On his return Ciss took 7 for 86 in the match against Derbyshire and a handsome dividend of 14 for 123 against his old county Yorkshire in the next; bowling Lancashire to victories on both occasions. Such performances were enough to win Parkin an invitation to represent the Players against the Gentlemen at The Oval. He would represent the Players in the fixture twice in 1919 and three times in 1920, a turn of events that would lead to further disapproval from the quarters of Lord Hawke. The Yorkshire President's problem was that during 1919 and 1920 Parkin had not been freely at Lancashire's disposal. Ciss, in 1919, had accepted an offer to play for Rochdale in the Lancashire League on a weekly salary, with a £100 guaranteed benefit and an under-the-table £20 signing fee; an admirable set-up for a league professional at the time. This commitment to Rochdale meant that his availability for Lancashire was limited to only four appearances in 1919 and five the following year. As such, his inclusion in the Players' ranks flew in the face of the MCC resolution of January 1919 that warned against the selection of players for representative matches who were not fully available for their county side. This state of affairs rankled Hawke to such an extent that he used the soap box of a Yorkshire County Committee meeting to broadcast his "strong disapproval" of Parkin's selection. The Yorkshireman's feathers must have been further ruffled, then, when, still tied to Rochdale, Cecil Parkin was included not only in further Players' XIs but also in England Test match sides for away and home Ashes series in 1920 and 1921. It would not be until 1922 that Parkin forwent his league commitments and pledged his availability to Lancashire full-time.

As a bowler, he possessed a box of tricks. Commonly listed as an off-break bowler, it was a label that hid more than it revealed, especially in the earlier part of his career. Measuring over six feet, Parkin would stand tall at the top of his run before beginning a curved path to the wicket. Into his delivery stride, it was anyone's guess as to what would come down. Bowling at a good fast-medium pace he could break the ball to the leg or off (his long fingers imparting great spin), deliver an accurate yorker and a cunning slower ball. At times it seemed Parkin was on a mission to bowl six different types of ball an over, a trait that led Plum Warner to complain that it was often impossible for a captain to set a field to him.

He quickly became a crowd favourite, not simply for his invention and wicket-taking ability but also because of his antics in the field and at the crease. For Parkin cricket was, and should be, fun and he was not afraid to show it. One of his favourite tricks of flicking a rolling ball from foot to hand was captured by the Pathé cameras and replayed in slow motion for cinema audiences to admire. Parkin's joie-de-vivre was not appreciated by all observers. *The Times*, in the run up to the 1924 South African series, described him as a "buffoon" good for those who "persist in regarding a cricket match as a jollification." Even his local *Manchester Guardian* complained of the effect Parkin's larking had on his batting performance, asking why he did not "put away his motley for a while and get to a studious cultivation of his unmistakeable talent for making at least a score of runs an innings?" *The Observer* followed in a similar vein, arguing that Parkin could be good for fifteen or twenty runs if he could just "regard the wicket as a wicket rather than a music hall stage." Such grumbling meant that disquiet was never far away where Parkin was concerned and, despite his obvious ability, his place in the England side was frequently a subject of criticism and debate in the press, often ending with a grudging acceptance that there was no one better for his place.

Still, his wicket-taking ability, especially on sticky-wickets, was not in doubt. Parkin's first full county season of 1922 saw him pick up 189 wickets at an average of 17 and a half; bettered only by Parker of Gloucestershire, Kennedy of Hampshire and Freeman of Kent. The following year he passed 200 first-class wickets for the first time with an even lower average, only beaten by his future England team-mate, the great Maurice Tate. Unsurprisingly, the 1924 *Wisden* almanac included Parkin alongside Tate and Gilligan in its 'Five Bowlers of the Year', remarking there was "something fascinating in his ceaseless experiments", though adding it was "a misfortune that he has never yet had the advantage of playing under a great captain." The issue of how Parkin was managed on the field was about rear its head again.

* *

Coming on first change for Gilligan in the second South African innings at Edgbaston, however, Parkin could find none of his usual zip,

The Times noted "his changes of pace were detected readily, and his faster balls did very obviously break." *The Manchester Guardian* was harsher in its assessment, "nobody who has not witnessed the game will understand from Parkin's analysis how utterly harmless his attack had seemed." Parkin was showing no sign of achieving any breakthrough and his mood would not have been improved when he dropped an easy chance from Commaille, having unusually (and oddly) found himself fielding in the slips. His captain, Gilligan, made up his mind that Ciss was a sticky-wicket bowler alone and, after a fruitless 16 overs all bowled on that second day, consigned county cricket's leading wicket-taker to fielding duties for the rest of the match.

Unfortunately for Gilligan, he did not have much luck with his bowling changes at either end as Percy Fender proved expensive and Roy Kilner economical but unthreatening. It was only when Gilligan turned again to Maurice Tate that the first wicket fell. After seeing two chances missed off his bowling, the Sussex man took a fine low return catch to dismiss the captain, Taylor, for 34.

On this occasion, one did not bring two and, despite the loss of their skipper, the South African batting continued largely unaffected; Fred Susskind joining Commaille at the crease. Susskind was a former Middlesex and Cambridge University batsman with a somewhat cramped style, whose use of the pads to stiffen his defence brought criticism from some quarters. He could also play some "capital" shots and his abilities were fully on display at Edgbaston as he took a more attacking approach to the innings than his resilient compatriot at the other end. The second wicket partnership pushed the score past one hundred before Commaille's resistance was finally broken, edging Tate to the slips for a gritty 29. Joined by the powerful and attacking left-hander, Dave Nourse, Susskind soon raised his bat for an attractive fifty but was cleaned up by a snorter of a delivery from Gilligan shortly after; the pair having added a half-century of runs. Nourse followed his partner back to the pavilion, accounted for by Gilligan for the second time in the match, this time caught behind. At 161 for 4, England looked firmly back in charge. Though only a little more than an hour remained on the clock, England must have harboured hopes of wrapping up the match within two days.

The two new batsmen – Bob Catterall and Jimmy Blanckenberg – had other ideas and took about the attack with gusto. Both used the drive frequently and effectively; Catterall employing it with style, Blanckenberg with power. With shots being played at both ends and the England attack looking toothless beyond Gilligan and Tate, the scoreboard ticked along; over one hundred runs added in the last hour. They were not faultless innings, especially for the Capetonian Blanckenberg, and Tate saw two further chances missed off his bowling. When stumps were finally drawn with the total at 274 for 4, both men had posted unbeaten half-centuries and South Africa had made its highest score in a Test match in England. It had been an admirable recovery and, while talk of a shock South African victory was fanciful, at only 134 runs behind, the tourists threatened to at least make England bat again.

Tuesday 17 June 1924
Day three

A moderate sized crowd – no doubt again a result of the high entrance fee – gathered for another sun-blest Birmingham day. England may have been in an overwhelmingly dominant position and expectant of emerging with the spoils of victory but, as play got under way, the story that began to emerge was of the brilliance of Bob Catterall's batting.

Catterall took up from where he had left off the evening before. The young South African drove strongly, his power based on exquisite balance and timing as much as natural strength. His wrists were quick, allowing balls that were angled into the body to be turned late to square-leg and anything dropped too wide was dismissed by a "hammer blow" of a square cut. He faced six English bowlers in his innings and only Tate could be said to have caused him any trouble. It was a display that drew plaudits from around the ground and across newspapers the next day.

At the start of play, things had not looked so good for Catterall or the South African team. Jimmy Blanckenberg was first to take strike, facing Gilligan from the Pavilion End. Gilligan's first ball was ill-directed and a wide was quickly indicated by the umpire. His next was more like it – on target, a touch of out-swing – caught the edge of the bat and flew high to the right of Percy Chapman at second slip. A shorter man would have watched the nick sail by, but Chapman, an excellent fielder standing six feet three inches tall, pulled off a spectacular one-handed catch with the ball almost past him. Blanckenberg had gone for a well-made 56.

Matters did not improve for the visitors when Nummy Deane, who had been limping since he emerged from the pavilion nine runs earlier, was unwisely called back for a fourth run by Catterall and promptly run-out by Wood via a strong throw from Hobbs. Deane's replacement, Buster Nupen, was soon on his way LBW to Tate for 5 and, at 295 for 7, it looked like Bob Catterall was going to run out of support before he could reach three figures.[7]

Relief came in the form of the doggedness of wicketkeeper Tommy Ward and the weaknesses apparent in England's change bowling. Ward supported Catterall ably, defending or leaving anything around or outside off and picking up runs on the leg-side. He used his feet well, even advancing on the speedy Gilligan; a tactic which prompted his

---

[7] There is confusion in contemporary reports over the dismissals of Nupen and Pegler, with some (but not all) newspaper articles describing Pegler as the LBW victim and Nupen caught by Hobbs. I have relied on the official scorecard here.

English fellow 'keeper to showcase his impressive reactions by faultlessly standing up to the quick bowler.

Gilligan, however, was tiring and after a couple of fast half-volleys had been returned with interest to the boundary, he decided it was time for a change. It was a sign of the lack of confidence he had in the abilities of his previous change bowlers, however, that, when the switch was made, Parkin, Kilner and Fender were overlooked it favour of the left arm of Frank Woolley. It was not one of the captain's more successful decisions. Catterall took a liking to the new man and, after the second six from the Kent all-rounder's bowling had bounced off the pavilion roof, Woolley was relieved of duties.

It took the return of Gilligan to finally undo the partnership and, with the score on 350, got a delivery to evade bat and make its way, via pads, onto the stumps. With only Pegler and Parker to come, the game as a contest was up. The only question that remained was whether those last two batsmen could stay at the crease long enough for Catterall to make a deserved century. The South African was not going to wait to find out and, facing the formidable Tate, hit three crisp boundaries in an over that allowed him to celebrate an impressive ton. The Edgbaston crowd, which had been cheering him on as his score neared the hundred, rose as one in acclaim. It was not only a doughty and admirable feat given the events of the first innings but also made Catterall the first South African to have reached three figures in England.

For his team, however, the end was nigh. Pegler had done his job supporting Catterall to his century and was soon out mistiming a drive straight to Hobbs. Parker emerged to immediately demonstrate that he had been included in the side for his bowling. Parker's flat-batted flail at his first ball sent a warning to Catterall that time was not on his side and the century-maker responded by hitting out at almost every opportunity. His luck lasted for a short while – seeing easy catches dropped by Woolley and Kilner off successive balls – before the next chance was accepted by Hobbs to end the innings and the match. Catterall out for 120, England had won by an innings and 18 runs.

While England had won the match, the plaudits went to the South Africans for what was considered a brave recovery and Catterall, in particular, for his splendid innings. The press was less kind to the English effort in the second innings with writers sharpening their pens to skewer England's fielding and the quality of the change bowling, given that (one run-out aside) all South African wickets in the match had fallen to either Gilligan and Tate.

As most of the England team celebrated their victory, one of their eleven appeared to be less than satisfied. Ciss Parkin was reported to be furious. Having had a miserable game – left un-bowled in the first innings and barely used in the second – it seemed that, not for the first time in his career, he felt undervalued and mismanaged by his captain.

In his regular column for the *Weekly Dispatch*, Parkin let rip:

> "On the last morning of the Test match...it was necessary for the England captain to make many bowling changes. During these changes I was standing all the time at mid-off, wondering what on earth I had done to be overlooked. I can say that I never felt so humiliated in the whole course of my cricket career.... Mr Gilligan bowled himself, he used Tate; he called up Frank Woolley; he went on again himself; he called back Tate; he asked Roy Kilner to bowl. And all the time I was standing there wondering how I had ever managed to get to the top of the English bowling averages this season. I admit that on Monday I was not at my best, but why should Mr. Gilligan have assumed that I would be worse than useless on Tuesday?...Beside his duty to his side, a captain has a

duty to his bowlers, who have their feelings. I can take the rough with the smooth with anybody, but I am not going to stand being treated as I was on Tuesday. I feel that I should not be fair to myself if I accepted an invitation to play in any further Test match. Not that I expect to receive one."

It was an amazing outburst. He had voiced criticism of a previous England captain, J W H T Douglas, following the disastrous 1921-2 tour of Australia, but not in such stinging terms and not of his serving captain in the middle of a series. More astounding still, Parkin would later claim that he neither wrote the offending column nor had prior knowledge or approval of the words attributed to him. In his 1936 memoir, Parkin recalled being "astonished and alarmed" on discovering the content of the article published under his by-line. He argued that at no time "either jocularly or otherwise" had he criticised Gilligan and that the whole story had been invented by a journalist on the paper who he had asked to ghost-write the column on this occasion. Ciss, though, was not minded to name the offending pressman for fear of getting him into "hot water." If Parkin's account is correct and a ghost-writer had taken it on himself to effectively announce the end of a cricketer's international career without consulting him, it was an incredible turn of events.

Regardless of who actually wrote the controversial article, they did have a point. While he may have been ineffective with the ball on the second day, as a front-line bowler (certainly not included for his batting prowess), Parkin had every right to expect another chance as the South Africans' innings grew and to have it before the ball had become too soft. Even Tate, who had secured what would have been Parkin's openers berth, admitted "he had reason for his grouch at not being asked to open the bowling with the skipper", though pointed to his successful partnership with Gilligan at Sussex as reason for the captain's choice of opening bowler.

Gilligan's reluctance to use Parkin had been seen before. During the Test Trial, *The Times* correspondent had complained that "those people who have quite rightly a high regard for Parkin's bowling were disappointed to see that the old habit of not calling him up until several others had failed was once more in evidence." While it was widely agreed that Parkin was at his most effective with the new ball, Gilligan's decision to award that privilege to Tate and himself was understandable given their success on the second morning. However, Parkin was understandably aggrieved when he was then passed over at first, second and third change. That Gilligan had concluded that Parkin could not be trusted on dry wickets was made clear on his parting remarks after the Edgbaston match, when he cheerfully bid his bowler farewell, saying, "I'm sorry you haven't bowled much to-day Ciss, but I hope you will get some sticky wickets soon."

Whatever the truth regarding the origin of the controversial piece, a few days later Cecil Parkin was moved to make an apology via the Press Association. His column, he pleaded, "was not meant to convey any feeling of animosity against Mr Arthur Gilligan. Far from that, I have a great opinion of him as a sportsman and gentleman. My object was to protest against his policy in not asking me to bowl." He also wrote privately to the captain expressing his "sincere regret to you for giving you any pain." On his part, Gilligan accepted the apology gracefully and said they remained friends despite the incident; a cordiality that extended to Gilligan agreeing to write the forward to Parkin's autobiography. Inevitably, it was not enough to save his place in the side and Parkin was dropped for the second Test; replaced by his Lancashire teammate Dick Tyldesley. Although his fate had probably been sealed by the forthright nature of the criticism alone, it did not help Parkin's case that in April of that year the MCC Board of Control had agreed a proposal that any player's selection for England should be conditional on their not contributing "a report or a statement of any kind to the Press, until the end of the season, as regards any Test match for which he is selected."

Parkin would famously clash with Hawke again in 1925 when, in the *Weekly Dispatch*, Ciss offered his view on the captaincy of the MCC party that was touring Australia without him. Free of the hope of selection, Parkin doubled-down on the earlier criticism of Gilligan and argued that the captain's form should see him dropped from the side. If an amateur must captain the side, opined Parkin, then the MCC should appoint Percy Chapman but that he should lead the side "under the supervision of Hobbs." The professional Hobbs, said Parkin, was the best captain he had played under. On hearing of Parkin's intervention, Hawke was furious. "Here is a professional criticising an amateur all this distance away", thundered the Chairman at Yorkshire's annual meeting. "If he had been a Yorkshire professional...I do not think that Parkin would ever step on another Yorkshire cricket field", adding as a final shot, "pray God no professional will ever captain England." Words that would come to follow him around.

Hawke was not alone in his outrage. Pelham Warner let his displeasure with Parkin be known on several occasions, including a letter to the *Morning Post,* written in defence of Lord Hawke. In it he recalled Ciss's criticism of Gilligan the previous summer which, according to Warner, had "offended deeply the instincts of all true cricketers" and had "hardly faded away when we see him again in the limelight with an effusion in equally bad taste." Parkin, he said, was a fine bowler but "his opinion on cricket matters is not on the same level of excellence... [and he] is not regarded by cricketers themselves as a reliable critic." Given the standing of Hawke in the MCC and that Warner was soon to become Chairman of Selectors, it took no clairvoyant to see that, if Parkin's international prospects had been damaged before, they were now dead. He never played representative cricket again and was released from his Lancashire contract a year later.

It was a sad end to the career of one of cricket's most entertaining characters and a true talent with the ball.

As for England, while it was not recognised at the time, this match was a turning point. On a rudimentary level, it was England's first home Test match victory since 1912, a fact that was of satisfaction in itself. However, while a victory had been secured and the series was eventually won 3-0, this did not mean that English cricket was in rude health; the subsequent away Ashes tour would be lost 4-1. What we instead see in 1924 was the planting of the seeds which would result in an Ashes victory in 1926 and the re-establishment of England as a competitive international force. There was the return of Hobbs, whose presence alone made any team a greater threat. Not only was nation's cricketing talisman back but Edgbaston had seen the establishment of, perhaps, England's greatest opening partnership – Hobbs and Sutcliffe. In 38 innings they would go on to score 3,249 runs together (including 268 for the first wicket in the first innings of the very next match), post 15 century stands (a number only Greenwich and Haynes have bettered) and end their partnership with a first wicket average of 87.81 (a figure that continues to dwarf any other opening pairing in the history of the game). A team cannot live by bat alone, however, and, while 1924 would prove to be Arthur Gilligan's international swansong, it was the start of Maurice Tate's wonderful England career. The trio of Hobbs, Sutcliffe and Tate would play 24 Test matches together, winning half of them and losing only five. The road from 1914 had been a long one for English cricket but, by the end of 1924, the patient was back on his feet

England v South Africa
Edgbaston, Birmingham
14th, 16th, 17th June 1924 (3-day match)

Toss: South Africa

Umpires: HR Butt, W Reeves

England first innings

JB Hobbs	lbw	b Blanckenberg	6
H Sutcliffe	b Parker		64
FE Woolley	c Ward	b Parker	64
EH Hendren	c Nourse	b Parker	74
APF Chapman	b Parker		8
PGH Fender	c Taylor	b Blanckenberg	36
R Kilner	c and b Pegler		59
MW Tate	c Taylor	b Parker	19
*AER Gilligan	b Pegler		13
+GEC Wood	b Parker		1
CH Parkin	not out		8
Extras	(4 b, 11 lb, 1 nb)		16
Total	(all out, 124 overs)		438

Fall of wickets:
1-136, 2-164, 3-247, 4-255, 5-315, 6-356, 7-386, 8-407, 9-410, 10-438

Bowling	Overs	Mdns	Runs	Wkts
Parker	37	2	152	6
Pegler	36	8	106	2
Blanckenberg	32	5	95	2
Nupen	18	2	66	0
Nourse	1	0	3	0

South Africa first innings

*HW Taylor	b Tate	7
RH Catterall	b Gilligan	0

MJ Susskind	c Kilner	b Tate	3
AW Nourse	lbw	b Gilligan	1
JMM Commaille	not out		1
JM Blanckenberg	b Tate		4
HG Deane	b Gilligan		2
EP Nupen	b Gilligan		0
SJ Pegler	b Tate		0
+TA Ward	b Gilligan		1
GM Parker	lbw	b Gilligan	0

Extras	(1 b, 7 lb, 3 nb)	11
Total	(all out, 12.3 overs)	30

Fall of wickets:
1-1, 2-4, 3-6, 4-14, 5-20, 6-23, 7-23, 8-24, 9-30, 10-30

Bowling	Overs	Mdns	Runs	Wkts
Gilligan	6.3	4	7	6
Tate	6	1	12	4

South Africa second innings (following on)

*HW Taylor	c and b Tate		34
JMM Commaille	c Hendren	b Tate	29
MJ Susskind	b Gilligan		51
AW Nourse	c Wood	b Gilligan	34
RH Catterall	c Hobbs	b Tate	120
JM Blanckenberg	c Chapman	b Gilligan	56
HG Deane	run out		5
EP Nupen	lbw	b Tate	5
+TA Ward	b Gilligan		19
SJ Pegler	c Hobbs	b Gilligan	6
GM Parker	not out		2

Extras	(4 b, 18 lb, 6 nb, 1 w)			29
Total	(all out, 143.4 overs)			390

Fall of wickets:

1-54, 2-101, 3-152, 4-161, 5-275, 6-284, 7-295, 8-350, 9-372, 10-390

Bowling	Overs	Mdns	Runs	Wkts
Gilligan	28	6	83	5
Tate	50.4	19	103	4
Parkin	16	5	38	0
Kilner	22	10	40	0
Fender	17	5	56	0
Woolley	10	2	41	0

4. RACE AND EMPIRE

West Indies versus MCC
Georgetown, Guiana, Feb 21-26, 1930

Saturday 8 February 1930

As dawn broke over the port of Georgetown, British Guiana, a sleek luxury liner sat quietly in dock awaiting the usual morning activity. Despite the early hour, the temperature was already making its way into the mid-70s and the rain clouds that had affected the region over the preceding weeks looked to have stayed away. The RMS Lady Drake was a familiar sight in these parts; one of a trio of Canadian steamships that serviced the eastern route of the Caribbean before returning to chillier climes. The Lady Drake had arrived from Trinidad in the early hours of the morning but let its 208 passengers sleep on before inviting them to breakfast and disembarkation.

For the members of the MCC party aboard, it had been agreeable way to travel. The 'Lady' ships had a reputation for excellent service; the staff were well-trained, the food outstanding and the liquor ran freely. Dinner was always a formal affair and breakfast catered for all tastes. For the adventurous, delicacies such as pawpaw, fillet of kingfish or devilled beef bones could enliven their morning meal, whereas more conservative passengers could stick with orange juice, corn flakes, or eggs and bacon. Once breakfast was concluded, the cricketers on board returned to their cabins to ensure their bags were fully packed and to ready themselves for the third leg of their winter tour.

One of their number, Freddie Calthorpe, had more on his mind than most. Disembarkation was scheduled for 08:30 when the MCC team were to be formally greeted by a large reception committee that had already gathered on 'Booker's No.1' wharf. Speeches would be made, welcomes extended, and Freddie would be required to reply on behalf of the tourists with the usual niceties. That was all to be expected. Where a more difficult diplomatic path would need to be taken was in the requisite interview with the local press. There were two issues he knew would be coming his way and with both he had to be less than forthright. The first was the use of matting wickets in the matches played at their last island stop of Trinidad. Freddie detested matting as a surface to play cricket on and was not a man to pretend otherwise, however he would speak of the playing conditions being the same for both sides and offer the concession of matting being conducive to games reaching a positive conclusion. That enquiry would be easy to brush aside. The other – questions surrounding comments he had somewhat rashly made while in Barbados and had followed him ever since – could not be dealt with so creatively and instead, Calthorpe decided, would need to be played with a dead bat; to simply decline to address the issue further and declare it closed.

The Barbados controversy surrounded an issue that would continue to be intertwined with the England-West Indies cricketing rivalry throughout the twentieth century – the bouncer. The use of short pitched deliveries (or 'bumper' in the parlance of the day) had been an accepted part of the game since the late nineteenth century but the question of when the frequency or target of the delivery crossed a line into behaviour that was unacceptable was purely in the eye of the beholder. For Freddie Calthorpe, the West Indies and, particularly, fast bowler (and fellow passenger on the Lady Drake) Learie Constantine had done just that during the first Test in Barbados. During that Test, many of the English batsmen had found the pace of both Constantine and Herman Griffith difficult to handle on the quick Bridgetown pitch but Calthorpe had taken particular issue with the number of leg-side bumpers dealt out by Constantine. In fact, Calthorpe had reportedly said, he considered Constantine's bowling to be so dangerous that he would not be prepared to bring another team to the West Indies if the Trinidadian continued in such a manner.

While one might uncharitably suggest that Calthorpe's outburst had something to do with the fact that, in his only time at the crease at the Kensington Oval, his stumps had been spread-eagled by a lightning bolt from Constantine, it was not the first time the two men had crossed swords in this way. During the previous MCC tour of the Caribbean in 1926, Constantine had launched a barrage of short deliveries at the Englishman until he was implored to stop by his teammates. That he was only handing out the same treatment that had been administered by the English bowlers to West Indies captain Harold Austin seemed to be beside the point. The contest was imbued with the politics of empire, class and race; a fact Constantine's 1926 teammates had been acutely aware of when they pleaded "Stop it, Learie! Do not bump the ball at that man. He is the M.C.C. captain, captain of an English county and an English aristocrat...if you hit him and knock him down there'll be a hell of a row." There lied the nub of the controversy in both 1926 and 1930. Learie Constantine was a black professional West Indian cricketer and Freddie Calthorpe – or, to give him his full title, The Honourable Frederick Somerset Gough-Calthorpe, son of the 8th Baron Calthorpe – was a white amateur aristocrat and captain of the touring MCC team.

The history of international cricket is inextricably linked with the rise and fall of the British Empire and the relations between the different peoples and races contained within. At its most obvious, it is inescapable that, until the 2017 admittance of Afghanistan (along with Ireland) to the Test arena, all nations (other than England) who were allowed by the International Cricket Council to hold Test status were former British colonies. For a sport with global pretentions it remains a fact that, at the highest level, competition has been limited to places in the world that were once coloured pink on the map.

As Dominic Malcolm has argued, the circumstances surrounding the emergence of cricket as a force in different parts of the Empire cannot be told in a single storyline. However, with the indulgence of many caveats, a picture emerges of imperial cricket not just as a game played across the countries Britain claimed as its own but as an institution that reflected British attitudes towards itself and its colonies and, later, the attitudes of the colonised to Britain and the British.

Because of the meaning that cricket came to assume within an imperial context, it is tempting to imbue the arrival of the game in the colonies with the purpose of a deliberate export designed to implant British values on non-British peoples. While the perception of the sport as a means of spreading social norms would become a powerful one, the immediate reality was far more mundane. Cricket appeared across the Empire simply as a matter of Englishmen settling in the newly annexed territories and bringing with them their favoured pastimes. The nature of the earliest arrivals in newly found colonial lands varied from place to place but in common were the presence of military and merchant settlers. The earliest available report of a cricket match in the West Indies was between the Officers of the Royal West Indies Rangers and Officers of the Third West Indian Regiment in Barbados, 1807. While other sports were carried overseas, the fact that cricket was favoured by the officer class, businessmen and, later, (public school trained) government officials gave the game particular status in the colonial dependencies.

This status, along with the intertwining of the game with notions of Englishness in the Victorian period, gave cricket a notable role in the emerging hierarchies of the colonial lands. It became as much a social, even political, institution as a sporting one. Here lies a world of contradiction and nuance, as cricket was both an arena in which local populations could participate and adopt the practices of the elite, yet one in which the separation of races and classes was keenly maintained.

For the Imperial elite, maintaining an active cricket presence served several purposes. It was a symbol of home in a foreign land, a sign of loyalty to the British ideal, a place where they could mingle among their own, a demonstration that the hotter climes had not diminished their physical prowess and a way of imbibing the local population with those (English) values that cricket was supposed to stand for. The Trinidadian writer and activist C L R James, in his peerless text *Beyond a Boundary*, wrote of his exposure to cricket at school that, "as soon as we stepped on to...the cricket field, all was changed. We were a motley crew.... Yet rapidly we learned to obey the umpire's decision without question, however irrational it was. We learned to play with the team, which meant subordinating your personal inclinations, and even interests, to the good of the whole. We kept a stiff upper lip in that we did not complain about ill-fortune.... We lived in two worlds."

Indeed, as Brian Stoddart has argued, the power of cricket as cultural imperialism "came from the sport's voluntary imposition by its new converts rather than from an arbitrary imposition by the imperial masters." In that way, it became a shared set of values rather than entirely imposed ones.

Those values, though, were implicitly not just English ones but *white* ones that other races, it was presumed, could aspire to but were not imbued with. Writing in 1934 about former England captain J W H T Douglas, Patsy Hendren offered praise by saying, "How often we apply the words "white man" slackly, and without meaning them in full. I use them about Johnny Douglas in the fullest sense. His first thought was always about his team."

For some in the Empire, the transmission of cricketing morals was not simply a desirable goal but something that would give an indication of the maturity and trustworthiness of indigenous groups. Lord Harris, former Governor of Bombay and MCC President, opined that seeing select groups of Indians successfully adopt the norms of cricket was a signal of their readiness for some political responsibility.

It is worthwhile pausing for a moment to acknowledge the issue of the terms 'British' and 'English' in this story. We have no time to prod the hornets' nest that is the debate over the relation between the English, Scots and Welsh and notions of Britishness in this period, save to say that imperial power throughout this time led back to Westminster via the hallways of Eton, Harrow, Oxford and Cambridge. The locations were English as were many, but certainly not all, of those who held serious office. For a discussion on cricket, however, we are certainly talking about an English game that was perceived as representing and upholding supposed English values.

So, for indigenous people who wanted to move closer to the centre of power (or, as we shall see later, who wanted to challenge it), cricket provided an opportunity to join in with the leisure practices of the ruling elite in a way that would have been impossible with other activities popular with the upper-classes such as polo, horse racing or shooting. To participate in the sport, that is, but, for all but the rare exception, not to do so as part of the same side or as an equal. While cricket was looked to as a means of transmitting desirable standards of conduct it was not seen as an arena where the classes or races would freely mix. A distinct local hierarchy of cricket was maintained. James described a pecking order in early twentieth century Trinidad where each cricket club maintained strict expectations as to the sort of player they catered for. Queen's Park was open to wealthy whites and a few mixed-race Trinidadians from well-established families, Shamrock accepted mostly white Catholics, Maple was for the brown-skinned middle-class player, Shannon fielded a black lower middle-class team, and Stingo was the club for lower-class black cricketers – the "plebians, the butcher, the tailor, the candlestick maker, the casual labourer, with a sprinkling of unemployed." In Barbados, the first non-white club (Spartan) allowed to compete in sanctioned island competition emerged in the 1890s and was restricted to lawyers, civil servants and other roles with high social status. The next was not permitted until

1915 and was a break-away from Spartan itself. Such narrow attitudes of who was allowed to compete continued despite clear evidence of great enthusiasm for the game in the local population, both in terms of playing in pick-up games and cheering on the elite teams.

Such attitudes towards race and class in English domestic cricket were fully on view in the case of the prolific England and Sussex batsman Ranjitsinhji; one of the superstars of the Golden Age of cricket. A true great of the game, he mastered back-foot play better than anyone who came before and, with a remarkable wrist speed, became a pioneer in the use of the leg-glance. In terms of class, 'Ranji' was a natural fit with the cricketing establishment. He was an amateur, Cambridge educated, a member of the ruling family of Nawanagar, and would later become Maharaja Jam Saheb of Nawanagar (a position he acceded to with more than a little help from the British imperial elite). Such breeding and undoubted cricketing prowess saw him move smoothly into county cricket, not only representing Sussex with distinction but captaining the side for four years. For many, the colour of Ranji's skin, rather than being an obstacle to his acceptance into the county circuit, added an element of the exotic to his performances.

Ranji, though, was one of very few non-white cricketers in English cricket. Other notable exceptions were Ranji's nephew, Duleepsinhji, and the Nauwab of Pataudi (Ifitikhar Ali Khan). All played as amateurs. Indeed, no non-white cricketer was employed as a professional in the county game up to the outbreak of the Second World War. It seemed that class was a determining factor as to whether non-white cricketers were accepted into the fold. Also noticeable was the fact that when non-white players did take the field for a first-class side in this period, they were all of Asian heritage. Those cricketers from Afro-Caribbean stock who came to England to find a club who could benefit from their skills found the path to first-class cricket much more troublesome. When the great Learie Constantine moved to England to ply his trade, he found a welcome home as a professional for Nelson in the Lancashire League.

His performances caught the eye of some at Lancashire County Cricket Club and, with Constantine's approval, a proposal was made to employ the Trinidadian. The idea was soon quashed by some members of the Lancashire Committee who, according to Constantine, "could not tolerate my colour." No such barrier had existed for some other cricketers from the Caribbean, such as Constantine's compatriot Sydney Smith. Smith had shone with bat and ball for the West Indies touring party of 1906 and, after the tour, remained in England to qualify for Northamptonshire, for whom he would make over one hundred appearances. Sydney Smith, of course, was white.

There were, for some, limits to inclusion whatever a player's background. While Ranjitsinhji would go on to represent England 15 times in Test matches, his selection proved problematic for some in the establishment. Publicly, at least, the arguments used against Ranji's inclusion in the national side were presented as one of qualification; that his Indian birthplace made him ineligible. The problem with this reasoning, however, was the collection of non-English born cricketers who had previously earned an England cap without similar controversy (notably, Trinidad born Lord Harris who had been an influential voice in opposing Ranji's selection). While an alternative case could be made concerning Ranji's Indian lineage – Harris and other non-native born England cricketers had English-born ancestry – the clear subtext in the debate was one of race and of the politics of empire. Simon Wilde has argued that there was a distinct political context to the dispute; that not only was there a fear that inclusion would set a precedent that suggested Englishmen were interchangeable with other races but it occurred at a time where there was a growing concern surrounding Indian involvement in British domestic affairs. For others, though, it was just that his face did not fit. When, in 1896, the selection panel were finally moved by public clamour and the on-field needs of the England team to allow one of the game's finest practitioners to be included in an

XI, one MCC member was famously heard to remark that England didn't need "a nigger showing us how to play the game of cricket."

Attitudes towards how race defined nationality was seen in 1868 when the first team of Australians arrived in England for a cricket tour. Over six months the tourists played 47 matches, winning 14, losing 14 and drawing 19. Their first fixture at The Oval was said to have attracted a crowd of 20,000. The reason, though, that record books insist the first "Australian" cricket tour to England took place in 1878 was that the cricketers who took to the field ten years before were not white. They were Aboriginals and, as such, were only viewed as a curiosity and, by a few, with distain. On their visit to Kent, the *Maidstone Journal* marvelled at "the great novelty of seeing men of colour play (a thing thought at one time impossible)." *The Times*, on the other hand, was distinctly unimpressed. While, during the initial Oval match, the newspaper's correspondent begrudgingly hoped that "some of [their cricketing] defects will be overcome by the practice with good players during their stay in this country", by the time of the fixture against the MCC, he had decided that the spectacle had been "a travestie upon cricket at Lord's." The reception which greeted the first white Australian team to land in Britain ten years later was very different. It is not lost to the modern eye that in the latter *Times* report, the Aboriginal Australian team were only referred to as "the Blacks".

Throughout the empire, ideas of race and class intersected and supported each other. An Asian (in India) or mixed-race Afro-Caribbean (in the West Indies) could, through education, employment, or wealth, access some of the preserves of the white imperial elite in a way that would be impossible for the working-class white. In the West Indies such social climbing was harder as a person's skin darkened. Thus, while recognising the ultimate distinction of white versus non-white which still prevailed, race became another complication to the Victorian (and post-Victorian) class structure. As James pointed out, "it is not too much to say that in a West Indian colony the surest sign of a man having arrived is the fact that he keeps company with people lighter in complexion than himself." This was particularly the case in cricketing circles, where local factors of hierarchy also came into play. Stoddart explains, "Plantation owners, merchants, bankers, clerks and civil servants came to competition matches categorized by their place in the hierarchy of sugar production, and cricket was a powerful instrument in the preservation and promotion of that hierarchy."

As cricket developed in the West Indies, the upper-classes transported their own norms of behaviour to the colonies, particularly in their attitudes towards the participation of men from lower social stock. While in England, title, wealth, education, employment, and the Gentlemen-Players distinction all determined a person's place in the game, in the colonies race was added as a dominant factor. The relationship between white cricketers on the Caribbean islands and their black counterparts had distinct echoes of that between amateurs and professionals in England. When black cricketers were allowed on the cricket grounds of the elite clubs, it was as practice fodder. They were the bowlers, the fetchers and carriers. When inter-island competition first began, the early representative teams were chosen from the ranks of white cricketers alone. When black and white men crossed on the field of play in later island or West Indian teams the 'Gentlemen and Players' distinction remained. Black cricketers were viewed as the most likely bowlers, the whites more suited for batting, and the colour of the captain's skin was never in doubt. The first two assumptions were clearly a fallacy and the last would become the great controversy.

British touring sides began visiting the Caribbean islands as early as 1895, organised by well-to-do amateur cricketers, including, in 1897, future MCC president Lord Hawke. The visiting sides hardly consisted of the finest cricketers England had to offer; teams were made up of acquaintances of the organisers and men who could afford the time to take an extended vacation to sunnier climes. The first team to visit the islands was led, in early 1895, by Robert Slade Lucas, a 'Jobber' on the London Stock Exchange who played as an amateur for Middlesex. The tourists would play island, local and services teams but no fixture against a combined West Indies side was arranged. Amongst Lucas' ranks was one man – Hugh Bromley-Davenport – who would go on to earn four England caps, but outside of him and Lucas, the other eleven men who played on that tour, would only accrue 134 total first-class career appearances between them. Even so, contemporary accounts of the tour reported the visitors being received by scenes of great excitement and when Barbados scored a record 517 runs against the tourists (albeit in a losing cause), the local press celebrated the feat exuberantly.

The idea of a combined West Indies side had already been seen as far back as 1886 when an (all-white) West Indian team toured Canada and the United States of America; winning five, losing five and drawing three. Two years later a combined West Indian team played its first home match, in Georgetown, against the Gentlemen of the United States of America; the visitors emerged victorious in an extremely low scoring game. No West Indian played in the combined sides of both 1886 and 1888. It would not be until 1897 that another group of cricketing tourists, under future Liberal MP Arthur Priestley, provided the opposition for the West Indies' next home fixture; a three-day game at Queen's Park, Port of Spain, Trinidad, which the home team won by three wickets.

While a group of ex-patriots from the Caribbean had played as 'West Indians' under the captaincy of Pelham Warner in July 1897, the first genuine West Indies' tour to England occurred in 1900. Inevitably, the issue of whether the touring side would be an all-white one raised its head but, on this occasion, was resolved with the inclusion of five black players. Two factors were prominent in this decision. Firstly, the argument for selecting a more inclusive team had found powerful advocates among the white elite, particularly in Plum Warner, and, secondly, the evidence from local and inter-island matches was becoming unanswerable: all-white sides were demonstrably weaker than those which included black cricketers. And so, Delmont 'Fitz' Hinds, Tommie Burton, Charles Ollivierre, Joseph 'Float' Woods and Lebrun Constantine (father of Learie) were included in a party of 15 who set sail that May.

In terms of results on the cricketing field, the tour got off to a poor start. The first ten games saw the tourists suffer eight losses – six of those being innings defeats – and two victories (a narrow victory against a combined minor counties side and a morale boosting rout of Leicestershire). The remaining seven games were far more encouraging and saw the West Indians avoid adding any further to the loss column. Matches were drawn against Derbyshire, Staffordshire, Liverpool & District, and Yorkshire; victories were notched over Hampshire, Surrey (by an innings and 34 runs) and, in the final fixture of the tour, Norfolk. This later run of results had done much to salvage the reputation of the West Indians as competitive cricketers. It was notable that the black cricketers had largely been the mainstays with both bat and ball. Ollivierre led the scoring with 879 runs, Lebrun Constantine coming in third, with white Barbadian Percy Cox sandwiched between. The bowling statistics were similarly led by Burton and Woods who took 150 wickets between them; 70 more than all the other bowlers combined. That Burton and Woods took most scalps was little surprise given that they bowled more than 60 percent of the overs sent down in the tour. They were no mere work-horses, however, as both men also topped the tourists' bowling averages with returns of under 22.

For many of those in authority the tour was about more than the seventeen matches. It marked another step in the growth of cricket and those values associated with the sport, and of the Empire itself. At a farewell dinner for the visiting side held at the Grand Hotel on Charing Cross, Lord Harris addressed the tourists in a manner that sat somewhere between paternalistic and patronising. He praised the courage of the West Indians to "beard the lion in his den" and the sportsmanlike spirit in which they had approached the game; "a way which we in England...wished to see it played." He added that he hoped the players, personally, had learned something "not only as to cricket, but as to the advantage of Empire." Following Lord Harris was William Palmer, second Earl of Selbourne, then at the Colonial Office. Selbourne noted that some had said the West Indies lacked a common interest, that they were akin to "unbound sticks" that might have been a "bundle of faggots." He urged them to follow the example of the Australian colonies who had become united into a "great commonwealth" and wondered what part the process of selecting a united cricket team played in that.

It was not until the West Indies' second tour to Britain, in 1906, that some of their matches were granted first-class status. The touring side had also made another step forward in terms of integration. The majority (and captain) were still drawn from the ranks of white West Indians but the divide had come closer to parity, with seven black cricketers – Burton and Constantine returned, plus Dr John Joseph Cameron, Archie Cumberbatch, Oliver Layne, Richard Ollivierre and John Parker – contained within a squad of fifteen. As far as results were concerned, as in 1900, the tour started badly but improved in time. Of the 19 matches played, the tourists lost ten, won seven and drew two. While most of their successful performances came against minor sides, the West Indians ended the tour able to boast victories over both Yorkshire and Northamptonshire. Sydney Smith starred with bat and ball, leading with 1,107 runs and 116 wickets. Smith, adopted by Northamptonshire, would later play against the West Indies for two touring MCC sides.

The 1900 and 1906 tours were of importance for two reasons. Firstly, although not unequivocal successes in terms of results, by posting wins against county sides late in each tour, the West Indies had shown themselves to be a growing competitive force on the field of play.

Secondly, the case for an integrated team was now indisputable. Even if one were to put aside the moral arguments for a non-racial selection policy, the individual performances on both tours showed that it was the presence of the black players that was largely responsible for the competitive nature of their cricket.

The next indication of English cricket's gradual recognition of the West Indies came via MCC tours to the Caribbean in 1911 and 1913. On each tour, three games were arranged against combined West Indies teams with the MCC winning two of the three in each case. The West Indies secured one victory; the second match of 1913. War came, and it would not be until 1923 that a West Indies side would grace the cricket fields of England again. Much like the two earlier tours, the West Indians took a while to adjust to English conditions and initial results were not entirely encouraging. However, as in 1900 and 1906, the tourists eventually found their feet. By the end of the tour in September, the West Indians had notched up 13 wins out of 28 matches, losing seven and drawing eight. Five first-class counties – Essex, Somerset, Surrey, Sussex and Warwickshire – were amongst their victims.

One notable opponent was missing from the tour schedule – England. To this point, international matches – Test matches – had been restricted to the three members of the Imperial Cricket Council: England, Australia and South Africa. In 1926, the ICC had only its second post-war meeting. This time, representatives from the West Indies, India and New Zealand were invited to attend and, at a second meeting later in the year, they were confirmed as members of the ICC. This formal acceptance of the three new cricketing powers opened the way for international fixtures and tours to be scheduled; in effect, the granting of Test status.

Of the three new ICC members, the West Indies would be the first to see that status confirmed on the field of play in the form of a recognised Test match. That was finally obtained at Lord's on 23 June 1928; the first of three Tests scheduled for that summer. In purely cricketing terms it was not a happy time for the visiting West Indian team, struggling with both bat and ball. All three Test matches were lost by an innings, with Clifford Roach high scoring for the tourists with 53 in the final fixture (one of only three half centuries from West Indians) and only Herman Griffith notable in the bowling returns – taking 11 of the 28 English wickets to fall to a bowler. At a reception held by the West Indian Club to mark the team's departure, little could be done to hide the disappointing nature of the cricketing performance, but each speaker tried to find something positive. Sir Robert Rutherford, Chairman of the Club, noted that the tour was a financial success and had been entirely free from any form of friction. Former England captain Henry Leveson-Gower said that he did not think it too long before the West Indies were invited for a five-match series, and Plum Warner suggested that the fast bowling of the tourists was the best seen in England since the Australians had last visited. The biggest cheer of the reception was reserved for the West Indian captain, Karl Nunes, when he protested that he had not been disturbed by the criticism received from the West Indian press; an indication of the level of unhappiness back home.

A little under a year and a half later, the West Indies got the chance to play their next Test series, once more against England – in their touring guise as the MCC – but, this time, on Caribbean soil.

English cricket in this period had an ambivalent attitude towards overseas tours. Noticeable was the fact that the creation of the Ashes, following the infamous *Times* death notice "in affectionate remembrance of English cricket", occurred not after the first Test defeat at the hands of Australia but the first home loss. It was indicative that between the first Test match in Australia in 1877 and the same tour one hundred years later, England teams toured as the Marylebone Cricket Club. Consequently, while the matches in 1930 between the MCC and a combined West Indies side were referred to throughout as Tests by media and players alike, there were some who questioned their status.

Wisden, for instance, continued to avoid the title, insisting on the official designation of 'representative' matches (only later would they universally be acknowledged as Tests). The discussion rumbled on sufficiently during the 1930 tour to prompt the Chairman of the Jamaica Cricket Board of Control, Sir William Morrison, to remind all those at the Island's farewell dinner for the MCC tour party that the ICC, on which he sat, had bestowed Test status on the West Indies and consequently matches between the nations were to be counted as Tests. It is noteworthy that *Wisden* had no difficulty in referring to the previous year's overseas fixtures between MCC and Australia as 'Test matches'.

MCC touring teams, often for logistical reasons, were rarely full-strength England sides. Amateurs could not always afford the extended period away from their livelihood and even professionals would sometimes find a reason not to tour. 1930 was a perfect example of this. Of the 23 cricketers who had represented England in the 1929 home series against South Africa, only eight travelled overseas that winter. Included in the list of tour absentees, preserving their energies for the upcoming home Ashes series, were the eminent names of Sutcliffe, Hammond, Leyland, Tate, Larwood and Hobbs. Normally, such a roll call of talent staying at home would have meant a weakened England/MCC team taking to the high seas. In 1930, however, it meant two weakened teams setting out on tour.

In their enthusiasm to bring Test cricket to the furthest reaches of the Empire, the MCC had accepted invitations from both the West Indies and New Zealand to tour in early 1930. Whether this also reflected a low opinion amongst the MCC of the expected standard of competition from the newly promoted nations or a lack of concern as to the ultimate result of the tours, they seemed content to send out two diluted teams to compete on behalf of England simultaneously. This situation was not unwelcomed by the receiving nations, indeed a common view in the Caribbean was that the most desirable team to visit the new Test-playing nation was one which was neither too weak to give the West Indies a game or "so strong that all interest would cease after the first encounter."

Of the two touring sides, the party en route to New Zealand was the most inexperienced. The inclusion of cricketing heavyweight Frank Woolley aside, the squad was one of novices. Sussex's Ted Bowley travelled with two Test caps under his belt; Duleepsinhji, Geoffrey Legge, Eddie Dawson and Fred Barratt had a solitary England game each. The other six men would need to make their debut against New Zealand.

Amongst those travelling to the Caribbean, however, all but three had previous Test experience. One of the uncapped tourists was the captain, Calthorpe; though he had led a previous MCC (non-Test playing) side. By far the most experienced of the party was the legendary Wilfred Rhodes, aged 52, still bowling his left-arm spin more than thirty years after making his debut in W G Grace's 1899 England side. It had been over three years since his previous Test match and he had only made a single appearance in the preceding eight years. Alongside the experience of Rhodes, both Gunn (age 50) and Sandham (39) travelled with eleven and ten England appearances under their belt, respectively. Two other players, while inexperienced in terms of England caps – Nigel Haig & Ewart Astill – were over forty, and the marquee name on the team-sheet, with 32 England caps and 1,869 international runs at an average of 42, was forty-year-old Middlesex professional Patsy Hendren. With only Bill Voce and Les Ames under the age of 25, this was not a young team. It was, however, a team respected by their opponents. The *Trinidad Guardian* reported the side arriving on its shores as "the strongest MCC team which has ever toured the West Indies." Writing about the series sixteen years later, Learie Constantine recalled the tourists as a "cracking good side."

The tour party aboard the SS Carare, docked at Bridgetown, Barbados, on 27 December, having spent Christmas of 1929 at sea. Time to become re-accustomed to land was short as, only four days later, the first game of the tour was scheduled to get underway at the Kensington Oval. Opportunities to practice in that short time were limited as, while they may have escaped the chill of the British winter, the tourists had brought wet weather with them. With temperatures high in the region, the rain clouds also meant that the atmosphere was humid.

Despite the odd downpour, thanks to the practice of covering the pitch and the intense Bajan sun, the first leg of the tour was played on true, quick wickets. Two drawn matches against the colony gave captain Calthorpe reason to be confident in his team's batting and fielding but brought doubts about how well his bowlers were adapting to conditions.

The star of the show from the tourists' perspective had been Patsy Hendren. Going into the first Test, he had batted only twice but notched up 434 runs without being dismissed; 223 in the first match and 211 in the second. He dealt with the short pitch ball with ease – cutting and pulling freely – and showed that he could bat equally well in whichever style he chose. In the first local match he was the careful run-accumulator, playing each delivery watchfully despite his first century already secured, a drawn match certain and the cries of an impatient crowd: "hit the ball, Patsy, we know you can do it." In the second, Hendren went for the jugular, hitting a hundred runs in the session before lunch on the third day in an eventual seventh wicket partnership of 323 with Leslie Townsend (who was out for 97). His efforts were widely celebrated, with even a poem by "K S W" published in the *Barbados Advocate*:

To Patsy

T'would please us greatly, my dear Pat,
For you to hit much less than that
And give a chance.
Too straight you wield a Hendren bat,
It's bad enough with young Wyatt
To make us dance,
Then you appear right on the scene,
"Cockspur" our bowlers to the screen,
Cause them to prance
Balls going there and everywhere;
Scare Flannigan from off his beer;
Your fame enhance

. . . .

A thousand runs are in your sight
But half a season gone
A hundred hundreds by your might,
We think, to you are one
So here's good health, long life to you
And all god wishes true
Choice of the girls for wife to you
You blazing good true-blue.

* *

Elias Henry "Patsy" Hendren was born in Middlesex, in 1889, to Dinah and Denis Hendren; his father a plasterer born of Irish parents. Short but stocky with powerful forearms – powerful enough to turn a forward defensive push into a run-producing drive – Patsy's batting talents were spotted early by none other than W G Grace. By 1905 he had been taken on to the Lord's ground-staff where, along with batting and net-bowling duties, he could be found selling scorecards around the ground on match days.

His Middlesex debut in 1907 was a great disappointment as rain prevented any chance of Patsy coming to the crease. It was not until the following season that Hendren had his second chance under the captaincy of Pelham Warner, although a score of three from his only innings was not a great improvement (though he did take a wicket). By the time war came, Patsy was an established county cricketer, having racked up 144 first-class appearances for Middlesex, MCC and other representative sides; though only six centuries in those fixtures gave little indication of the player he would become.

It did not take Hendren long to get back into his stride when cricket resumed 1919. 85 in his first innings, a century in his second match, 214 in the third and 201 in his fifth. Fearless against the short-pitched delivery, he could hook and pull with venom, yet quick on his feet against the slower bowler, Jack Hobbs called him "my ideal batsman." A rock-solid fielder who took 759 career first-class catches, he was an immensely popular cricketer amongst his peers, full of humour both on and off the field of play. Hendren was also talented on the football field and, although he would not make the same mark as he did in the world of cricket, he was good enough to appear for the first teams at Manchester City and Coventry City.

By the time of his retirement, Patsy Hendren could legitimately be ranked among the great batsmen of all time. In terms of sheer weight of runs, only Hobbs (naturally) and Frank Woolley could boast more that Hendren's 57,611 (a state of affairs that remains the case today) and his first-class average, at 50.80, was the highest of those three batsmen. In 21 summers he passed 1,000 runs, of those 15 passed the 2,000 mark and, in 1928 and 1933, two thousand became three. Add to that thousand-plus run winters on tour with the MCC on four occasions. If that was not enough, Hendren's 170 first-class centuries stand second on the all-time list, bettered only by Hobbs. For England, Patsy's record was also one to be proud of: 51 Tests, 3,525 runs at an average of 47.63, including seven centuries.

* *

While Hendren shone in Barbados, it was not an entirely one-man show. A century for Andrew Sandham ("always delightful to watch"), two half-centuries for Bob Wyatt, one for George Gunn, and decent lower-order support from Wilfred Rhodes and Calthorpe himself, would have left the captain confident that the English batsmen had the measure of the Barbados pitch.

The bowling was a different matter. There had been some encouraging signs. In each of the preliminary matches when the pitch was fresh and the bowlers the same, the opening pair of Bill Voce and Nigel Haig had picked up early wickets. Voce, particularly, used pace and bounce to unsettle batsmen still getting their eye in. The slow bowling of Wilfred Rhodes, Ewart Astill and Jack O'Connor also held up well in conditions not normally conducive to spin. However, even the wiles of Rhodes et al were not going to run through a home side on Caribbean pitches and, once the quicks began to tire, the ball grew old and the surface baked in the sun, the Bajan batsmen made merry. Voce seemed to wilt in the heat, delivering an alarming number of no-balls and, on the fourth day of the second match, had become so frustrated with his lack of impact that he tried his hand as a slow bowler. The Bajans took full advantage and centuries were posted by Percy Tarilton, Teddy Hoad and a seventeen-year-old schoolboy who had initially been only called up as wicket-keeping cover, Derek Sealy.

When the opening day of the first Test arrived, the weather gods were kind; the clouds remained high, the temperature warm and the trade-wind brisk. The West Indies won the toss, elected to bat and began to make good use of the conditions. England's bowling woes seemed to have continued, as opener Clifford Roach punched his way to a rapid, faultless century and, after a couple of wickets had fallen, was joined by Frank De Caires who passed fifty in a far more cautious manner. When De Caires eventually departed – brilliantly caught by Sandham one ball after receiving a viscous head-high bouncer from Voce – the West Indies' score sat comfortably at 303 for 4. Finally, though, the English attack found its mojo. Voce, while expensive, peppered the batsmen with threatening short-pitched deliveries and Rhodes, ever the miser, tied down an end allowing only 44 runs from 163 balls bowled. The unlikely hero for the tourists was Greville Stevens who took five wickets with his leg breaks (albeit at a cost of 105 runs) and finished off the innings early on the second morning for a total of 369. The West Indies knew they should have made more.

The opening of the MCC's innings was in marked contrast to the display with which Roach had treated the crowd. Gunn and Sandham, facing the speed of Constantine and Griffith, took their time. No run was accrued for the first 16 minutes and, when rain brought an early lunch at five minutes to one (some 70 minutes into the English reply), the batsmen had inched their way to a total of 33 without loss. The contest had been intense and the bowling accurate but, the odd body-blow received from the hand of Constantine aside, the batsmen had not appeared to be in any serious trouble. The crowd, who were known to voice their disapproval of slow play, appeared instead to be engrossed in the battle between opening batsmen and bowlers.

To an extent, there seemed to be an acceptance that this was just the way English teams played cricket; to blunt the new-ball attack before making hay when bowlers and ball were tired. The *Barbados Advocate* put it more poetically by attributing the sometimes painful caution of touring batsman to "the bulldog emblematic of English tenacity, first fight resolutely for his grip and having once secured it, he squeezes his rival into complete submission." Still, the technique was effective and by the end of a rain-interrupted second day the score stood at 233 for

2, with the form pair of Sandham (111 not out) and the much freer scoring Hendren (65 not out) at the wicket.

The third day's play was to see no heroics, with both sides trading blows. Hendren fell twenty runs short of his century (caught Constantine off Edwin St Hill) while Sandham departed (LBW Constantine) having made 152. Decent contributions throughout the card from O'Connor, Haig and Calthorpe lifted England to a respectable final total of 467. A lead of 98 runs. For the West Indies, the wickets had been shared between their all-seam attack of the quicks Constantine and Griffith and the medium pacers St Hill and 'Snuffie' Browne. Oddly – given he had only bowled four overs in the first innings – skipper Calthorpe decided that his right arm medium pace would open the bowling with Voce when the MCC took the field again. It appeared to have been an inspired decision as, with only six runs on the board, he picked up the wicket of his West Indian counterpart Teddy Hoad for a duck. George Headley and Clifford Roach saw the home side safely through to the close.

The next day was all about George Headley. Compact in stature and light on his feet, the Panamanian born Jamaican was a superb back-foot player with a precise touch. Alongside his overnight partner, Headley helped move the score past 150 and, when Roach departed, he and Frank de Caires pushed the total beyond three hundred. 360 runs were on the board when Headley was finally dismissed, by Rhodes, for a score of 176. It had been a brilliant innings by the twenty-year-old, at times cautious given the match situation but, with rapid foot movement and bat speed, he had the ability to change his shot at the very last minute, making him a wonderful player of both spin and pace alike. When, on the fifth and final day, the West Indies had been dismissed, England faced a deficit of 286 with under four hours of play left. Gunn and Sandham set off at a pace and, scoring at a rate in excess of a run a minute, the chase looked on. However, by tea, with the openers back in the pavilion and the bowling and fielding tight, the batsmen stopped chasing the ball and settled in for a, now, inevitable draw.

England had been frustrated. They had shown again that, with the likes of Sandham and Hendren in the side, large totals could be amassed but unless the bowling attack could prevent Headley, Roach and company from doing the same, victory would remain elusive. Captain Calthorpe was quick to point to the fact that he had been without three of his bowlers for part of the second innings (Voce had managed only three overs having left the field with a knee injury on the fourth day, Stevens, who finished the match with ten wickets, was also absent for a period, as was Jack O'Connor), arguing that "probably but for that misfortune we might have won". In truth, the performance continued the story of the earlier 'colony' matches.

If the post-Test conversation should have revolved around the brilliance of Headley or Roach or Sandham, Calthorpe had other ideas. During a reception to mark the end of the first leg of the tour, the MCC captain used his speech to criticise the bowling of Learie Constantine. His short-pitched bowling, particularly those delivered to a packed leg-side field, caused batsmen problems and one leg-side bumper had struck Andrew Sandham. Such tactics, Calthorpe loudly proclaimed, were not only dangerous but ineffective. He opined that the bowler would be much more efficient if he bowled at the wicket with three slips and a gully in place. This, on top of his remarks concerning his potential reluctance to lead another MCC tour to the Caribbean if such tactics were to continue, amounted to an astonishing outburst. However, it fitted into a widely shared assumption by many (on both sides) that the MCC were in the Caribbean not just as opponents but as educators, or, in Calthorpe's words, "to help them in cricket." Accordingly, when asked to speak, members of the England party willingly gave forth on issues such as matting wickets, covered wickets, the advantages of English coaches or the size of the stumps used.

As for the legitimacy of his criticism of Constantine, Calthorpe was on shaky ground. The MCC team, particularly Bill Voce, had not been shy in delivering a barrage of bouncers at West Indian batsmen when thought necessary, hitting several and, during the first match of the tour, striking the Barbados batsman Clifford Inniss over the heart; a blow that many viewed as the cause of his subsequent lack of confidence and form that led to his omission from the Test team. Writing later, Constantine argued that the ball which hit Sandham only did so because the batsman had moved a foot outside of leg-stump; the intention of the ball was to be out of the reach of the batsman in the cause of bowling for a draw rather than to hurt him. The irony of the controversial use of leg-side bouncers by the MCC team which toured Australia three winters later in the notorious 'Bodyline' series was not lost on the West Indian.

Furthermore, it seemed that Calthorpe and others in the party were not content to let the matter rest with a public outburst. When the teams met for the second Test, Harry Mallett, a notable figure in West Indies cricket who was serving as the manager of the MCC tour party, strolled up to Constantine, announced that the English batsmen felt the bowler was trying to hurt them and told him that he must not use so many leg-side bumpers. An astonished Constantine, wary of generating any ill-feeling, "cheerfully" agreed. The fact that any emissary from the MCC team felt he could walk up to a West Indian cricketer and issue instructions as to how he could or could not play – an unthinkable situation were the nationalities of the teams (or, especially, races) reversed – gave further indication of the nature of the relationship between England and the colonies. It would not be the last time in Constantine's career where short-pitched balls to English batsmen would provoke debate.

The criticism directed at Constantine was unfortunate in its timing as the MCC were due to sail to the fast bowler's home island of Trinidad next and face him on the unfamiliar surface of matting wickets. Even without such controversy it promised to be a difficult encounter.

At the close of play on day one of the first local match against Trinidad, things looked a lot rosier for Calthorpe and his MCC side. The bowlers – Rhodes and Stevens particularly – had taken a liking to the matting surface and, despite being without the recuperating Voce, had skittled the home side for 150. Especially pleasing for the tourists was that one of the thorns in their side from the first Test – Clifford Roach – had been back in the hutch for single digits. When the umpires drew stumps on the first day, the MCC had reached 63 for 1, with the dangerous pair of Sandham and Hendren still at the crease.

It proved a false dawn. Scoring was difficult in such alien conditions and, by ten minutes to three on the second day, the MCC innings was over, all out for 167; seen off by the slow left arm of Puss Achong, the occasional medium pacers of Ben Sealey, along with some outstanding catching by Constantine. If they hoped to win a low scoring affair, England were to be disappointed. Rhodes bowled well once more, adding six wickets to the four he took in the first innings, but he could not prevent the Trinidadians reaching a comparatively daunting score of 333. Wilton St Hill led the charge with a century (for which he was awarded the prize of a bicycle by the acting Governor of the island), ably supported by knocks from Sealey and Mervyn Grell.

Faced with over three hundred runs to win the match, Hendren fought hard but it was to be a lone battle. When the Middlesex man was cunningly caught by Constantine (the Trinidadian had noticed Hendren eyeing up the gap between himself at gully and first slip and had sneaked to second slip before the next ball was bowled), Hendren departed with some "very violent language" directed towards the fielder, four short of a century, taking his team's hopes with him. While Astill put up some resistance down the order, St Hill, Achong and Grell cleaned up the tail for a famous Trinidadian victory. At the fall of the final wicket, the large crowd poured onto the field in celebration.

Things were not getting better for Calthorpe. Stung by defeat in the first game, there was only one day's respite before the next match began with another MCC struggle on the matting wicket; all out for 142 in the first innings (Hendren top-scoring with 30) and for only 118 in the second. At last, however, the bowling fired and, with Voce (slowing to a medium pace to better exploit the surface) and the leg-breaks of Stevens operating in tandem, the tourists knocked over the home team for innings scores of 108 and 130. An MCC win by 22 runs. Their first taste of victory on the tour.

So, despite a bout of ptomaine poisoning that struck half of the squad, Calthorpe's men entered the second Test with more reason to be confident than they would have a week before when their frailties on the matting wicket had been fully exposed. Furthermore, the West Indies side they were to face looked, on paper, significantly weaker than that which had taken the field in Barbados.

The task of selecting an all-West Indian XI was delegated to the host island's cricket committee for each match, which meant that local biases, along with the regular unavailability of some players from other islands, could produce locally dominated teams. The first Test of 1930 was a fairly even spread from across the Caribbean: four Bajans, four Trinidadians, two from British Guiana and George Headley, the Jamaican. Three weeks later the West Indian side for the Trinidad Test consisted of eight Trinidadians and one apiece from Barbados, British Guiana and Jamaica. The local nature of the side did not go unnoticed and attracted criticism even from Trinidadian voices. A regular complaint was that no place in the XI was found for the promising Derek Sealy – who had performed so well previously – despite having made the trip to Trinidad. That was not to say local cricketers were guaranteed a place and the omission of Trinidadian Edwin St Hill, who had held a place in the previous Test, caused consternation in the dressing room. Whether one could argue that, given the difficulties the English batsmen had in adapting to Trinidadian matting wickets, a side dominated by locals well practiced on such surfaces was a wise tactical choice, it was difficult to see a team missing the talents of Sealy, Browne and Edwin St Hill (his brother Wilton was selected) as anything other than diminished.

The captain from the previous Test, Teddy Hoad, was also absent. One of the other consequences of having locally based selection committees was the habit of installing a local (white) cricketer as captain, leading to a complete absence of continuity of leadership. With the captaincy decision deliberated before every match, the choice was regularly the source of widespread and heated debate. Matters had been further complicated before the second Test in 1930 by rumours that the Bajan Hoad had been approached to continue as captain in Trinidad. Whether there had been any truth in those stories, it was not to be, and the normal convention prevailed: Hoad was out and Nelson Betancourt was in.

At first, it seemed that the Trinidadian selectors had done their job well, as an unchanged MCC side had their familiar problems on the matting surface. Sandham saw his off-stump removed by a smart Griffith off-break, Gunn was run-out attempting a second and Stevens edged a quick, lifting, Constantine delivery to second slip. The score stood at 12 for 3. Half an hour into play and only thirteen runs had been posted by the tourists. As usual, the English hopes rested on Hendren and he, alongside Jack O'Connor and (when O'Connor departed to a good catch in the deep by Headley) Les Ames, began to steady the ship.

Hendren appeared to be the sole Englishman comfortable with either the sharp spin or jumping deliveries coming from the wicket; cutting, hooking and pulling with intent. While Constantine had agreed to the request to restrain his use of leg-side bouncers, there was no way he would have removed the short ball from his armoury completely and Hendren receive his share. The hullabaloo concerning Constantine's tactics threatened to flare up again when, during the afternoon session, Hendren mistimed a pull off Constantine and was struck on the head.

A nervous four minutes later, the Middlesex batsman declared himself fit to continue and the game resumed. When Hendren was finally dismissed, playing the ball onto his stumps off Achong for 77, the score was on a somewhat precarious 142 for 5, but some dogged work by Ames pushed the score to 208 before he was last man out. Not an intimidating score but, given their previous difficulties on matting, it at least gave the bowlers something to work with.

During the West Indian reply, the advantage swung back and forth between the two sides. It was the perfect start for the visitors when Roach mistakenly left an off-break from Voce alone and was bowled before any score had been registered. The West Indies fought back with wicketkeeper Errol Hunte (promoted from number eleven in the previous Test to open) and Wilton St Hill moving the score to 89 before the latter was trapped in front by Astill who, along with Voce, continued to chip away at the home side. When the two bowlers combined to pick up the wicket of Joe Small (c. Voce b. Astill) the score stood at 160 for 7 and the tourists had high hopes of a first innings lead. Once more Constantine proved the thorn in their side but, this time, with the bat. A quick-fire half-century powered the West Indies to 254; a small but potentially crucial lead.

That lead looked even more threatening when England's top three, Gunn, Sandham and O'Connor, were back in the hutch with their team on 52; a lead of only six. If this was not to be another embarrassment for the touring side, they needed the heroes of the first innings, Hendren and Ames, to stand up again.

And stand up they did. When Ames was caught off the bowling of Small for 105, they had taken the score to 289. The wicket of Hendren proved beyond the reaches of the West Indian bowlers and he left the field unbeaten on an imperious 205 as, with rain showers eating up time, Calthorpe declared the innings closed on 425 for 8. It was Hendren's third double century of the tour, completed on his 41st birthday. Between him and Ames, they had racked up more runs than the entire side had managed in any one innings on the Trinidadian matting previously. For their efforts, Tour Manager Mallett rewarded Hendren with 50 pounds and Ames with 25. The local authorities presented the pair (along with the captain) with walking-sticks in recognition of their efforts.

With a lead of 379 and four sessions remaining in the game, the MCC would have felt confident of leaving the island one-nil up in the Test series. Voce made sure they were not to be disappointed. While the West Indies fought hard, establishing partnerships all the way down the order, they eventually succumbed some 167 runs short. Voce, who had found his new slower pace highly effective on matting, finished the innings with 7-70, giving him eleven wickets in the match. There is no record of the Nottinghamshire man being rewarded with talent money or walking sticks but, as often the case, such was the lot of the bowler.

* *

Bill Voce – so often (unfairly) recalled as a supporting cast member to Harold Larwood and Douglas Jardine in the 1932/3 'Bodyline' tour of Australia – was a fine pace bowler in his own right. Though one whose career at the very top would be kept relatively short by injury and war. A miner by trade, Voce was spotted playing local cricket by Nottinghamshire's Fred Barratt and, in 1926, was taken on to the county's staff. Initially a slow left-armer, his county debut came in 1927 and he made an immediate impact by claiming a five-wicket haul against Gloucestershire in his debut innings. He repeated the trick a few weeks later against Essex (including picking up former England captain Johnny Douglas for a duck) while conceding very few runs in the process. In 1928, having experimented with swinging the ball the previous year, Bill Voce made the decision to switch to seam bowling. A decent season followed but his real breakthrough came the following year when he took 120 first-class wickets at an average of a shade over

17. That performance helped Nottinghamshire to the County Championship title and saw him invited to join the tour to the West Indies.

Not quite as fast as his county teammate Larwood, Voce still bowled a brisk fast-medium, using his notable strength and height to generate an awkward lifting ball. As he learnt his craft, Voce moved from being a predominantly round-the-wicket bowler to using the other side of the crease just as effectively. Add in a quick, accurate bouncer that he would not be reluctant to deploy, the left-armer became a threat to the best batsmen the game had to offer. Following his success in 1929, Voce took over one hundred first-class wickets in each of 1931, 1932, 1934, 1935 and 1936. The following year came a knee injury that meant he was never quite the same bowler again. His batting was largely restricted to hard-hitting lower order cameos but in 1933 he topped one thousand runs for the season and ended his career with four first-class hundreds; one, against Glamorgan in 1931, made in only three-quarters of an hour. Bill Voce played first-class cricket up until 1952 (though only occasionally post-second World War) and took 98 and 97 wickets in the seasons of 1938 and 1939, respectively, but it was that period between 1929 and 1936 that the Nottinghamshire man was truly at his best. He was named one of the *Wisden* cricketers of the year in 1933.

It was a shame, then, that the same period was such a turbulent one for English cricket and that Voce saw his opportunities in Test cricket reduced as a result. Chosen for the Ashes tour of 1932/3, captain Douglas Jardine employed Voce, along with Larwood, as his shock weapons in the leg-theory ploy that became known as Bodyline. Playing four of the five Tests in the series (he missed the fifth through injury), Voce picked up 15 wickets at a respectable average of 27. That, along with his domestic feats, should have been more than enough to see him selected for the return series in 1934, but both Nottinghamshire bowlers were omitted for diplomatic, rather than cricketing, reasons. As if to underline the injustice of the policy, Voce took 8 for 66 in the first innings when the Australians took on his county and did not spare the bouncers.

So frustrated was he by his treatment at the hands of the MCC that he declared himself unavailable for selection for the 1935 Tests against South Africa but relented a year later. Despite taking few wickets in his solitary Test of 1936, Bill Voce found himself back on the boat to Australia in 1936/7 for another tour. Under the leadership of Gubby Allen – who had refused to bowl Bodyline on Jardine's tour – there was to be no repeat of the leg-theory tactics; a policy which Voce agreed to after some hesitation. Bowling to a conventional field, he had an exceptional series. In the first Test Voce took ten wickets in the match and, bowling in tandem with his captain, knocked over the Australians in the second innings for 58 in the space of 12.3 (eight ball) overs for an England victory by 322 runs. His performance in the second Test was similarly noteworthy. Just the seven wickets this time but he set the tone for the eventual innings victory by blowing away the Australian top order in the first innings. By the end of the third over the hosts were wobbling, three wickets down and only one run on the board. Bill Voce had taken them all in the space of four balls, including Bradman, caught by Allen for a golden duck. A back injury would seriously curtail his effectiveness for the final two tests of the tour, yet he still returned home with a haul of 26 wickets at an average of under 22.

The knee injury he picked up playing for England the following year meant that Voce's international career could not continue upwards. He was selected for three Tests after the war but was nowhere near his best and took only one wicket in those matches. After retiring from playing, he turned to coaching and died, in his native Nottinghamshire, in 1984, aged 74.

* *

Back in 1930, the MCC party – players, manager, umpire Joe Hardstaff (who also acted as baggage-man) plus Mrs Calthorpe – boarded the Lady Drake just hours after the second Test had drawn to a close to set sail for British Guiana, with high hopes of wrapping up the series on the comfort of familiar turf wickets.

Bourda, Friday 22 February 1930
Day one

On the first morning of the third Test, Freddie Calthorpe strolled out to the middle, bathed in beautiful Demerara sunshine. The pitch looked a perfect batting track; fast but true. In such conditions a drawn Test was widely anticipated – an outcome that the MCC captain would not have found upsetting given his men's series lead – but Calthorpe had reason to feel quietly confident of an even better result. This was to be his third match on the Bourda pitch and the two warm-up games had resulted in thumping innings victories for the touring side. The local team had reason to claim they were undercooked seeing that the weather had seriously curtailed their opportunities to practice but, for Calthorpe, the all-round performance of his players must have given satisfaction regardless of the state of readiness of the opposition. Pleasingly, all his bowlers had played well, sharing in the wickets, and contributions with the bat had been made up and down the order. It had often not been pretty ("unimaginative, unenterprising, unimpassioned", according to one local newspaper) but most of the batsmen seemed to have the measure of the pitch. Most importantly, England's big guns continued to fire, with centuries for Sandham and Ames. And then there was Hendren. The magnificent Patsy. 254 not out in the first Guianese match, 171 in the second. With the Middlesex man in such form, it was difficult to see how they could be beaten. A few clouds had loomed for Calthorpe: Greville Stevens and vice-captain Ronald Stanyforth had left the island with illnesses, and Jack O'Connor had been injured when hit by a beamer from Merrill Anthony in the second local game. At least, with only eleven fit players at his disposal, the captain had no selection dilemmas; something which could not be said for his opponents.

Following defeat in the second Test, the Caribbean had been awash with arguments over selection for the combined team. Widely held was a view that the omission of Edwin St Hill and Derek Sealy in Trinidad had been a mistake and one that needed to be rectified in Guiana. Questions were raised about which, if any, Guianese men should be added for their home Test. Perhaps the biggest decision for the selection committee, however, was over the place of opening batsman Clifford Roach. Roach, a centurion in the first Test, had struggled with the bat since, with a run of scores that read: 2, 13, 9, 0, 0 and 0. To drop such a key member of the West Indies side – especially as an invitation had been extended to him before the extent of his bad trot had become evident – would have been a bold and controversial move; possibly too controversial for an island board other than his native one. Realising this, the magnanimous Roach sent a cable to Guiana offering to stand down for the Test.

It was not an offer that the Guianese selection committee took him up on. Roach remained in the side while Derek Sealy and Edwin St Hill returned. The captaincy, to no-one's surprise, went to the skipper of the British Guiana team, Maurice Fernandes; a batsman who had been on the 1928 West Indies tour of England, featuring in the Lord's Test. He led a side of five Guianese, four Trinidadians, two Bajans and one Jamaican. Once again, practicalities and politics had chopped and change the West Indian line-up. The notable absentee on this occasion was the Bajan quick, Herman Griffith, who had been unavailable to travel on to Guiana due to commitments at home.

At 11:30 the teams followed umpires Hardstaff and Hill onto the field to an enthusiastic reception from the crowd of only a few hundred. Attendances had been an issue at all of the tour matches at the Bourda.

The second local game, in particular, was played to a conclusion in front of fewer than fifty people. Complaints were heard about the prices being charged for admission and, consequently, in attempt to swell the crowds for the Test, prices for the 'rails' had been reduced from 16 cents to 12 cents and 'season' tickets for some seats in the stands were also brought down. Local schools were instructed to reduce the length of their day to four hours so that the children could attend the later sessions of the match. Once various local dignitaries' hands had been shaken, the toss took place. Calthorpe called incorrectly and Clifford Roach walked to the wicket alongside Errol Hunte to open the innings for the West Indies.

The pressure was on Roach to find his form and find it quickly. He had spoken to an early coach of his, George John, prior to the match and had revealed his intentions regarding the innings. "I am going to fight for the first hundred", said the batsman, "and if they let me get that, then I am going to get my own back in the second." This promise would mean a dramatic change in style. Roach was never one to spend too long playing himself in; it would be quite a stretch for him to do so for one hundred runs.

Bill Voce opened the bowling from the Northern End. While the track was expected to be batting friendly, it also promised to give a bowler like Voce some early bounce to work with and the Nottinghamshire man would not be hesitant to use it. He knew, though, how the crowd would react to any bumpers he sent down. It was clear from the first local match that they had not forgotten the words of Calthorpe in Barbados and let Voce know it whenever he dropped short. On this morning, however, he settled onto a good length, letting the natural lift of the hard Bourda pitch do the work. Roach was not to be tempted. True to his word, he began watchfully, letting the ball pass over the stumps. When, on the fifth ball of the match, Voce pitched one up, Roach found himself in trouble as the ball thudded into his pad.

Fortune was on the side of the Trinidadian and Umpire Hardstaff was unmoved by Voce's appeal.

When Nigel Haig began the next over from the Southern End he found Roach's partner, Errol Hunte, in a similarly cautious mood. Both men were respectful to anything straight, waiting for the bowlers to err in line before they cut and drove through the off-side or leg-glanced for the occasional run. Voce and Haig were followed by Les Townsend and the veteran Wilfred Rhodes – another right-left arm combination – and, with less pace on the ball for the batsmen to work with, the scoring remained slow. When lunch was taken, the score sat at a very un-Caribbean-like 38 for no wicket. While wicketless, the English attack would not have been displeased by their morning's work. The only real blemish had been when Hunte had edged Haig to Voce standing close in at gully and the fielder grassed the relatively simple chance. The duel between Roach and Rhodes had been the centrepiece of the session. The wily spinner held as tight a line as always, but he was played expertly by Roach; the West Indian danced down the wicket to Rhodes' good length balls, smothering them at source, and then, when Rhodes changed his length, sat back in the crease to work the runs that would break the shackles of the over.

Following lunch, it looked as though the slow pace would continue, as the Roach-Hunte partnership resumed its watchful brief against Voce and Haig. It was when Calthorpe rang the changes, turning to first Astill and Rhodes, then himself, Les Townsend and Bob Wyatt, that the game livened. The batsmen had seen themselves in and decided it was time to up the pace. As the drives, cuts and hooks began to appear in increasing regularity, England's fielding began to look ragged; two more dropped catches off Hunte, overthrows, a ball trickling through Townsend's legs for runs, a missed stumping and wicketkeeper Ames suffering the misfortune of being hit by an errant throw from Wyatt at square-leg. At one point, as the score mounted, the tactics smacked of desperation, with Astill bowling half-volleys to Hunte in the hope he might miscue one. Hunte was in no mood to oblige and patted the inviting deliveries back to the bowler, much to the amusement of the growing crowd. Finally, with the score on 144, the breakthrough came. Hunte, three runs after having reached his half-century, hit Wyatt straight to extra cover where Townsend took a comfortable catch.

Roach was joined by one of the heroes of the first test, the impressive Jamaican, George Headley, who was in no mood to settle-in slowly and drove his first delivery from Voce through the off-side for a single. Roach, however, had started to struggle with cramp in his left arm and, after some treatment on the field, hooked a short ball from Voce for four and cramped up again. Calthorpe generously agreed to take an early tea to allow the batsman, who had reached 87, some rest.

Roach, however, had no intention of allowing the bowlers any rest when play resumed. He may have told his old coach that the first hundred would be hard fought but, clearly, 87 had been sufficient and the batsman took after every one of the MCC bowlers. The first two overs after tea saw Roach take a leg-side boundary from each; a glide and a hook off Wyatt and Voce, respectively. Back on strike for the fourth ball of Wyatt's next over he took to the Warwickshire man, hitting him for three consecutive boundaries – an off-drive, a leg-glance and a hook – the first of which brought Roach his deserved century. It had taken him 193 minutes. The Trinidadian was good to his word and, the first hundred up, he set about getting "his own back" in the second. Calthorpe rang the bowling changes regularly, took the new ball when available, but to no avail. Roach's scoring rate continued to rise, hitting to all parts of the ground, including sixes off Astill, Rhodes and Haig. When the hundred partnership was raised, Headley's contribution had been just 25. The Jamaican had not been playing slowly, it was Roach who had been the express.

The onslaught continued from both ends with Roach and Headley pulling or hooking the quicker bowlers and driving the spinners, while being able to see out an over with a dead bat when required. Only 74 minutes after celebrating his first century, Roach danced down the wicket, drove Rhodes to cover point for a quick single and raised his bat to acknowledge his second. It had been a brilliant batting display that had utterly dismantled the MCC attack. Shortly after, Roach made his first real loose shot of the day and cut Townsend too close to cover-point, where Haig made no mistake. Gone for 209, including three sixes and 22 fours, the batsman left the middle to a tumultuous ovation. Headley was not far behind, 60 not out, as stumps were drawn with the score on 336 for 2. With the heat having reached over 80 in the shade during the day, the tired and battered English team dragged themselves to the sanctuary of the pavilion.

Saturday 22 February 1930
Day two

The first day had undoubtedly belonged to Roach and the West Indies, but Calthorpe's men had no reason to be downcast. It had been a flat wicket. A batman's track. One on which high scores were to be expected and they would get their chance to fill their boots later in the day. The task for the second morning was simply to make sure the total did not grow too large. And that meant getting rid of George Headley.

While Roach and Headley had complimented each other in their skill and range of shots, Headley and Fernandes were a contrast. Headley, the artist with poise and touch; Fernandes cramped and cautious. While the Jamaican was quick to use his feet to dictate the length of the delivery and play the ball away with the full face of his bat, the Guianese captain tended to sit back in the crease, waiting for a bad ball, with his pads a regular second line of defence.

At first both looked comfortable against the English attack, using the speed of Voce and Haig against them to keep the scoreboard ticking; 36 runs coming from 25 minutes of pace bowling. It was when Calthorpe made a double change, taking the pace off the ball by introducing Astill and Rhodes to the attack, that scoring started to slow. Fernandes found it difficult to get the ball away and the run of dot balls started to frustrate Headley who, finding an early single, would be forced to watch most overs from the non-striker's end. Eventually the pressure got to Fernandes and he hit out, punishing a full-toss from Astill with a leg-side boundary; a shot that received a large ovation from the crowd. With 400 on the board, the skipper tried to be similarly as adventurous against Rhodes but mistimed his hook and was caught behind by Ames. 400 for 3.

Derek Sealy was next in, but the young batsman's return was not to be a triumphant one. A few overs passed with Headley keeping the score moving but, facing Rhodes, Sealy tried to leg-glance, mistimed the stroke and provided a simple caught and bowled via a leading edge for a duck. Guianese Vibart Wight, making his second (and final) appearance in the Test arena, was determined not to hang around and after hitting Townsend for a couple of boundaries, was clean bowled by the right-armer for ten. At 417 for 5, England's tails were up but they had still not dislodged Headley who continued to find the boundary with sumptuous cuts and drives and, shortly before Wight's departure, brought up his century with a rare streaky nick through the slips for four.

The crowd knew who was in next and, as Learie Constantine stepped from the pavilion, the air filled with the loudest ovation. Constantine, hard hitting, so often the hero with the ball, was a popular enough figure across the Caribbean already and the latest run-in with Calthorpe had simply enhanced his folk-hero status.

* *

Learie Constantine's role as chief antagonist of Calthorpe and the England side tapped into an aspect of the colonial cricketing story that was at odds with the intentions of the Imperial elite. While, for them, the growth of this most English of all sports was part of spreading British values and encouraging the assimilation of local populations, in the Caribbean the success of West Indian – particularly black West Indian – cricketers was an indicator of exactly the opposite. Success, particularly against English teams, symbolised pride, independence, self-determination; to stand toe-to-toe with the imperial oppressors and beat them at their own game. That Constantine did so with fear-inducing aggression that so upset the likes of The Honourable Frederick Somerset Gough-Calthorpe, gave extra piquancy to the fight; a theme that would have resonance right through the twentieth century.

Victory on the field of play was not only one in the eye for the rulers from the masses but a direct challenge to contemporary British notions of racial hierarchies. Such upsetting of the ideas which ran through the veins of the Empire came into sharp focus with the rise of batting talents such as George Headley. Assumptions – which were still being voiced by notable figures late into the twentieth century – had grown about the success of black West Indian fast bowlers being a result of racial physiology; that they were simply born with bodies that allowed them to do so. The West Indian as bowler also fitted nicely into existing ideas of the lower status of the bowler that came from the amateur/professional divide in the English domestic game. That someone like Headley – black, professional – could reach the same heights of the game with the bat as men like Bradman or Hobbs was no small matter.

A further issue was that of the captaincy of the West Indian side. That only white cricketers were considered for the position, drew an unbreakable line where any challenge to racial hierarchy would stop. As the West Indies gained Test status, showed they could compete against English sides and did so predominantly by the cricketing talents of their black players, agitation for the leadership of the side to be taken from exclusively white hands grew. C L R James, through the pages of *The Nation,* led calls for a change in policy, arguing the case for George

Headley to take command. The calls were eventually successful – albeit for a single Test – when the Jamaican led the West Indies against England in 1947. It would not be until 1960, however, that black captaincy became a more permanent feature. The groundwork for this eventual change was laid in series such as 1930 by the likes of Constantine, Headley and Roach.

* *

On this occasion, however, Constantine's stay at the crease would be short. After a few singles, twos and one boundary, he missed a leg-break from Wyatt and was stumped by Les Ames, in fine form behind the stumps. Adding to Constantine's misfortune, a few overs before, he and Headley had attempted a too ambitious second run to Gunn on the third man boundary. The Nottinghamshire man sent in an accurate return to Ames who completed the run-out with Headley feet from his crease. It had been a beautiful innings and one which no doubt should have gone on to even greater heights. Still, 114 was a worthy return. With Headley and Constantine gone, England were into the tail at 446 for 7.

Resuming after lunch, the crowd, taking advantage of further reductions in entrance fees, had grown considerably. They were briefly entertained by Snuffie Browne hitting out against Voce's pace, before the bowler sent the batsman's off-stump cartwheeling out of the ground. The tail – Charles Jones, George Francis and Edwin St Hill – offered little resistance and the West Indies innings closed just twenty minutes into the afternoon session with 471 runs on the board. It was a strong total but the feeling in the ground was that they could have got more and that, with Hendren, Ames and Sandham reaching for their pads, the MCC were more than capable of matching it.

As in each of the previous Tests, Gunn and Sandham were to open for England. It was to be Francis and Constantine for the West Indies with the ball. From the start, the home team's tactics were clear – it was to be fast and often short. The very first ball fired a warning shot across the MCC's bows when a lightning-bolt from Francis not only beat Gunn for pace but wicketkeeper Hunte also. The opening batsmen were not to be cowed and took the fight to the bowling with square-cuts and leg-glides. Gunn particularly looked up for the battle until, when on just 11, having been struck a painful blow on the thigh, was pushed back too far in the crease by the pace of Francis and stepped on his own wicket. Bob Wyatt, batting at three, did not relish the pace of the bowling or the wicket as much as the man he had replaced and, before he could trouble the scorers, blindly fended off a short Constantine rocket and was snaffled by Francis in the gully. The crowd erupted and, at 20 for 2, England were in trouble.

Help was at hand. The large, reassuring figure of Patsy Hendren emerged into the Guianese sunlight to try and steady the ship. Captain Fernandes was determined to keep his bowlers fresh and, after eleven overs, made a double change. St Hill, sharp but not quite as quick as Constantine, came on to bowl, followed by the medium pace of Browne. Hendren immediately looked comfortable and began to work both men for runs. Sandham was finding life more difficult, especially off Browne, who gave the opener less pace to work with and, after batting for an hour, had only nine runs to his name. Finally, trying to force the pace a little, Sandham went for a cut off Browne and was sharply taken by Hunte close behind the stumps. 33 for 3.

It was time for the partnership that had performed so well in the first two Tests – Hendren and Ames – and they saw England safely to tea. On resumption, the batting assumed a peculiar character. On the one hand both men looked confident against the attack, taking the score into three figures; on the other they repeatedly flirted with danger. Ames was dropped twice, Hendren played the ball perilously close the wicket on a couple of occasions and had some near-misses in the field. In one such instance, Francis took a one-bounce return catch and jokingly held it aloft. Hearing the cheers from the hoodwinked crowd, Patsy played along and started to trudge to the pavilion before stopping, smiling, and returning to the crease.

Ames's luck did not hold. Francis, returning to the attack, drew a mistimed pull from the Englishman that skied the ball and presented Hunte with the simplest of chances. The wicketkeeper did not disappoint. Townsend, the new man, barely had time to adjust to the light before he nicked the same bowler behind and was walking back to the pavilion having scored three. 107 for 5 and the responsibility to try and nudge the score to respectability – at least to avoid the ignominy of following-on – looked like Hendren's alone.

Pushing on, Hendren had brought up his half century when cricketing disaster struck. Facing Constantine, the batsman had been treated to a couple of slower balls before the Trinidadian sent down a quicker one; short but delivered with a lower arm. The ball did not get up as much as Hendren anticipated, the attempted hook missed, and he was clean bowled. The crowd erupted. Particularly raucous was the noise coming from the stand reserved for schoolchildren. A few days before the match, Patsy had given some local schoolboys advice on batting and had voiced his opinion that a good batsman was rarely bowled. Those boys now at the Bourda had a lot of fun with that and, as Hendren departed with his stumps in a mess, "behaved very badly."

'Very badly' was also how it was going for the MCC. The remaining batsmen could not cope with the ferocity of Constantine and Francis and soon crumbled. 120 for 7 at stumps; all out for 145 early the next morning, a deficit of 326. The two bowlers shared eight of the wickets evenly between them. Only Astill, who had been run out for a duck while backing-up, could consider himself unlucky. The others had simply been outclassed.

Monday 24 February 1930
Day three

Sunday being a rest day, the players gathered next on the Monday to resume their contest at an overcast Bourda. The English innings was wrapped up within 35 minutes; only the captain Calthorpe showing anything close to resistance. All eyes turned to Fernandes for a decision regarding the follow-on which, he announced, would not be enforced.

The decision caused a fair degree of consternation and argument within the crowd, many of whom were clearly hoping to see Constantine and Francis get about the English wickets. Perhaps even force a win later that day. For some, Fernandes was taking a risky path with the possibility of rain coming to the rescue of the Englishmen if the match was extended unnecessarily. The more conspiratorially minded of observers suggested that, given the MCC tour had not been the bonanza sell-out that the Guiana Cricket Club may have hoped for, Fernandes (a G.C.C. member) was ensuring there would be cricket on the fourth and fifth days for the paying public to watch. A more charitable interpretation of the decision to bat again was that the skipper wanted to give his fast bowlers some rest before unleashing them again on the English batting order and was trying to avoid the prospect of chasing even a small total on a potentially crumbling wicket. Whatever the reason, the animated discussions amongst crowd members were still carrying on when Roach and Hunte emerged to start the second innings; so much so that there was hardly a reception for the opening pair.

As expected, Voce, in partnership with Haig, took the new ball. The Nottinghamshire bowler, remembering his success in Trinidad with slower deliveries, began by taking pace off the bowl, focusing instead on getting the ball to swing and move off the wicket. The tactic did not work so well this time and, often bowling to a packed leg-side field, both he and Haig found themselves milked easily for runs. The latter bowler also put down a caught and bowled chance giving Roach, of all people, a second life.

Calthorpe did not wait long before changing his attack. With only 19 on the board, Rhodes replaced Haig at the Southern End; Townsend for Voce at the Northern. It worked. The runs began to dry up and, with the score on 23, a breakthrough came, though not without a measure of controversy. Hunte, facing up to Townsend, swung hard at the fourth ball of the over, missed, looked back to see a bail dislodged and, assuming he had hit his own wicket, walked back to the pavilion. The scoreboard read 'hit wicket' but, for many of those watching, that had not been the case at all – it had been Ames who had removed the bail in an effort to enact a stumping. Furthermore, it was suggested, had Hunte realised and stood his ground, it was highly unlikely that Umpire Hardstaff, standing at square-leg, would have raised his finger as the batsman appeared to be safely in his crease. If the fielding captain was aware that he had not been given out stumped and Ames had indeed removed the bail, the gentlemanly thing to do would have been to call Hunte back before he reached the boundary. Whether Calthorpe was unaware or unwilling, Hunte was gone and the West Indies were 23 for 1.

George Headley joined Roach – a dangerous combination – and looked in fine nick, finding the gaps despite Rhodes bowling to a packed off-side field. Ominously for England, both batsmen appeared unthreatened by the bowling and took the home team through to lunch with the score on 42.

During the luncheon interval, Calthorpe came to a decision. With the West Indian lead fast approaching 400, he wanted to slow things down, dry up the run-rate, frustrate the batsmen and take as much time out of the game as possible. So began a sometimes tortuous afternoon session. Rhodes was to be Calthorpe's main weapon. Bowling again to a packed off-side, the veteran spinner pitched his leg-breaks outside off-stump into the foot-hole worn into the crease by Voce, turning them further away from the batsmen's reach. From the other end Astill, though less consistently, placed his off-breaks outside leg-stump in a similar effort to 'hide' the ball. It had the desired effect as maiden overs mounted, only broken by the odd single when the bowler erred. The tactics were not well received by the large crowd. The rails were now thronged and in full voice, letting Rhodes, in particular, receive the full force of their displeasure. Calthorpe further enraged the watching public with his deliberate slowing of the pace between balls. Fielders moved at a leisurely speed around the field, consultations between bowler and captain were frequent and drink intervals were called for on several occasions. While everything was played within the laws, questions of the spirit of the tactics were raised, particularly given the self-proclaimed role of the MCC tour of educating the colonies in the ways of cricket. The word 'contemptable' was thrown at the fielding team more than once.

Finally, it was Roach who cracked. Reaching to drive a ball from Astill, the batsman missed and was stumped by Ames. His 22 had taken two hours to make. Fernandes was next in and, as in the first innings, played a cautious counterpart to Headley's attacking intent. The West Indian captain stood as virtual spectator when facing Rhodes, listening to the barracking of the crowd and watching as ball after ball passed wide outside his off-stump. After 32 minutes at the crease he went after one from Rhodes, skied it to cover-point where Bob Wyatt made a mess of the chance. The batsmen crossed, and Fernandes had scored his first run.

George Headley was not content to let the bowlers hide the ball away, taking what he could off Rhodes and going after Astill, using his quick feet to get to the ball. By tea, the pair had moved the score on to 99 for 2. Only 57 runs had been managed in the session. On resumption, Headley continued to attack when he could, threading the ball through the, often, eight man off-side field and even lifting Rhodes for six into the College Stand on one occasion. It was, though, becoming a lone stand as wickets started to tumble at the other end. Fernandes, brilliantly caught by Calthorpe at long on; St Hill, having been let off by the MCC captain off Rhodes, disposed of his batting gloves and was promptly bowled by Astill; and Constantine departed for a duck two balls later. All had gone hitting out in an attempt to up the scoring rate. It appeared that Calthorpe's controversial tactics of frustration had borne fruit and, when bad light brought a premature end to the third day, the home side were on 150 for 5. Headley with a hard fought 70 not out.

Tuesday 25 February 1930
Day four

Most pleasing for the MCC captain was not the five wickets captured but that his approach on the third day had the slowed the rate of scoring considerably. Indeed, during the previous evening session, it would not have suited him for the West Indians to have collapsed; that would have just given the MCC more time to bat to save the game. The lead by stumps was 476 and thoughts of an unlikely second innings chase had long been banished. As the temperature rose on the morning of the fourth day's play, the task for Calthorpe's men was set. Whether by five wickets falling or a declaration, the MCC would have something close to five sessions to see out for a hard-earned draw. So inevitable was the scenario that there was little point in pursuing the tactics of the day before which had brought such public disquiet. Instructions were passed to his bowlers that normal service could resume.

For the gathered spectators the morning was all about Headley and whether he could become only the fifth man to register a century in both innings of a Test. There was no question that Headley had the talent and the temperament to do so, it was more a question of whether his partners would hang around long enough to allow him time. The question became even more pertinent when, off the fourth over of the day, the youngster Sealy tried to lift Rhodes over the in-field and was caught by Hendren at mid-off. Equally as ominous for the prospects of a Headley century were signs that the pitch was starting to misbehave, with the occasional delivery keeping low.

There was no need to worry. The next man in, Vibart Wight, instantly calmed any nerves and the two took the score beyond 180 and Headley to the verge of his hundred. Then, with a sumptuous late cut off Rhodes, the deed was done and the crowd, along with the batsman, could celebrate an impressive knock. The Jamaican was warmly congratulated by the English fielders.

All that was left was for the batsman to push the score on as quickly as they could, ready for the declaration. The attack was taken to Haig and Voce, quick runs being more important at this stage in the match than preserving wickets. Perhaps inevitably, Headley's innings soon came to an end, slashing Haig towards cover-point where Townsend pulled off a one-handed catch. Headley left the field to a well-deserved ovation; out for 112.

With Headley gone, the English bowlers may have thought that the end of the innings was little more than a formality. They cannot have anticipated the havoc that the Bajan tail-ender Snuffie Browne was about to wreak. His first nine balls were a sedate affair – two singles and seven dot balls – but then his bat started to swing, consistently beating the field. By the time he ran out of partners, Browne had scored an undefeated 70 in 50 minutes, including ten fours and a six. The West Indies, all out for 290 on the cusp of lunch (though captain Fernandes came in for some criticism for not declaring earlier). Ewart Astill had finished with four wickets and his bowling partner Wilfred Rhodes with two; the Yorkshireman with the remarkable return of 23 maidens from his 51 overs, largely as a result of his unpopular tactics from the third day. The target for an MCC victory was 617 but, realistically, their task was to bat out five sessions to save the match.

The crowd were full of anticipation for what was going to be a fascinating finish and gave Gunn and Sandham a rousing welcome when they took the field. Nineteen balls later the crowd were back in full voice as Sandham made the return journey before a run had been added by either batsman; caught and bowled Constantine. If Bob Wyatt had been intending to come in and calm the nerves of his compatriots, he did not start that way; surviving an LBW decision from his first ball from Constantine and then edging Francis through the slips in the next over. It was apparent that Wyatt was finding the pace of Constantine too hot to handle. Facing the second ball of Constantine's fourth over, the Trinidadian sent down a slower ball, the umpire called it a no-ball and Haig took the opportunity to deposit the fast bowler over the southern boundary for six. It was not difficult to predict what was coming next and, even though Wyatt would have been as ready as everyone else, he struggled to duck out of the way of the rising ball, fended it with his bat, which was promptly knocked from his hands by the ferocity of the delivery. Credit to the Warwickshire man, despite looking increasingly uncomfortable in the face of a Constantine barrage, he continued to chance his arm against the bumper and, three balls later, made enough contact to sky one over the slips, just out of reach of the chasing Derek Sealy.

What happened next was the subject of hot debate across Guiana for the rest of the day. The crowd must have been rubbing their hands at the prospect of another roughing up of Wyatt at the hands of Constantine. When Constantine began his next over with an errant line and was easily put away to the leg-side boundary by the Warwickshire right-hander, those gathered would have been justified for fearing for the health of the batsman. Yet the anticipated salvo did not arrive. The batsman played out an over of good length balls and, before the duel could resume, Constantine was replaced by Edwin St Hill, only five overs into his spell. For some at the ground it was patently clear that the change had been political; that Fernandes had instructed the fast bowler to reign in his bouncers so not to cause further incident with their visitors. Such theories were given more credence when, later returned to the attack, Constantine did not resume his aggressive line.

Others more charitable to the West Indian captain argued that Fernandes was trying to keep his premier bowler fresh for Hendren and Ames and that, by pitching the ball up, Constantine was more likely to take the wickets his team needed for victory.

With both Constantine and Francis resting, the excitement levels dropped. The batsmen looked unthreatened by the medium pace of St Hill and Browne, defending anything on target and milking the odd single when they could. They were in no hurry to move the scoreboard along and, with the maidens racking up (St Hill's analysis read eight overs, six maidens, no wicket for seven runs), Fernandes called his opening pair back into the attack. Much to the disappointment of the crowd, when Constantine sent down his first over back, he did so at medium pace off a shortened run. When he finally returned to his usual run-up and pace, the masses roared their approval. Still, the English batsmen were in no mood to take any risks and the score crept along at a snail's pace. When tea was taken, Gunn and Wyatt remained unbeaten at 47 for 1.

Fearful that the pattern of the afternoon session would repeat itself in the evening, Fernandes tried every change he could to try and find a breakthrough. Straight after the break, the slow left arm of Charles Jones was given its chance, opening the session with Snuffie Browne. With Jones not looking like breaking the partnership, he was quickly replaced by George Headley to bowl his occasional leg-breaks. Soon normality resumed and Constantine replaced the part-time bowlers, partnering St Hill at the other end. Again Constantine, to the irritation of the crowd, would restrict himself to medium pace.

It may have been the fact that this fearsome quick was serving up medium pacers that emboldened George Gunn. Whatever the reason, he decided to come out of his shell and dispatched Constantine for 14 runs in an over. Bob Wyatt, who may have been annoyed by an attempt by the bowler to run him out while backing-up at the non-striker's end, decided to join in the fun. After missing a vicious pull-shot off

Constantine he tried to repeat the trick to the next ball and pulled it straight into the hands of Charles Jones at mid-on.

82 for 2

Time for Hendren to try and work his magic. If he was to do it, however, it would have to be with Les Ames again, as, seven balls after Hendren arrived at the crease, Gunn nicked the newly recalled Francis behind, where Hunte took a stunning catch.

82 for 3

Fernandes continued to ring the changes, rotating his bowlers with regularity and experimenting by allowing Vibart Wight his chance with the ball. It was to no avail and, at 5:10, bad light ended the day's play with England on 102 for 3.

Wednesday 26 February 1930
Day five

The fifth and final day of this controversial Test match dawned with the equation at its most simple. The home team needed seven wickets to register an historic win; the visitors, with victory beyond them, to bat the day for a draw. One complication loomed, and it favoured the visitors – the weather. Not only had bad light caused a premature end to the previous day, but rainclouds were about the region and threatened to play their part in the drama. Indeed, such was pessimism of many about the ability of the home side to force anything than a draw, that the crowd was noticeably smaller on that final morning.

One other reason for Calthorpe to remain optimistic was that Hendren and Ames, England's stalwart partnership throughout the tour, was still in place. There were no surprises as to who would open the bowling on that morning: Francis and Constantine. As with the previous day, however, if the spectators were hoping for fireworks from the quicks, they were often disappointed. Constantine mixed it up and bowled just as many medium pacers and lobs as quicker deliveries. The Trinidadian quick may have been reigning in his arm but was no less effective and, having registered a maiden for his first over, struck in his second. It was a curious prod outside the off-stump that Ames offered to a Constantine slower ball and the gift was gleefully accepted by Francis in the gully. A jubilant crowd saw the England wicketkeeper back to the pavilion.

106 for 4

The new man Townsend initially looked all at sea to Constantine, narrowly missing a fielder with the first ball received and subsequently edging one though the slips. He somehow managed to survive until Fernandes gave the fast bowler a rest. Much more of a contest was Constantine's duel with Hendren. Rising to the challenge, the Trinidadian cranked up his pace and showed no reluctance to drop the ball short or aim high tosses at the Middlesex man. Hendren was equal to the task, standing up to the barrage with hooks and pulls. It was an engrossing battle between two masters of their arts.

Francis and Constantine were replaced by Browne and St Hill, but the new attack looked ineffective. The batsmen were in no hurry – wicket preservation was the top priority – and runs came at a leisurely rate. Trying to force matters, Fernandes made another of his surprise bowling changes, entrusting Roach with the ball to try out his leg-breaks at one end and the return of the part-time bowler Jones at the other. It made little impact and made Fernandes appear somewhat desperate as he rotated through Constantine, Francis, St Hill, Wight and Roach in search of the next wicket. Matters were made worse when wicketkeeper Hunte had to leave the field with an injured finger, handing the gloves to Sealy. The West Indies were so close to victory but the England pair stood firm and the frustration of the home captain grew. Hendren soon registered his, seemingly obligatory, half-century and, soon after, lunch was taken with the score on 157 for 4.

It was difficult to say who would have been most pleased with their morning's work. England had managed to survive with only a single wicket lost but that wicket was the valuable one of Ames and the West Indies had seen from the first innings how the English lower-order was able to collapse.

One danger for Hendren and Townsend to navigate was that, under the agreed playing regulations of the time, the West Indies – in particular Francis and Constantine – would have the luxury of a new ball when the score reached 200. Keen to delay that eventuality, their rate of scoring ground to a halt and, after taking a couple of singles off the first two balls of the session, began to turn down even the safest of runs. So doggedly did the batsmen implement their stonewalling tactics, were it not for the occasional wide or no-ball, the scoreboard would have remained undisturbed. Constantine, probing for a breakthrough against passive opponents, ran through his repertoire of balls from the low round-arm skidder to the chest-high bumper. In response, Townsend adopted the approach of quickly taking body and bat out of the way of any delivery that appeared not to be heading towards his stumps. It worked – for a while – but it was perhaps inevitable that Constantine would be too good and, when the bowler hit a perfect length, which the Englishman misjudged, the ball knocked the bails to the ground.

162 for 5

With Nigel Haig at the crease, the partnership may have been new but the negative tactics remained the same. Captain Fernandes sensed another change necessary and threw the ball to Snuffie Browne.

Hendren took a single to keep the strike but, apart from that, the only runs accrued were four byes and a wide. When Haig finally faced up to the Bajan, he proved no match and, on the last ball of the over, failed to keep out a googly. Bowled for a duck.

168 for 6

Hendren decided that the tactics had to change. He could no longer sit back and watch the maidens rack up as his lower-order partners were skittled by the skills of Constantine and Browne. His response was immediate and Constantine was dispatched for two boundaries in the next over. The problem for Hendren was at the other end and he watched in alarm as the new man Astill was bewildered by Browne's googlies. Taking matters into his own hand, Hendren called his partner through for a sharp single and saw the spinner off himself. Two misfortunes then befell the Englishman. Firstly, he failed to find a single off the last ball of Browne's over, which would have let him keep the strike. Secondly, Astill decided that he would follow Patsy's lead and have a go at Learie Constantine. It worked, once, but having played the bowler to the leg-boundary he decided to repeat the shot, stepped back to hook a short ball and promptly trod on his own stumps.

181 for 7

England were in trouble. Freddie Calthorpe walked to the wicket aware that he was staring down the barrel of becoming the first man to lead a team to defeat in a Test match against the West Indies. The MCC skipper was not the sort of man to go down without a fight and, with the reassuring figure of Patsy Hendren at his side, Calthorpe took about his task with confidence and purpose.

For Fernandes, the apparently resolute partnership of Hendren and Calthorpe would normally have been considered a temporary problem.

There was still ample time left in the day to create enough opportunities to force a win. On that day, however, it was not so simple, as another problem loomed. Ominous looking clouds had begun to gather over the Bourda, making any calculation of exactly how much time was left to take those three much needed wickets uncertain. Fernandes had enough of the slow progress towards a total of 200 and the new ball and decided to force matters along. Eight byes from one Browne over, four overthrows, another four byes from Constantine's next plus a couple of helpful boundaries off the bat and the new, hard, ball was in hand.

While the recent sudden drop in fielding standards had been part of a plan, the subsequent lapse was certainly not. Almost immediately after Constantine had been armed with the new ball, he forced an error from Calthorpe. The batsman mistimed his shot and sent the ball steepling towards a waiting Fernandes at square-leg. It should have been the simplest of catches but the West Indian skipper, perhaps with other things on his mind, let it slip through his fingers to the turf. All knew how costly that error could be and, as if to underline the mistake, Calthorpe started collecting quick boundaries. Bad went to worse for Fernandes when, three overs after his drop, rain began to fall and the players trooped back to the sanctuary of the pavilion. Hendren undefeated on 73, Calthorpe on 24. 230 for 7.

Fortunately for the home side, it proved to be a brief shower and fifteen minutes later they were back on the field for Francis to complete his interrupted over. With the field up, any shot that pierced the in-field would most likely race to the fence and Calthorpe took full advantage, hitting five boundaries in the delayed over. Nothing seemed to go the West Indies way as edges began to fly over the slips' heads or just out of reach of frustrated fielders. As rain began to drizzle, the batsmen continued to play positively, happy to collect the runs on offer. Fernandes, as he had all day, changed the attack regularly, turning to the occasional bowler Roach for a third time. Calthorpe watched his first over with respect before deciding that his second was ripe for runs.

He hooked Roach's third deliver for four, took two byes off the fourth, edged the fifth through the slips for another boundary before hitting the last straight to mid-on, where Jones made no mistake. Out for 49; 48 of them scored after being dropped by Fernandes. The partnership with Hendren worth 88. It had been a gutsy knock by the captain, though, perhaps too aggressive at the end. With only Rhodes and Voce left to bat, it seemed only the weather could save England.

269 for 8

Wilfred Rhodes was no rabbit. This was a man who had, in his pomp, opened the batting for England alongside Hobbs. However, at 52 years of age, those days were long gone, and the West Indies may have thought that the Yorkshire veteran would not delay them long.

Tea was taken and when the players emerged again from the pavilion all eyes were cast upwards. Dark clouds had gathered, and the crowd sensed the possibility that the victory which had started to look inevitable might be snatched away by the elements. That threat was palpable when at 3:50, five minutes into the evening session, the players were back indoors, sheltering from the rain.

By five past four the rain had relented sufficiently for play to resume. Although the scheduled finish was half past five, given that play had ended at 5:10 the previous day due to bad light – and that had been without the presence of rainclouds to darken the skies further – the West Indies might only have an hour to remove two of the last three batsmen. And that was presuming there be no more interruptions.

The Englishmen were alert to the possibility of a weather assisted escape and emerged determined to do all they could to assist that. On taking the field, both batsmen immediately complained to the umpires that the wicket at the northern end had been covered later than the other and as such was wet and unsuitable for play. Umpire Hill told them to play on. They obliged, but as slowly as they could. Conversations between the batsmen became frequent. At one point Hendren felt it necessary to pat down the pitch at the striker's end with his bat in the middle of the over (something that would have been unremarkable were it not for the fact that it was Rhodes who was batting) and even held up St Hill by taking time to wipe water from the stumps. The time-wasting tactics were blatant and led to the crowd growing increasingly agitated. Their humour was not improved when Rhodes survived a loud appeal for LBW; West Indian umpire George Westermaas – a late replacement for the Englishman Hardstaff who had been indisposed at the start of the day's play – the man to shake his head.

The official was less obliging to the batsmen when, at the start of the following over, Hendren appealed for bad light. No matter though as, one ball later, the rain returned and another fifteen-minute delay further frustrated the home team.

When the players took the field again, Hendren and Rhodes received the full force of the crowd's displeasure as to the tactics they were so obviously pursuing. They were more generous when, off the first over on resumption, Hendren notched up the runs needed to take him to yet another century. The congratulations over, things were starting to look bleak for the West Indies. The clock was ticking its way to 5 o'clock and the light was starting to dwindle.

Then, shortly before the hour, a breakthrough came. Hendren, trapped in front by St Hill, looked up to see Umpire Westermaas raise his finger. The West Indies had not only got a wicket but had *the* wicket – Hendren. After nearly seven hours at the crease, he was out for 123 but was not going anywhere quickly. First, there was time for some fairly light-hearted remonstrating with the wicket keeper over the appeal (Hendren, it seems, had got some bat on the ball before it hit his pad), then there was the walk to the pavilion – a long, slow, circular walk that used up as much time as possible. It should have been a moment for the crowd to show their appreciation for another great innings by the Middlesex man but, not only did his ponderous walk from the wicket enrage the locals, his interplay with the fielders had not been seen as friendly by many of those watching and he left the field to a chorus of insults. The clock stood at two minutes to five by the time Voce arrived at the wicket.

326 for 9

Edwin St Hill, roared on by the excited spectators, came in to Voce but the batsman kept the delivery out. Francis, from the other end, had no success with the tail-enders and when his over was successfully navigated by Rhodes and Voce, Fernandes threw the ball to his main weapon, Constantine. With the light closing in, the West Indies were hurrying their overs; unlike Rhodes who took his time in readjusting his pads and refitting his gloves before facing up. The Yorkshireman was calmness itself and watchfully saw off the over; four byes the only score.

The time had gone five past five and the West Indians crowded round Voce as Francis pounded to the crease. Two dot balls came and went. The third forced a stroke and caught the edge but somehow managed to avoid the hands of those fielding behind the wicket. No run off the fourth ball. For the fifth, Francis pitched one up, straighter this time, which missed the bat of Voce and thudded into his pads. A huge appeal rang out and every eye in the Bourda turned to look at Umpire Hill who, without much hesitation, gave his verdict – out.

The Bourda erupted in joy. Celebrations continued long in Georgetown and across the island. In New Amsterdam, some 60 miles away, a large crowd had gathered throughout the afternoon at the telegraph office to keep abreast of the score as it was relayed to them. Roach, Headley, Constantine and Browne (the latter also took the opportunity to announce his retirement from international cricket) were presented with souvenirs to mark their achievements. The West Indies had registered their first Test match victory and had done so against the MCC, the touring guise of the islands' colonial masters. England had literally been beaten at their own game. The margin of victory – 289 runs – was large but belied how close it had come to a draw. Within fifteen minutes of the final wicket falling, rain swept across the Bourda.

Although much can be forgiven in victory, many would not forget the chicanery by which a drawn game was so nearly achieved. The English time-wasting with both bat and ball and the erroneous dismissal of Hunte in the second innings still rankled. How many times over the years had the colonists been lectured about the ethics of the gentleman's game, the importance of them learning and abiding by the spirit of cricket, those English values that were held so high? Why, even on that tour, had not the MCC captain felt it proper to lecture the jewel in the West Indian's bowling attack on the appropriate way to approach the game? The correspondent for *The Daily Chronicle* of Georgetown gave vent to such feelings. The Test, he angrily proclaimed, "was not played in accordance with the highest traditions of the game", indeed, he continued, if that was the spirit in which such matches would be contested, then better to not have them at all, lest the islands' young players be corrupted. It had been a "disgusting" affair "that taught British Guiana nothing uplifting." "The English team", he concluded, "were disgraced not only in cricketing and strategy...but also in the moral quality of courage which makes cricket the great game it is."

It would have been understandable if Freddie Calthorpe had wanted to board the boat to Jamaica as quickly and as quietly as possible. However, whether by desire or duty, the MCC captain had further counsel for the islanders. Speaking to *The Daily Chronicle*, Calthorpe mused on the Guianese teams his men had faced in the earlier local matches and expressed a withering opinion on their performance. He was, Calthorpe said, "disappointed" in their efforts. "You did not attack the bowling at all", he complained, "you seem to have been 'cowed' as it were, but after all, one of the best means of defence is attack." While he understood that the weather had hindered the Guianese team's preparation, Calthorpe surmised that he "expected you to do better." He advised that they would benefit by employing an English coach. The comments were extraordinary considering the negative tactics the MCC had employed in the third Test. Pressed on the matter of the time wasting at the Bourda, Calthorpe dismissed the criticisms by insisting that he "employed, rightly or wrongly, the only tactics which anybody who knew anything about cricket would have used." With at least a nod to conciliation, the Englishman complemented Learie Constantine's performance on the tour, describing him as "the best bowler and fielder in the world", although he could not let the moment pass without adding that Constantine could become the world's best all-rounder if he would only, "curb his methods of batting." It was not an unfair comment, just perhaps unfortunate in its timing.

Calthorpe and his team sailed to Jamaica for the tour's conclusion. The final Test, scheduled to be 'timeless' (played until a result was obtained), eventually finished after nine days as a draw simply because the MCC team needed to catch their boat home. So, the series was drawn 1-1 but, in truth, only did so because of misfortune or misjudgement, depending on how charitable one was to the decision of Freddie Calthorpe not to enforce the follow-on in the final match. The MCC's first innings in Jamaica was remarkable, finishing on 849 all out, with a world record-breaking 325 by Andrew Sandham; an innings which included 28 fours, one five and one seven. He also added a half-century in England's second innings; a knock which was to be Sandham's last in Test cricket.

After spending more than two whole days in the field, the West Indies – fielding a side with nine changes from the victorious Guiana match – could not get close to England's first innings score. Bowled out for 286, with only captain Karl Nunes registering a half-century. With the follow-on at Calthorpe's disposal and a lead of 563, it should have been a relatively simple matter of asking the West Indies to bat again and, with no concern about time running out, departing the Caribbean with a series win. It was the timeless nature of the match that lulled Calthorpe into a false sense of security and he, perhaps understandably, opted to give his bowlers a rest from the heat by electing to bat again. The English batsmen played positively, moving the score along at a rate of just under three and half runs an over, and, by the time they declared, nine wickets down on the morning of the sixth day, the lead stood at an unnecessarily large 835. The sixteen runs added on the morning of the declaration were particularly puzzling.

There were two things missing from Calthorpe's calculations: the first was the weather, the second was the brilliance of George Headley. On Saturday 12 April, the ninth day of the match, Freddie Calthorpe and his men sat helplessly watching the rain soak the outfield and wash out the last possible day's play before the liner Changuinola set sail for Dartmouth Harbour with the MCC party on board. The West Indies were still on 408 for 5, Headley having made an impressive 223.

As the MCC sailed for home, it was clear which of the two sides would have been the happier. The West Indies, despite all the chopping and changing of personnel so common of combined island teams of the period, had emerged with huge credit. A tied series result and their first Test win. It had taken only six Test matches to register a victory; a figure which would go on to compare very favourably to South Africa's 12, India's 25 and New Zealand's 45. The tour had also seen the Test debut of the incomparable George Headley. The Jamaican would play 22 Tests for the West Indies, registering ten centuries (two of them doubles) and 2,190 runs at an average in excess of 60. The West Indies would not wait too long for their second victory – their first away from home – when, a year after Guiana, another Headley century inspired them to a narrow win against Australia in Sydney. Their first series victory would come in 1935, winning a four Test home series against an England side captained by Bob Wyatt, 2-1.

While the defeat of England in Guiana and a hard-fought draw for the tied series in the last Test were celebrated across the islands, it is difficult to assess exactly what the feelings were amongst the English, either returning from the Caribbean or back home. Little was made of the result in the British press and what reporting there was of the Guiana Test match often focused on the battling qualities of Hendren's second innings effort. The *Daily Express*, for instance, led its report of the West Indian victory with the headline "Heroic Hendren"; The *Daily Mirror* limited its report to two sentences, one of them informing their readers of Hendren's score. The *Athletic News*, at least, remarked on a "red letter day in the history of West Indian cricket." Even *Wisden* gave the series perfunctory coverage, describing it as "a most enjoyable tour." Perhaps most tellingly of the lack of importance attached to overseas tours – or at least this particular overseas tour – is that one of the two men in Calthorpe's party to subsequently write a memoir of their career, Patsy Hendren, did not consider his time in the West Indies in 1930 worth mentioning. Despite racking up 1,765 runs on the tour, featuring six centuries, four of them doubles, and finishing with a tour average of 135, Hendren's exploits in the Caribbean are completely absent from his 1934 book *Big Cricket*.

The English view of cricket remained Anglo-centric or at least Anglo-Australian centric. Cricketing history played its part here, but the role of race cannot be ignored. Indeed, it would take some time – perhaps West Indian victory on English soil at Lord's in 1950, perhaps the emergence of Garry Sobers as the greatest all-rounder, perhaps the gaining of political independence by the island nations from 1962 onwards or even the emergence of the all-conquering side of the 1970s and 80s, that the English establishment would be forced into the realisation that cricket was not an Englishman's – a white Englishman's – gift.

Marylebone Cricket Club in West Indies 1929/30 (3rd Test)

Venue: Bourda, Georgetown on 21st, 22nd, 24th, 25th, 26th February 1930 (5-day match)

Toss: West Indies

Umpires: J Hardstaff, RDR Hill

West Indies first innings

CA Roach	c Haig	b Townsend	209
+EAC Hunte	c Townsend	b Wyatt	53
GA Headley	run out		114
*MP Fernandes	c Ames	b Rhodes	22
JED Sealy	c and b Rhodes		0
CV Wight	b Townsend		10
LN Constantine	st Ames	b Wyatt	13
CR Browne	b Voce		22
CEL Jones	c Ames	b Voce	6
GN Francis	not out		5
EL St Hill	st Ames	b Haig	3
Extras	(3 b, 11 lb)		14
Total	(all out, 148 overs)		471

Fall of wickets:
1-144, 2-336, 3-400, 4-406, 5-417, 6-427, 7-446, 8-459, 9-464, 10-471

Bowling	Overs	Mdns	Runs	Wkt
Voce	26	4	81	2
Haig	23	7	61	1
Townsend	16	6	48	2
Rhodes	40	8	96	2
Astill	28	3	92	0

Calthorpe	6	0	23	0
Wyatt	9	0	56	2

England first innings

G Gunn	hit wkt	b Francis	11
A Sandham	c Hunte	b Browne	9
RES Wyatt	c Francis	b Constantine	0
EH Hendren	b Constantine		56
+LEG Ames	c Hunte	b Francis	31
LF Townsend	c Hunte	b Francis	3
NE Haig	b Constantine		4
WE Astill	run out		0
*FSG Calthorpe	c Headley	b Constantine	15
W Rhodes	b Francis		0
W Voce	not out		1

Extras	(11 b, 2 lb, 2 nb)	15
Total	(all out, 61.3 overs)	145

Fall of wickets:
1-19, 2-20, 3-33, 4-103, 5-107, 6-117, 7-120, 8-126, 9-141, 10-145

Bowling	Overs	Mdns	Runs	Wkts
Francis	21	5	40	4
Constantine	16.3	6	35	4
Browne	10	2	29	1
St Hill	14	4	26	0

West Indies second innings

CA Roach	st Ames	b Astill	22
+EAC Hunte	hit wkt	b Townsend	14
GA Headley	c Townsend	b Haig	112
*MP Fernandes	c Calthorpe	b Rhodes	19
EL St Hill	b Astill		3

LN Constantine	b Astill		0
JED Sealy	c Hendren	b Rhodes	10
CV Wight	b Haig		22
CR Browne	not out		70
GN Francis	lbw	b Astill	2
CEL Jones	b Townsend		2
Extras	(9 b, 5 lb)		14
Total	(all out, 127.3 overs)		290

Fall of wickets:

1-23, 2-76, 3-135, 4-138, 5-138, 6-155, 7-209, 8-248, 9-281, 10-290

Bowling	Overs	Mdns	Runs	Wkts
Voce	16	4	44	0
Haig	10	1	44	2
Rhodes	51	23	93	2
Townsend	7.3	2	25	2
Astill	43	17	70	4

England second innings

G Gunn	c Hunte	b Francis	45
A Sandham	c and b Constantine		0
RES Wyatt	c Jones	b Constantine	28
EH Hendren	lbw	b St Hill	123
+LEG Ames	c Francis	b Constantine	3
LF Townsend	b Constantine		21
NE Haig	b Browne		0
WE Astill	hit wkt	b Constantine	5
*FSG Calthorpe	c Jones	b Roach	49
W Rhodes	not out		10
W Voce	lbw	b Francis	2
Extras	(30 b, 5 lb, 3 nb, 3 w)		41

Total   (all out, 158.5 overs)   327

Fall of wickets:
1-0, 2-82, 3-82, 4-106, 5-162, 6-168, 7-181, 8-269, 9-320, 10-327

Bowling	Overs	Mdns	Runs	Wkts
Francis	26.5	11	69	2
Constantine	40	17	87	5
Browne	33	15	32	1
St Hill	33	15	61	1
Roach	9	2	18	1
Headley	2	0	8	0
Jones	10	7	5	0
Wight	5	1	6	0

5. WAR, ONCE MORE

Sussex versus Yorkshire
Hove, 30 August-1 September 1939

The more things change, the more they stay the same.

It had only been twenty-five years since the start of the devastating conflict that had become known as The Great War and Britain was staring down the barrel of a gun once more. Twenty-five years. Shorter than the Test career of Wilfred Rhodes. The blink of an eye.

And how was this England that stood on the brink of another great battle? Look one way and it was far from the England of 1914. Look another and it seemed not to have changed.

As in life, as in cricket. This was not the same game played by Blythe or Fry or the Grand Old Man Grace. Yet, in another light, it was just that.

The more things change, the more they stay the same.

* *

Many of the changes in English society, politics and economics that took place in the inter-war years were continuations of trends that pre-dated the Great War. Britain, by 1913, had lost its place as the world's leading manufacturer, and that relative decline continued in the post-war world to the point that by 1939 its share of world manufacturing had fallen to 9 per cent; behind the United States, Russia and Germany.

At home, changes to the social fabric would move on a pace, yet the diminishing control of British political institutions by the aristocratic class in the inter-war years was but an extension of a movement that dated back to the Great Reform Act of 1832 and continued through further extensions of electoral suffrage, the taming of the House of Lords in the Parliament Act of 1911 and the rise of the Labour Party.

Such social disruption reached the highest political office. The resignation of the Marquess of Salisbury from the post of Prime Minister in 1902 marked the last time a member of the House of Lords would occupy number ten Downing Street. Men of aristocratic heritage would lead governments again, but never while in possession of their inherited title. The early twentieth century also saw men from the lower-classes promoted to the top job in party politics. Liberal Prime Minister David Lloyd George was raised by his mother Elizabeth and her brother Richard Lloyd, a cobbler and Baptist minister; Labour's first Premier Ramsay MacDonald was the illegitimate son of a crofter.

Who was or was not part of the British elite was in flux, much to the dismay of some from the old aristocracy. Industrialists or, worse, 'war profiteers' were taking their place at the top table through marriage or the purchase of land. Even the House of Lords, that bulwark of the British aristocracy, had seen an influx of new money, including some who had directly purchased a title from the government of Lloyd George; knighthoods could be bought for £10,000, a peerage would set you back over £50,000.

The intangible feature of English aristocratic life known as 'society' was similarly changing. The Country House, such a staple of the pre-war social calendar, was under threat as many landed aristocratic families faced pressing financial straits which could lead to the sale of parts of, if not the entire, estate. The stabilisation of the food supply after the end of the conflict led to a drop in the prices of wheat, barley and oats and helped contribute to a collapse of land values during the 1920s that, along with a sharp fall in agricultural rents, presented huge financial challenges for those whose family wealth was tied to rural land ownership. Rising taxes challenged them further. A war-time super-tax on annual incomes over £10,000 was retained and assessed on gross income rather than net – a particular problem for landowners with larger than average outgoings due to the demands of property upkeep. Inheritance taxes added to the pressure on landed gentry to sell-up; in 1919, estate duties on properties valued at over £2 million were set at 40 per cent, by 1930 that figure was 50 percent, by 1939, 60 per cent. Further financial strain was felt in families where the male head of the household had been killed or seriously injured during the war and, in some cases, the wives and widows of these men found themselves having to work to sustain the lifestyle to which they had become accustomed.

The effect of this was an increasing metropolitanisation of the upper-class as families looked to uncouple their fortunes from landed estates and other property – adding to and caused by the wider inter-war change from a British economy based on land and international finance to one centred on commerce and manufacturing. Some land from aristocratic estates was rented out, some sold to tenant farmers, and other parts were snapped up by the nouveau riche in an attempt to cement their social status. "England" lamented *The Times*, "is changing hands."

Also changing were the attitudes of many of the young aristocracy towards their expected place in society and how they should be seen to behave. For some of that younger generation, the certainty and stability that came with their social position had been torn apart by the war and they looked to carve out a new freedom from themselves, often very publicly.

The antics of these so-called 'bright young things' and the dazzle of high society remained attractive to newsreel cameras and newspaper editors. However, while the young aristocrats of the 1920s and 30s retained their social cache, they increasingly shared the limelight with the equally glamorous stars of cinema screen, stage and gramophone. The criteria for inclusion in this new elite was becoming one of fashion and glitz rather than simply title or breeding. Nightclubs became an increasingly popular place for the young upper-class to let their hair down. Even the Prince of Wales was seen in the nightspots of Bond Street and Piccadilly.

If the upper-classes appeared to be in danger of losing their footing, the middle-class seemed to be on the rise. After a few rocky years immediately after the war, middle-class Britons began to enjoy a more prosperous time, particularly when compared to those both below and above them in the social strata. A combination of a lowering of the cost of living in the 1920s, relative stability in the level of pay for those in salaried professions and comparatively low middle-class unemployment (even during the years of the Great Depression) saw those in professional and management roles having by far the best of it. The extra spending power allowed people to enjoy more fruit, vegetables, eggs, milk and sugar; many children able to relish in the arrival of new chocolate brands such as Mars Bars, Milky Ways and Smarties. New technologies were also making their way into the home, with luxuries such as the wireless and the refrigerator becoming affordable objects for many. Even the motor car was no longer the preserve of the rich.

One of the largest changes in inter-war British life was the rise in the levels of home-ownership. The up-lift in middle-class spending power, together with slum clearance programmes and increased house building, opened the possibility of owning a home for more people than ever before. If Britain did not completely shift from being a nation of renters to one of owner-occupiers, the proportion of the population who lived in their own property increased from ten per cent at the outbreak of the first World War to 35 per cent on the eve of the second.

While the 1920s and 30s were good for some, those in waged or casual employment faced a much more difficult time. From the start of the War until about 1920, wages increased all round, particularly for unskilled workers. Unfortunately, this would not last and, between

1920 and 1923, wage levels fell quickly; those working in the mines hit especially hard. When earnings began to stabilise from 1923 onwards and prices continued to fall, many workers saw an up-tick in their spending power. The problem here was, for that to happen, they needed to be in work and many were not. It was a sad fact of the inter-war period that most working-class Britons experienced unemployment at one point or other – something most middle-class families did not. In 1931 alone, at any chosen time, one fifth to one quarter of the lower-class was out of work. Those who had relied on industries such as coal-mining, ship-building, heavy engineering and textiles suffered more than most and, given that such ways of life were overwhelmingly based in the North of England, West of Scotland and South Wales, these regions suffered most too.

With wages decreasing and industry facing pressure, it was not a surprise that industrial strife followed in its wake. In the first few years of the 1920s, with trade unions looking to prevent a fall in workers' pay, the nation saw more strike-action than at any time previously. There was an irony in that the decline in the number of strike-days lost in the later years of the 1920s and the early 1930s was partly due to the rising levels of unemployment, especially in areas and industries with a strong union history. Employment, after all, was an essential condition for a strike. When unemployment began to fall in the later years of the 1930s, levels of industrial action rose once more. In industrial relations, however, all industries and areas of the country were not equal, and the mining and textile communities of South Wales, Yorkshire and Lancashire were more strike-prone than many others. Even in 1926 – the year of the General Strike – over 90 per cent of the total days lost to industrial action were a result of miners' strikes.

By the time of the outbreak of the second great war, these patterns – at least as far as the middle and working-classes were concerned – began to reverse themselves. As the need for rearmament increased the demand for labour, manual wages began to rise precisely when middle-class spending levels stalled. In terms of industry, much of the damage was already done, and mining, shipbuilding and textiles struggled to meet the new demand brought about by the needs of a nation preparing for another long conflict.

In so many ways, then, the interwar years were a time of flux for all social classes. Yet, the Britain of 1939 was, in many other ways, the same as that of 1918. It was still a predominantly working-class country; the middle-classes had grown and had seen the stirrings of change in their character, but any greater shift would need to wait for the effects of another war to take hold. Organised industrial action was a notable feature of the period, yet a majority of workers still did not belong to a union; membership levels kept low partly because of the difficulty unions appeared to have in attracting women.

Indeed, the plight of women in the workforce typified the tensions between the old and new. Progress was clear: full electoral suffrage was won in 1928, the American born Lady Astor had already become the first female Member of Parliament in 1919, and the 1929 General Election saw 14 women take seats in the House of Commons. Having seen many previously male-dominated avenues of employment open up during the First World War, Parliament, in 1919, passed the Sex Disqualification (Removal) Act to ensure that civil employment could not once again be closed to women. Yet, in the inter-war period, there was no noticeable increase in the proportion of women in employment, and the number working on equal terms with men saw a decline. Of the 1.3 million women who entered employment during the war, the vast majority were no longer in work by 1921. Some returned to the home voluntarily, others were the victim of a backlash in traditionally male industries. Marriage would often see the end of employment, with many employers still only willing to engage unmarried women; including in the public sector where such a policy was supposed to be unlawful. Rising levels of unemployment, particularly in the textile industry, forced many women out of work; often the first to be disposed of. In 1933, Sir Herbert Austin, the motor company chief, actually suggested that sacking women would be an ideal remedy for unemployment. So, despite some post-war optimism that traditional gender roles in work had started to be challenged, fundamental imbalances remained and the most popular avenue of employment for the semi-skilled female worker continued to be domestic service.

For the upper-classes, they remained an indisputable social, political and financial elite. Despite financial challenges and the infiltration of their ranks and families by new money, very little of the redistribution of wealth that occurred in this period was from upper to middle-classes. Most of the movement of money was within the elite and by 1939, the richest one percent of the population still held well over half of all Britain's wealth. Despite the fears of the demise of upper-class society, when George VI ascended to the throne in 1937, London still resounded to the sound of aristocratic balls and social events. Richer or poorer, the face of the aristocracy would continue to be upheld. In the words of Loelia Ponsonby, Duchess of Westminster, "One dressed for dinner though the skies fell."

* *

As in life as in cricket. The game in this period was essentially the same played by Grace and Abel, still awash with the expectations and traditions of class – of the player and the gentleman – but change was tugging the coat of this most conservative of all sports.

We saw in chapter three how war had taken its toll on the ranks of amateur cricketers. It was a trend that would continue. As the economic realities of the inter-war period began to bite, fewer amateurs could find the time to turn out for their county side, and teams began to rely much more on their professional players. In 1913, 30 percent of all county cricketers were drawn from the amateur class; by 1930 that figure had dropped to 20 per cent and kept around that level for the remainder of the decade. Not all counties were alike in this regard; Lancashire, Nottinghamshire and Yorkshire tended to field sides dominated by professionals, whereas for a county such as Somerset, the reverse was true. By 1939, however, the decline in the numbers of amateurs affected all counties, with only Kent seeing more than 30 per cent of their side unpaid.

Cracks were also beginning to appear in the customs which sustained the cultural barriers between amateur and professional. The tradition of the two cricketing classes changing in different rooms and entering the field of play was being chipped away at. The 1920s saw Surrey abolish separate entrances at The Oval and the MCC adopted a single dressing room for England teams. Formalities between the cricketing classes were starting to move. In the pre-war era, professionals would always address their amateur colleagues as 'Sir' or 'Mr'. While such niceties mostly endured in the inter-war period, it was increasingly common to hear an amateur captain being called 'skipper' by his professional charges. Some dared to go further. Gloucestershire's Wally Hammond shocked Surrey's captain Errol Holmes by hailing him as 'Errol'; an act which made the amateur wonder if he should report Hammond for such audacity.

Wally Hammond was one of a different breed of professional who were beginning to appear. Grammar School educated, he dressed and held himself with the air of an amateur, with Brillcreamed hair and a silk handkerchief peeping from his trouser pocket. He played golf, drove to training by car and would dip into his pocket to ensure his accommodation was of a higher standard than that which was usually experienced by a professional. Marrying into money - his wife was a Bradford wool-merchant's daughter – Hammond crossed the cricketing class boundary in 1938 and played the rest of his career as an amateur.

In his professional days, it also helped his earning power that Wally Hammond was one of world's best batsmen, but he was not alone. The cream of the professional crop – Hobbs, Hendren and others – earned the sort of money that comfortably put them in the bracket of middle rather than working-class; taking home more a year as a cricketer than they would as a GP. They were, however, the exceptions and most professionals still led the lifestyle of workers.

Professionals were establishing themselves in positions of authority in the national game, with Jack Hobbs and Wilfred Rhodes invited to join the England selection committee. Mostly, such professional influence did not yet extend to the formal reigns of captaincy. However, with fewer and fewer amateurs pulling on a county cap and the ranks of the professionals now supplying the outstanding cricketers of the day, the question of whether professionals should be permitted to captain a side continued to stir. Although largely unspoken, there was a growing recognition that captaincy was still being reserved for the amateur alone for reasons that had little to do with who was the best leader of a side on the field of play. This was evident by the number of professionals who were asked to deputise when their usual amateur skipper was unavailable. In 1926 Jack Hobbs led the England side in the absence of Arthur Carr; Ewart Astill captained Leicestershire for the entire 1935 season until the amateur Stewie Dempster qualified for the county the next year; and in 1927 Herbert Sutcliffe accepted the full-time captaincy of Yorkshire until pressure from dissenting voices prompted him to decline. There was an irony that Lord Hawke – the man who had denounced so strongly the idea of a professional ever captaining England – had been behind the offer to Sutcliffe in the first place. Yorkshire would be captained by amateurs right up until 1960.

Hawke's fellow cricketing peer of the realm, Lord Harris, was not so flexible over the issue of in whose hand a county's captaincy should reside. When Stanley Cornwallis, the captain of Harris's county of Kent was going to be absent from duty, the skipper suggested that James Seymour, a professional, step into the breach rather than one of the amateurs in the side. Hawke was outraged and sent Cornwallis a strong rebuke by letter, reminding the captain that the authority granted to him by the County Committee did not include the "revolutionary introduction of a professional to be Captain when an amateur is procurable." Seymour would never formally lead his county.

If there was to be a softening of the line of who held the reigns of captaincy it would be helped by the fact that age was catching up with cricket's old guard. Lord Harris, such a stickler for rules and tradition, passed away in 1932 and was followed six years later by Lord Hawke.

Change was occurring elsewhere in cricket. As we saw in chapter four, Test status had been extended to the West Indies, India and New Zealand; although of those three, only the West Indies managed to secure any victory before war forced a halt to international competition. On the domestic front, the number of teams competing in the County Championship rose to eighteen with the inclusion of Glamorgan in 1921, a move that meant it was no longer an all-English affair.

The laws of the game were also in flux during the inter-war period, with the MCC looking to find ways in which to redress the balance of the contest, which many felt had become too much a batsmen's game. 'Pad-play' had become increasingly common with batsmen often reluctant to offer anything other than a leg or a leave to balls pitching outside off-stump, some going as far as to kick the ball away. Bowlers grew frustrated and the spectacle did nothing for the entertainment value of the sport. To counter the trend, bowlers were awarded some new advantages: in 1927 the ball was made smaller, the stumps became larger in 1931 and, in 1937, the leg-before-wicket rule was amended to allow umpires to raise the finger for balls which pitched outside off-stump, as long as they hit the pad in-line with the stumps.

Less welcome to the bowling fraternity was another innovation designed to move the game along – the adoption, in 1939, of the eight ball over. This had been the standard in most Australian cricket since 1918, had more recently been adopted by South Africa and re-adopted by New Zealand. West Indies cricket made the change along with the MCC.

The 1939 English season began, eight balls in an over and all, with Yorkshire as reigning champions. It would have taken a brave person to bet against them repeating the feat, boasting as they did an opening partnership of Len Hutton and Herbert Sutcliffe, a bowling attack spearheaded by Bill Bowes and Hedley Verity, along with a supporting cast of Test-capped cricketers such as Maurice Leyland, Arthur Mitchell, Norman Yardley, Wilf Barber and Arthur Wood, led ably by their no-nonsense captain Brian Sellers.

Yorkshire's defence of their championship was a robust one, finishing with an identical win-loss ratio (20 to 2) as they achieved in 1938, increasing their point tally by four via the first innings points system and so upping their average point score – the statistic that determined who finished top of the table. Only a challenge by Middlesex kept the race alive into late August but, when they drew against Surrey at Lord's on 30 August, the title was Yorkshire's again. It was the twelfth time Yorkshire had been crowned champions in the 21 seasons played since the end of the First World War. Hutton ended the year as the County Championship's leading run scorer; Verity finished second in the wicket-takers list but managed to top the national bowling averages.

As in 1914, the season was played out under a gathering threat of war but, this time, the atmosphere was different. Memories of the last conflict were fresh and few were under any misapprehension of what another war would mean this time round; no more expectations of the boys being back home by Christmas. While, before, events had moved swiftly and caught many on the hop, now the writing had been clearly on the wall for some time. By the start of the 1939 County Championship in early May, German forces had already overrun Czechoslovakia, making a mockery of Prime Minister Chamberlain's assurance of 'peace in our time.' As Britain sought to reassure Poland of its commitment in the face of further Nazi aggression, steps were hurriedly taken at home to prepare for conflict. The pace of rearmament was increased and, on May 26, the day before Yorkshire and Lancashire took up the Roses battle at Old Trafford, Parliament passed the Military Training Act that allowed for the conscription of 20 and 21-year-old men into basic training and active reserve. Despite this, unlike in 1914, there were no calls for the immediate cessation of sporting contests. Instead, there was a sober realisation that, when war was declared, sport would stop but, until then, people would carry on as best they could.

In the darkness of early 9 August, a few hours before Sussex took on Worcestershire at New Road and Yorkshire played Leicestershire at Aylestone Road, householders across a great swathe of the country took part in a practice blackout. RAF bombers were called on to make a surprise mock attack, to be met by fighter aircraft; both flying low to check the effectiveness of the efforts of the population to extinguish or cover any light. Unfortunately, from an aerial viewpoint at least, bad weather contrived to frustrate those plans.

With war beginning to appear inevitability and the nation's preparations accelerating, the cricket season rolled on as normal. A Test series between England and the visiting West Indies passed without interruption. England took the three-match series 1-0; Hutton and Hammond leading the way with the bat for the home team, Bill Bowes and Derbyshire's Bill Copson with the ball. For the visitors it was the incomparable George Headley who predictably plundered the most runs; Learie Constantine the main bowling threat.

Soon after the conclusion of the final Test match, the West Indian tour party received notice from Kent that their fixture scheduled for 30 August was to be cancelled. The abandonment of this match prompted the tourists to decide that it would be preferable to make their voyage home before any outbreak of hostilities and, calling off their remaining five fixtures, left the British Isles on 26 August, catching the SS Montrose from Greenock to Montreal.

The news of the premature West Indian departure was not well received on the south coast, where the tourists were due to play at Hove on the very day they set sail for Canada. With only a day's warning of the fixture's cancellation, Sussex's captain, Jack Holmes, attempted some last-minute diplomacy in an ultimately futile effort to change their mind. "Essential to play tomorrow" he messaged the West Indian tour management, "keep the flag flying." John Nanson, the Mayor of Brighton, lent his weight to the efforts, admonishing the visitors with a warning that their early return home would "certainly give the impression that we are not putting up a united front."

It was to no avail. The tour was off and the majority of the West Indian team sailed to Canada, where a hurriedly arranged match was played against Montreal before the players went on home. The apparent haste in which the tourists made the decision to set sail at the first opportunity was not well received by many of the West Indian cricketers either; the batsman Jeff Stollmeyer reported that his captain, Rolph Grant, "nearly had a riot on his hands" when he relayed the news to his men. Their swift exit turned out to be a life-saver. Had they hesitated for another day before leaving, their next chance would have been aboard the SS Athenia, which departed Glasgow towards Montreal on 1 September. Two days into the journey the Athenia became the first British ship to be hit by a German U-boat during the Second World War. 117 lives were lost.

Hove, Wednesday 30 August 1939
Day one

It was a lovely day to be by the coast. The previous few days had been warm, bright – a little cloudy at times – and had been spared any of the thunderstorms rattling around more easterly and northerly parts of

Britain. As the players gathered on that Wednesday morning, they were greeted by clear blue skies and the promise of temperatures reaching into the mid-70s. One thing was clear – once the morning dew had evaporated, this would be a good day to bat. And so, when the coin fell Sussex's way, their skipper, Jack Holmes, had no hesitation in announcing his decision to do just that and soon the Sussex opening pair of Bob Stainton and John Langridge made their way to the crease.

It was an odd sort of occasion. It should have been one of celebration: the visit of the Champions; one final chance to catch sight of the talents of the likes of Hutton, Leyland, Verity and Bowes before the season's close. The fixture had been intended as the main attraction for the Brighton and Hove Cricket Week and, if that were not enough, it had been set aside to act as a benefit match for the popular Sussex professional Jim Parks.

Yet the context in which the match began gave little reason for joy. The spectators who strolled along Eaton Road to the gates of the County Ground, the sea glistening in the background, would have known that this was not only the last chance to see their Sussex side and those Yorkshire greats in 1939 but for a considerably longer time and, for some, perhaps ever.

Yet come they did and in good numbers. 4,000 on the first day. Perhaps they were spurred on by the knowledge that another opportunity for a long summer's day at the cricket may not come again soon; perhaps they came for a little light relief from the spectre of war; or possibly, the people of Sussex just wanted to show their support for Jim Parks.

* *

Jim Parks was a highly effective batting all-rounder for the south coast county. Although he made his first-class debut in 1924, he took a few years to fully settle and finally found his rhythm in 1927 when he recorded his first thousand-run season; picking up 44 wickets to boot. A stocky, brave opening batman, often in partnership with John Langridge, he would pass a thousand runs in all but one domestic season from 1927 to 1939. Batting was his bread and butter, but he ably supplemented it with dependable bowling spells – often picking up wickets with his slow-medium in-swingers – and a good pair of hands at second slip. While it would be fair to describe Jim Parks as a very effective county pro rather than a stellar one, there was one year in which he reached heights that very few cricketers scaled before or since. The year was 1937 and Jim Parks was unstoppable. 3,003 runs came from his bat that summer at an average of over 50, with eleven tons and another eleven half-centuries. If that was not enough, he picked up over a hundred wickets for only the second time in his career. This run of form was enough to give Parks a Test-cap. Against New Zealand at Lord's, he opened the innings with Hutton, scored 22 and 7 and took three wickets, His services were not required for the next Test and it would remain his only international appearance. Jim Parks was 34 years old when Yorkshire visited Hove for his benefit game. In normal times he could have expected to serve his county for another five, six years, perhaps more. But these were no normal times and Jim Parks would not play for Sussex again. He would pick up the bat after the war for Canterbury in New Zealand and Nottinghamshire's second eleven, playing until the fine age of 54, but, as was the case for so many, the coming conflict would rob him of first-class cricket.

* *

There was no denying that Parks's benefit match was taking place in a strange atmosphere. Every effort was made to make the day one of celebration – a band played on the lawn, teas were served by a group of volunteers led by Lady Eva de Paravicini – yet conversations inevitably drifted back to more sombre affairs. Throughout the day, groups of spectators would be seen gathered around parked cars, listening to wireless reports of the last, fruitless, efforts of ministers and diplomats. The Sussex professional George Cox reflected on the contrast. "The tension was awful", he said, "there was a feeling that we shouldn't be playing cricket. Yet there was also a festive air. We knew that this was to be our last time of freedom for many years and so we enjoyed ourselves while we could." Bill Bowes recalled the match being played in a "most strained atmosphere" where "people watched the match, but their minds were on the war."

Stainton and Langridge – amateur and professional, both twenty-nine years old – took their places at either end of the freshly rolled pitch. At this time of year, it was obligatory to pay extra caution even on a true surface in case the morning dew cause the odd ball to deviate and especially so when the man running in to open the bowling was Bill Bowes.

* *

William Eric Bowes was an unlikely looking cricketer. Standing tall at six feet four inches, bespectacled, blonde curly hair, with a clumsy gait, he did not resemble a professional athlete. Yet, with ball in hand, Bill Bowes was destined to become one of the best of his time. With no nursery established in his home county of Yorkshire, Bowes was dispatched to Lord's to learn his trade on the ground-staff under the watchful eye of Walter Brearley, and it would be his tutelage - along with Bowes' own insatiable appetite for improving his game - that would shape the young bowler. Every day at four o'clock, Brearley would bounce into Lord's to coach the Yorkshireman. Resisting the temptation to try and mould his young charge into an express quick, Brearley persuaded Bowes to cut down his run to ten yards, saying how he would really like to make it eight. Instead, he taught him the art of skilful fast-medium bowling; the use of the crease, of control, and swing through the air. Bowes would pound to the wicket in his usual ungainly style; a mostly side-on delivery and a quick veer away from the pitch in a follow-through that left him watching the batsman's reaction from over his shoulder. He was not rapid, but the ball came off the pitch much quicker than expected. Bowes, under Brearley, proved a willing student and by 1929 had made his Yorkshire debut.

One thing continued to elude him - the away swinger. It was, according to Brearley, "the ball you have to bowl" to fully reach potential. Despite his mentor's instructions, Bowes could not master it but refused to settle for being an in-swing bowler only and doggedly kept on seeking the magic formula. It took him three years of trying and, in 1931, he finally cracked it. A tip picked up in an obscure coaching manual about the position of a bowler's feet on delivery did the trick and soon Bowes was moving the ball both ways without any noticeable change in his action. He quickly became the leader of the Yorkshire attack, discouraged from paying too much attention to batting practice, exertions when in the field, or anything that might distract him from the job of taking wickets.

His evolution into an all-round swing bowler saw Bill Bowes given an England chance and, although he performed well - taking six wickets on debut - his international career would be one of fits and starts. That he lacked that extra yard of pace compared to the likes of Larwood, Voce or Allen made him susceptible to being the first of the attack to drop out when a change in balance or personnel was demanded. Even so, 68 wickets from 15 Tests at an average of 22 was respectable and, one suspected, would have been greater were it not for the interruption of war.

* *

At Hove, operating in tandem with right-arm medium pacer Frank Smailes, Bowes nearly got an early reward when he forced a false stroke from John Langridge, only to see the sharp chance go to ground at gully. As expected though, there were few demons in the surface and the Sussex openers knew that by playing with a straight bat, taking few risks and waiting for the hittable delivery, runs would come; something each proved with drives through the covers off the Yorkshire opening pair. Even on this pitch, though, this was a quality attack and, with only 26 on the board, Bowes drew Stainton into offering an edge that was snapped up by wicketkeeper Arthur Wood.

Next to the wicket was Harry Parks, brother of the match beneficiary Jim. A new batsman but no change in tactics from the Sussex pair; steady as she goes. It was low-risk cricket but, with the bowling taking on the air of a dead-rubber, runs still came at a steady rate. Bowes, particularly, seemed lethargic as he reeled off over after over for more than an hour. It would take a brilliant act of wicket-keeping and an inept piece of running between the wickets for Yorkshire to remove these cautious batsmen.

The breakthrough came after Yorkshire's normally sharp fielding let one get away. With the score on 81, Frank Smailes got Harry Parks to prod outside off, only to see the ball elude the hand of Arthur Mitchell low down at first slip. No matter, only eight runs later, Parks fenced at a ball from the same bowler and, this time, 'keeper Wood left nothing to chance; diving full length and low to take the catch in front of the slips.

It looked highly unlikely that the cautious John Langridge would be tempted into a similar fate and, at a quarter past one, he raised his bat for a watchful fifty. The Sussex score had moved into three figures some ten minutes before. The fact that Langridge would not survive to lunch was down to the eagerness of his new batting partner, George Cox. Cox had come to the crease with a clear intention of moving the score along with his usual gusto; driving Smailes through the covers for a boundary off the very first ball he received. Such forthright intent was welcomed by the home crowd but, in his keenness to take the attack to the county champions, Cox saw his partner off. Pushing a ball from Verity to Wilf Barber at mid-off, he called Langridge through for a single that was never there and the Yorkshireman made no mistake with his throw. Langridge, out for 60, the score on 133 for 3. On the way back to the pavilion he passed his brother James, bat in hand, making his way out to the middle.

* *

George Cox seemed to like batting against Yorkshire. In the 24 matches they were his opponent – 23 times with Sussex, once for the Royal Air Force – Cox averaged 43.41, with five fifties and six centuries, including one double; 212 at Headingley in 1949. When George Cox scored runs he was a joy to watch – powerful, inventive, yet no slogger – and while he was at the crease the scoreboard operator would get little rest. Such a carefree approach to his craft brought with it obvious hazards and George finished his career with a healthy 77 first-class ducks; 76 of them for his county. Not quite a Sussex record, but enough to put him comfortably in their top ten. The county's record for being dismissed without score – an impressive 126 times – was held by his father, the left-arm bowler George Rubens Cox.

While many would have liked to have seen it, George junior was never afforded the opportunity to don an England cap. He can consider himself somewhat unfortunate to be overlooked. It took a few seasons for his batting to flourish but, from 1937 onwards, he was a consistent performer for Sussex and had enough standout years to come to the selectors attention. In 1949 he scored 1,938 runs at an average of 40.37; the next year he passed the 2,000 run mark at average of 49 and a half. Perhaps the odd dip in form would scupper those chances – the standout years of '49 and '50 were sandwiched between seasons with averages in the low 20s, featuring a lone century each time. Or perhaps his attacking verve was seen as too much of a risky luxury for the Test arena. Whatever the reason, George Cox would finish his first-class career at the age of 50 with no international recognition, but with the plaudits of those who had seen him in full flow.

* *

When play resumed after lunch, George Cox had no intention of reigning in his attacking instincts. The batsman drove, cut and pulled with great power. Of course, he flirted with danger; the odd ball passed the edge of the bat and a few flew close to the outstretched hands of the slips, but the highly able Yorkshire fielding was mostly employed in an effort to prevent boundaries. It took Cox only ten minutes of the afternoon session to move from his lunchtime 22 to a warmly greeted half-century. At the other end, James Langridge – a quality left-handed batsman, capped eight times by England and who was one of *Wisden*'s Cricketers of the Year in 1932 – was almost a spectator, taking the occasional run but mostly content to let Cox go on his merry way. In what seemed a blink of the eye the partnership between Cox and Langridge had passed 50 and, at ten minutes to three, the Sussex score to 200.

200, though, meant the new ball was available and Yorkshire captain Brian Sellers had no hesitation in recalling his opening pairing of Bowes and Smailes into the attack. The hard, new cherry seemed to inject life into the bowling and soon the partnership was broken. Bowes found the edge of James Langridge's bat and Arthur Mitchell took the catch at slip with little fuss.

It was time for the match beneficiary, Jim Parks, to make his entrance. While the welcome to the middle would have been warm, his stay was brief. With only two runs to his name, Parks tried to carve a ball from Frank Smailes hard through the gully but only found the hands of Ellis Robinson who took a smart catch. In no time at all, 202 for 3 had become 205 for 5.

If the Hove crowd had been disappointed in Parks' misfortune, the sight of Hugh Bartlett with bat in hand would have raised their spirits. Bartlett was a dashing, hard-hitting left-hander who could produce spectacular performances, such as his onslaught against the Australians in the previous year where he reached 100 in less than an hour. That effort secured for him 1938's Walter Lawrence Trophy for the quickest century, pipping his equally free-scoring teammate George Cox. The prospect of Bartlett and Cox batting in tandem was always an enticing one.

On that afternoon, though, the anticipated fireworks did not come. With the Yorkshire bowling back to its normal high standard, Bartlett found it difficult to free his arms and Cox looked in difficulty when facing up to Bowes. Yet, despite some false strokes and near-misses, the batsmen managed to keep their wickets intact and runs began to accumulate. A couple of classic off-drives from Cox showed his rhythm returning, though it was a mis-hit that evaded the field which allowed him to reach a well-received century.

A century in the bag, George Cox began to swing his bat freely, taking runs from all bowlers but particularly having fun with Hedley Verity; driving one of the slow left-armer's deliveries for six and then getting down on one knee to pull another to the boundary later in the same over. Wickets began to fall at the other end, but such was Cox's haste that decent partnerships were built with little input needed from the tail enders.

First Bartlett went for an uncharacteristically restrained 24, bowled by one of Ellis Robinson off-breaks; the partnership worth 61. Jack Holmes came and went for only 11 – bowled Verity – but had hung around long enough for his partnership with Cox to have passed fifty. Tea was taken with the score on 331 for 7. 154 of them from the bat of George Cox.

On resumption, Cox took off from where he left, moving the score along as quickly as he could. His endeavour brought risks, of course, and it looked like his time was up when he tried to lift Verity over the infield once more, but only found Bill Bowes at mid-on, who spilled the head-high chance. Later in the same over, Cox's partner, Billy Griffith, was not so fortunate and Verity picked up his second of the innings thanks to a smart one-handed catch by Frank Smailes at mid-off.

At a quarter past five, all eyes were on the middle as George Cox faced up to Ellis Robinson, needing just two more runs for a thrilling double century. Robinson trotted in and served up the hittable delivery that Cox was waiting for − a touch short, a little wide, ripe for the cut. Unfortunately for the Sussex man, he failed to get on top of the shot and hammered the ball straight into the waiting hands of Arthur Mitchell. It had been a scintillating innings, warmly appreciated by the Hove crowd. His efforts had moved the Sussex score to 387 and there it would remain as Jim Wood, in at number eleven, lasted precisely one ball; the umpire's finger sent him off LBW and brought the innings to a close.

The south-coast sunlight was holding up and promised Yorkshire a full 90 minutes to eat into the Sussex lead. It was an unusual combination of opening batsmen who strode to the crease to begin the champions' reply: Wilf Barber and Len Hutton.

* *

That one can say Leonard Hutton was only just getting into his cricketing stride when war put halt to serious sporting competition, is an indication of the extraordinary heights his career would reach. For, when stumps were finally drawn at Hove, Len Hutton's record was already one to admire. Since making his Yorkshire debut as a prodigious seventeen-year-old in 1934 - he would be run out for a duck in his first time at the crease - Hutton had, by the end of 1939, racked up eleven and a half thousand runs at an average of a scratch under 49, including 36 centuries. England recognition came in 1937 against New Zealand at Lord's, though, as with his county debut, his first innings would end scoreless. His second in the match would not be much better; out with only one run to his name. Retained for the next match, Hutton, opening alongside Gloucestershire's Charlie Barnett, would register his first century. It would be his only score of note in the series, but the 21-year-old had given notice that he belonged at the highest level.

1938 brought the Ashes series that would secure Len Hutton's place in the history books. With a century already secured in the first match, the final match at The Oval would change everything. Only 29 runs were on the board when Hutton lost his opening partner, Bill Edrich, and was joined by the familiar face of Maurice Leyland. The Yorkshire pair put on an incredible 382 runs, breaking the English Test partnership record for the second wicket. When Leyland was run out for 187, Hutton ploughed on, often at a snail's pace. By the time he was out, the score on 770 for 6, Len Hutton, with 364 runs to his name, held the record for the highest individual score in a Test match. It would be a distinction he would hold for twenty years until the great Garfield Sobers bettered Hutton's score by a single run. It does, though, remain unsurpassed by any English cricketer today.

The pre-war Hutton was graceful yet determined; great touch allied with huge reserves of concentration. Bowling attacks could be taken apart, but many innings were characterised by a patient occupation of the crease that wore the opposition down. At times the runs came slowly but come they did. 1936 would be his first thousand-run season, 1937 brought 2,888 and, in 1939, only five runs fewer. He was poised for greatness, but war came and looked, for a time, to have brought a premature end to his cricketing days. It was not enemy fire that fell Hutton but an accident during a Commando training course when a mat slipped from under his feet, leaving the Yorkshireman with a fractured left arm. It was no simple recovery; operation followed operation and over a year later his arm was still in plaster. When the cast was finally removed, it revealed a shrunken limb that was permanently shorter than the other. When Len Hutton picked up a cricket bat again, the gap had been three and a half years.

That Len Hutton learnt to adapt to his altered physique, remain classically correct - though the hook would no longer feature in his game - and did so to a professional level was admirable enough. That he went on to become one of England's greatest players is extraordinary. 1946 began a run of eight consecutive thousand-run seasons, including two thousand runs in 1948, 1950, 1951, 1952 and 1953, and over three thousand in 1949. When Hutton retired from competitive first-class cricket in 1955 he could reflect on a career that had brought over 40,000 runs and 129 centuries, including 19 for England. Such was his impact on the popular imagination that Len Hutton became Sir Leonard Hutton soon after his retirement. He would also be the man who finally broke the symbolic line of class when, in 1952, playing as a professional, Hutton was appointed England captain. It was not the death knell for amateur captains - the honour reverted to the hands of amateurs immediately after Hutton - but the line had been crossed and, from that, there was no going back.

As with most openers, Hutton would be forever linked with the men with whom he shared the opening berth. For England it was Cyril Washbrook, whose combined 2,880 Test match runs sit eleventh on the all-time list. For Yorkshire, despite that their careers only crossed in the immediate pre-war years, the names that trip most easily off the tongue are those of Len Hutton and Herbert Sutcliffe. Both were from the small market town of Pudsey and it had been Sutcliffe himself who sold Hutton his first proper bat. When Hutton made his Yorkshire debut, Herbert Sutcliffe was firmly established in the England side and was the marquee name on the Yorkshire team-sheet. In four years of regularly opening together, they would score fifteen century partnerships for the County.

* *

On this sunny Hove afternoon, however, Herbert Sutcliffe was absent. As an army reservist, he was one of the first cricketers to be called up for service and, while his team-mates were seeing out the last rites of the county season, Herbert was joining up with the Royal Army Ordnance Corps. In his place Wilf Barber had been promoted to open. Barber, who had made his Yorkshire debut in the tail end of the 1926 season and had briefly represented his country against South Africa in 1935, was a classical off-side batsman with a sound defensive technique. He was no novice in the openers berth but had, throughout his career, moved up and down the order depending on the needs of the team.

Hutton and Barber settled quickly into their task and made both pitch and bowling look benign. Runs came easily from both ends with little sign of a Sussex breakthrough. Hutton, powerful from timing through the off-side, delicate when playing to leg. Half an hour into the Yorkshire innings and the fifty partnership had been posted, 22 from the bat of Wilf Barber. He would add no more. Attempting to late-cut a ball from the Sussex left-armer John Nye, Barber found himself cramped for room and edged it into the safe gloves of Billy Griffith.

The reliable Arthur Mitchell was next in. Thirty-six years old and capped six times by England, Mitchell had gained a reputation as a resolute on-side player, but he was no-less effective and such impressions often ignored the fact that he was more than able on the off-side when the match situation called for a more ambitious approach. At first, the Sussex bowling to Hutton and Mitchell was tight – keeping a good line and length – but as the shadows lengthened, the batsmen re-found their rhythm and, when stumps were drawn at seven o'clock, they had moved the score along to 112 for 2. Hutton's half century secured.

Thursday 31 August 1939

Day two

The contrast with day one could not have been greater. Gone were the blue skies and the sunshine. In their stead were heavy grey clouds and persistent rain; the remnants of a wicked storm that had swept across Sussex overnight. Unfortunately for Jim Parks and his benefit fund, the wet weather also meant the absence of the paying public who had shown such great support the day before. No cricket, no crowd, no gate receipts. The prospects did not look good either. Rain continued to fall throughout the morning and, although it relented after lunch, the effects on the playing surface did not bode well for a speedy resumption. For the players, all they could do was sit and wait, try to entertain themselves and leaf through the morning newspapers or turn on a wireless for some clue as to their country's future.

The news was not good. War, it seemed, had taken another step closer. In the early hours of the morning, the German Foreign Minister, Joachim von Ribbentrop, had met with the British Ambassador Sir Neville Henderson and handed him a list of demands regarding Poland; including the handing of Danzig over to German control and a plebiscite to determine the fate of the Polish Corridor. The Polish government were given to midnight to send an envoy with full power to negotiate an agreement. When the Polish ambassador, Józef Lipski, contacted von Ribbentrop later that day and declared that he could only receive the demands as an ambassador, with no authority to sign any agreement, Adolph Hitler took to the airways to declare that he considered his terms rejected. This announcement came only minutes after the ratification of the Nazi-Soviet pact which had cleared an important obstacle in the path of German eastward expansion. Given the obvious and imminent nature of German intentions towards Poland – a country both Britain and France had treaty obligations towards should it be attacked – the implications were clear. As a result, the British Government began to speed up its move onto a war footing. It took a decision to complete the mobilisation of the Navy, call up the remainder of the regular and supplementary army reserve, increase the call-up of Air Force volunteers and put into place ARP emergency measures, including round-the-clock work on public air shelter construction.

One further announcement on that wet Thursday brought the reality of a war-time Britain into sharp focus. Operation Pied Piper – the plan to evacuate a predicted three million children and other vulnerable people from those cities and towns considered most at risk from aerial bombardment – was set into action. The next day, September 1, from early in the morning, children were to gather at designated railway and London tube stations, carrying their gas masks, clothes and toothbrushes, names written on labels pinned to their coats, to begin the journey away from their families to, they hoped, safety. Some of the half a million London children who were to be evacuated on that first day would be heading to the south coast, including fourteen train-loads destined for Brighton station.

The rapidly developing crisis was not lost on the players of Yorkshire, sat in their hotel, waiting for the rain clouds to pass on by. Norman Yardley recalled that all morning, "we were feverishly discussing the cables from Poland and Germany. None of us had much attention to give to cricket."

Finally, in mid-afternoon, the sun made an unexpected, yet welcome, return and, at three o'clock, the umpires declared conditions fit for play; the contest to resume half an hour later. In cricketing terms at least, the Sussex players must have thought the gods were on their side – runs on the board, a lead of over 250 and now a wet pitch to make mischief on their behalf.

Determined to make the most of the changed conditions, Sussex skipper Holmes went on the attack. It was to be the left arm pairing of John Nye from the sea-end – both mid-on and mid-off in close, crowding the bat – and James Langridge from the other, two slips in place.

To what extent the pattern of the afternoon's play was because of or despite the pitch depended on whose report you believe. For the 'special correspondent' of *The Times*, the surface was 'easy' despite the earlier downpour. According to Jim Kilburn of the *Yorkshire Post,* the ball carried through sluggishly "and at varying and illogical heights." In Kilburn's view, any apparent ease was entirely due to the brilliance of Len Hutton. Hutton simply refused to allow whatever demons that might lurk in the pitch to have their way. Using his feet, particularly to the quicker deliveries of Langridge, Hutton denied the ball any chance to land, let alone spin, until the bowlers dropped so short that he could hang back and punish the resulting long-hop. It was a sumptuous exhibition of hitting, showcasing drives, pulls, square-cuts and late-cuts, and, after three-quarters of an hour, Hutton drove Jim Wood through the covers to notch his fourteenth boundary and a brilliant century.

It hadn't taken long for Jack Holmes to ring the bowling changes and after Parks, Nye, Langridge and Wood had chanced their arms, the Sussex captain turned to the hero with the bat on the first day of the match, George Cox. It was only the seventh time he had been thrown the ball that season, but it was a stroke of genius – or luck – and, with the very first ball he sent down, tempted a pull from Hutton which missed. The Yorkshire opener was on his way LBW. Out for 103, leaving his side handily placed on 175 for 2, 212 runs behind.

It had been no one-man show. Arthur Mitchell seemed to have few problems with the changing Sussex attack and had already passed fifty runs. Even without Sutcliffe, this was a strong batting line up – seven of the top eight had England experience – yet the departure of Hutton was an opportunity for Sussex. The obvious move for Holmes was to recall one of his frontline bowlers to have a crack at the new batsman; especially as the incoming Yorkshireman was the greatly experienced

Maurice Leyland, who at 39 years of age could boast over 32,000 first class runs, 41 England caps and nine international centuries. However, the Sussex captain stuck with his instinct and not only chose to keep Cox going with the ball but soon introduced another part-timer from the other end – himself. Given that, in seventeen years of cricket for Sussex, he had only taken seven first-class wickets, the decision had an end-of-term feel about it.

It worked. The Yorkshire scoring slowed and just before tea – scheduled for five o'clock – the skipper, with his first ball, picked up his eighth career first-class wicket; Arthur Mitchell mis-hitting one high in the air, easily taken by James Langridge close to the wicket for a bright 67. Tea was taken with the score at 204 for 3.

After tea, Maurice Leyland together with the young, talented amateur all-round sportsman Norman Yardley looked to push the score along with purpose. Leyland took some time to find his rhythm but soon both were scoring runs off each of the Sussex bowlers, making the pitch – which had promised so much for the home team earlier – look increasingly becalmed. Yardley gave one chance – a sitter dropped on the square-leg boundary – but, beyond that, the pair looked in total control. When stumps were finally drawn, the partnership had passed 100; Leyland on 62, Yardley 72 and Yorkshire 330 for 3. Only 57 runs behind. A good session for the visitors, yet any pleasure the Yorkshire dressing room had taken from the day's play was dampened by the news that the popular Scarborough Festival, scheduled for the coming weekend, had been cancelled owing to the likelihood of war.

Friday 1 September 1939
Day three

The players awoke to grim news. In the early hours of the morning, the German invasion of Poland had begun. It had started with pre-dawn bombing of Wieluń, escalated with the shelling of Danzig and, by eight o'clock, German troops had crossed the border. While it would take two days for Britain to formally declare war, the die was cast.

It was no time for cricket. Surrey's match at Lancashire was abandoned, Derbyshire's at Leicestershire went with a hand from the weather and the three games yet to start were cancelled. In Hove, Brian Sellers received a message from the Yorkshire committee suggesting they follow suit. Yet the captain demurred. Their match was being played as a benefit for Jim Parks and, not only was he an extremely popular cricketer with his peers, all knew the difference a decent pay-day could make to a professional, especially in times as uncertain as these. Who knew if he ever would get the chance again? So, after an exchange of views, the match was to continue.

With only one day's play remaining and Yorkshire's first innings not yet complete, Sellers decided they needed to move the game along. The remaining batsmen were to put quick runs ahead of preservation of their wickets, force a lead as soon as they could and then see what the Yorkshire bowlers could do on a pitch that was visibly cutting up.

Yardley and Leyland resumed for the visitors under a blazing sun and they quickly looked to make hay. The bat swung freely and risks were taken; an approach that brought runs and wickets. Twelve had been added to the overnight score when the first man was on his way back to the pavilion; Maurice Leyland attempting to launch Jim Parks out of the ground gave a steepling catch to the man at cover. Leyland had made a steady 64, part of a valuable partnership of 138 with Yardley.

If Norman Yardley was to push his team into a lead and his own score into three figures, he would need some support from the other end. At first it looked like that would come from his skipper, Sellers, but after a brisk 12 runs the captain suffered the same fate as Leyland and it was Hugh Bartlett who accepted the skied mishit in the covers. 363 for 5 and Yorkshire were still behind.

The remaining batsmen did not hang around long. Frank Smailes aimed a drive at a Parks delivery, made no contact, and was bowled for a duck. Arthur Wood managed to get off the mark but, with only two runs to his name, fell to an excellent running catch by his namesake Jim Wood on the square-leg boundary. Ellis Robinson missed one from Jim Langridge without troubling the scorers and, at 377 for 8, it looked as though even a small first innings lead might be beyond them; even more so when Yardley's fine stint at the crease came to an end with his team still one run shy of parity. He had, though, managed to raise his bat for an impressive century. Finally gone for 108.

If a lead was to be achieved, it would be up to Verity and Bowes; a somewhat unlikely pairing with bat in hand. They took to their task with purpose and, for the first time in the day, an element of caution entered the Yorkshire play. It paid dividend, to a degree, and when Bowes was caught by the match beneficiary, Parks, the score had crept to 392. Five runs ahead.

It was over to Sussex to play out the day and bring the 1939 English cricket season to a close. It would not be easy. The pitch did not look good. The combination of the rain of day two, the subsequent bright sunshine and marks left by the bowlers' feet had left a disturbed surface ripe for spin bowling. It would also be understandable if the batsmen's minds were on matters other than the cricket. Still, this was a pitch that had seen two Yorkshire centuries scored after the rainstorm, and so a drawn match was most likely.

The problem for Sussex was that such conditions were made for Hedley Verity.

* *

It is fair to say that Hedley Verity scaled the cricketing heights he did because of his single-minded determination to become a Yorkshire professional as much as his obvious natural talent. From an early age, young Hedley's passion was Yorkshire cricket and everything else came second. It was a mindset that not everyone welcomed and, in his last year of school, Verity found himself excluded from all sporting activity by his Headmaster; a punishment for playing truant in order to watch Yorkshire's second XI play a match nearby.

Fortunately, his parents were much more understanding. Having left school at fourteen, Hedley was being lined up for a career in his Father's coal business; working with a private tutor to learn secretarial and accounting skills. It was to prove a short-lived plan. "It's no use Dad" Hedley stammered, "you are wasting your money. I've made up my mind to some day play for Yorkshire." While he would continue with some office work at the coal depot, with his parents' blessing every spare moment was devoted to his true calling. Corners of the office and hallways in the family home became impromptu nets as Hedley honed his batting and bowling technique. The coal yard proved useful for Hedley in bulking up his build, as did the footpaths of nearby Cragg Wood where he would run and skip in heavy work boots to improve his stamina further.

Performances for his local team of Rawden and, later, Horsforth Hall Park brought him to the attention of Yorkshire but, when invited for a trial, opinion was not unanimously in his favour. He could play, no doubt, but for the watching Bobby Peel, Verity - operating as a seam bowler - was not fast enough, particularly for someone of his height. Still, the recently retired George Hirst saw something in the young cricketer and used his connections to secure Hedley a contract with Accrington, and then Middleton, in the Lancashire League.

The period playing hard league cricket gave Verity a fine grounding in the game, but it was a decision to change his bowling style that saw him take the biggest step towards finally getting the county recognition he craved. It had taken the intervention of a pair of Yorkshire greats - George Hirst and Wilfred Rhodes - to prompt the change. At a Yorkshire net session sometime in the late 1920s, Hedley was taken aside by the two and advised that if he continued as a medium-pace bowler he would face plenty of competition for a place at the county. If, however, he was to try his hand as a left-arm spinner, then, with Rhodes himself eyeing retirement, who knew?

With the support of his league club, the change was made and, after a few faltering steps, he had found his art. In 1930, aged 25, Hedley Verity made his Yorkshire debut, taking three wickets in a match against Sussex at Huddersfield. 1930 was but an introduction and the following season he hit his stride, taking 188 first-class wickets at an average of under 14, including 18 five wicket innings, four ten wicket match hauls and the rarest of all bowling feats – ten in an innings. It would not be the only time he would achieved that. In 1932, he surpassed the 10 for 36 he had registered against Warwickshire the previous year, with an incredible 10 wickets for 10 runs on a turning Headingley wicket against Nottinghamshire. His son, Douglas, has said that "he wouldn't reckon that ten for 10 as being as good as one for 60 in 40 overs on a batters' wicket. He only valued things which were difficult." Between 1931 and the outbreak of war, Hedley Verity would pass 150 wickets each domestic season – three times passing the 200 mark – and ended the 1939 season with a career wicket total of 1,956 at an average of 14.9. All this in a period of cricketing history that was widely viewed as a batsman's.

Verity's run up was quicker than many spinners but was still smooth – a glide to the wicket almost – and delivered the ball with a noticeable extra effort that pushed it through at near medium-pace. While he may not have spun it as far as some, he had full control; varying line, flight, curve, speed and spin to lure batsmen into the false stroke that would feed the slip-cordon. Frequently operating in tandem with his good friend Bill Bowes, the pair ran through many a county side. In the ten seasons they played together, Bowes and Verity accounted for over half of all Yorkshire wickets and were the backbone of the seven County Championship titles secured in that time. The two men were of a similar mindset when it came to working on their craft and spend long hours analysing the match gone by and plotting the downfall of the opposition in the next.

Another man Hedley felt similar affinity with was his England captain between 1931 and 1934, Douglas Jardine. Although Verity had little enthusiasm for the bodyline techniques employed on the 1932/3 tour of Australia, he was fully supportive of his captain. The respect was mutual and, on their return home from Australia, the skipper wrote to Hedley's father in praise of his son, calling him "a real friend and a grand help to me." Hedley Verity would have three sons. The first he would name after Wilfred Rhodes, the second after George Hirst, and the last would be Douglas, in honour of Jardine.

His England career would not be plain sailing. There were times that he faced questions over his effectiveness on flat tracks and would be omitted from the team on a few occasions but, by the time war came, he had racked up 40 caps and 144 wickets at an average of under 25. And no-one would dismiss Don Bradman in Tests more times than Hedley Verity.

* *

It was to be Jim Parks to open with James Langridge this time round; Bob Stainton having suffered a leg injury whilst in the field. Parks would have known that Verity could be lethal on a pitch that was cutting up and he saw off the first delivery watchfully. The second was a different matter, the match beneficiary failed to meet ball with bat and was heading off without scoring, LBW. 0 for 1

Sellers was a canny skipper and, while Bill Bowes could be a handful on any surface, this was a morning for the slower bowlers so, to open at the other end, he turned to the off-breaks of Ellis Robinson. The switch paid off and soon Robinson had a scalp – John Langridge; caught by the captain himself.

From then on it was Verity's show. Taking advantage of this most helpful of pitches and his vast reserves of skill and experience, he bamboozled each of the Sussex men with extravagant turn. Henry Parks, George Cox, James Langridge were all caught off his bowling; Hugh Bartlett, Jack Holmes and Billy Griffith, all bowled. The dismissal of Sussex captain Holmes exemplified the spell that Verity was weaving. The batsman watched a ball pitch outside of leg-stump, turn and clatter into off, with no shot offered. The final indignity for the home side was an avoidable run out when John Nye drove Robinson to Hutton in the deep and, as the Yorkshireman fielded the ball, Nye called Jim Wood back for an inexplicable second run. Wood was a long way from safety when the bowler completed the run out. With Stainton unable to bat, the innings was over. 33 all out in only 11.3 overs. Verity's return: seven wickets for nine runs. A master at work.

Verity's astonishing performance had guaranteed a Yorkshire victory, but it was not done yet. The last rites needed to be performed: 29 runs to secure the match. There was enough life left in the match for one last wicket to fall – Hutton out for one – but from then on it was straightforward and, shortly after lunch, Wilf Barber hit the runs that brought proceedings to a close.

A Yorkshire win by nine wickets but that did not seem to matter much. All present knew that more important things awaited. Handshakes were exchanged, the pavilion and changing rooms grew crowded as friends took the chance to wish the players farewell. Spectators purchased scorecards as a memento of the last first-class cricket for, well, who knew how long? It was a sombre scene. Len Hutton, in particular, was said to look very pale.

For Yorkshire, there was the practical matter of how to get home. The needs of evacuees moving south made travelling by rail impossible and many of the roads were out of use for the same reason. A green Southdown coach – a charabanc in the words of the time – was commandeered and the team climbed aboard for the long journey north. First along the coast to Havant, then up to Oxford and beyond; passing vehicles packed full of families along with most of their worldly goods searching for safety. As the sun set, an undisturbed darkness fell; a blackout in place across the land. Driving through the pitch-black the mood on the coach took a similar hue. Hutton remembered that, the further they went, "the deeper was our conviction that we would be lucky if we ever played cricket again."

Night time upon them, the decision was made to stop in Leicester. Time for one last meal together as a team; oysters washed down with champagne, no less. One by one the players retired to bed until two figures remained, continuing their conversation into the small hours. Bill Bowes and Hedley Verity, such good friends, sat contemplating where their lives would take them next. Wherever that was, they wanted it to be in each other's company and, given that Bowes's wife, Esme, was soon to give birth, they agreed that they would join the Air Raid Precautions until the child's arrival and only then pledge themselves to full military service.

It would be over six and half years before the County Championship resumed; first-class English cricket in other forms reinstated the year before. Despite this lengthy hiatus, 20 of the 22 who played in that final peacetime game at Hove would return to play first-class cricket again.

Not all would return for their counties. For Jim Parks, his benefit game would be his last in Sussex colours. It had netted him £734; an amount inevitably depressed by the circumstance and weather. He would play a handful of first-class matches in New Zealand and one final game on home turf, representing a Commonwealth XI against The Indians in Blackpool, in 1952.

For his captain, Jack Holmes, who was aged 40 when he led Sussex for the final time in 1939, it was no surprise that he would not be back. It was not the end of his cricket and he played various matches for the Air Force and other teams before finally packing away his pads in 1944.

It was also Hedley Verity's last. Good to his word, he and Bowes signed up to the ARP and awaited the arrival into the world of Vera Bowes. Safely delivered, the two friends arrived together at the Bradford recruiting office and signed up. At first, they were employed as lorry drivers – a difficulty in sourcing uniforms that fitted the pair solved by a call to Captain Herbert Sutcliffe who was in Ordinance – but soon a chance of infantry commissions came their way. Unfortunately, Bill Bowes was judged physically unsuited to infantry duties due to surgery that had been carried out on one of his knees. They had always pledged to stick together but, knowing how much his friend wanted to serve, Bill persuaded Hedley to go on without him. "This is war, Hedley" counselled Bowes, "when there has been a Test match and I've not been picked you have still gone and done your damnedest. It's the same way here." Thus Captain H. Verity joined the Green Howards at the end of 1939. Bowes was headed for the Officer Cadet Training Unit.

Verity soon proved himself as a natural leader with an aptitude for military strategy, studying the subject as keenly as he had learned his left-arm spinners. War took him first to India, then Persia and finally to Sicily where Hedley led a company in an attack on a German division holed up in a farm building in Catania. In the fog of battle, Verity's men found themselves ahead of the leading company and took the full force of the German guns. The Captain was among those injured and, when found the next morning, taken prisoner. He had been hit in the chest and was ailing. The German doctors worked hard to save him, operating to remove part of a rib that was causing him difficulty, but it was to no avail and Hedley Verity died on 31 July 1943, aged 38.

Bill Bowes had, by this time, also seen action and was himself a prisoner of war, first in Italy, then, following the Italian Armistice, in Germany. It was while in Chieti, Italy that Bowes heard the news. A recently captured Canadian airman had casually mentioned that he had seen "some cricketer guy" named Verity at a hospital in Caserta. "Do you mean that Hedley Verity was in hospital...?" asked Bowes. "Yeah, that's the feller" responded the airman "but he's not in hospital now. He was buried yesterday." As Bowes recalled, "I walked out into the deserted roadway through the camp. The wind was cold but I did not notice it."

In 1946 the County Championship began once more. Yorkshire away to Glamorgan in their first match. Brian Sellers returned as captain. Pulling on his county blazer, Sellers noticed a small sheet of paper in the top pocket. It had been given to him by the scorer, all that time ago at Hove. It read: Verity: 6 overs, 1 maiden, 7 for 9.

County Championship, 1939
Sussex v Yorkshire
County Ground, Hove
30,31 August, 1 September 1939 (3-day match)

Result: Yorkshire won by 9 wickets
Points: Yorkshire 12, Sussex 0

Toss: Sussex
Umpires: JJ Hills, CWL Parker

Balls per over: 8

Sussex 1st innings

RG Stainton	c Wood	b Bowes	14
JG Langridge	run out		60
HW Parks	c Wood	b Smailes	35
G Cox	c Mitchell	b Robinson	198
J Langridge	c Mitchell	b Bowes	17
JH Parks	c Robinson	b Smailes	2
HT Bartlett	b Robinson		24
*AJ Holmes	b Verity		11
+SC Griffith	c Smailes	b Verity	17

JK Nye	not out		2
DJ Wood	lbw	b Robinson	0
Extras	(b 3, lb 4)		7
Total	(all out, 75 overs)		387

FoW: 1-26, 2-89, 3-133, 4-202, 5-205, 6-266, 7-321, 8-361, 9-387, 10-387.

Bowling	Overs	Mdns	Runs	Wkts
Bowes	17	0	71	2
Smailes	12	0	48	2
Yardley	9	0	48	0
Verity	18	1	108	2
Robinson	15	2	87	3
Hutton	4	0	18	0

Yorkshire 1st innings

L Hutton	lbw	b Cox	103
W Barber	c Griffith	b Nye	22
A Mitchell	c J Langridge	b Holmes	67
M Leyland	c sub	b JH Parks	64
NWD Yardley	c & b J Langridge		108
*AB Sellers	c Bartlett	b JH Parks	12
TF Smailes	b JH Parks		0
+A Wood	c Wood	b J Langridge	2
EP Robinson	b J Langridge		0
H Verity	not out		7
WE Bowes	c JH Parks	b J Langridge	2
Extras	(b 3, lb 1, w 1)		5
Total	(all out, 95.4 overs)		392

FoW: 1-52, 2-175, 3-204, 4-342, 5-363, 6-364, 7-377, 8-377, 9-386, 10-392.

Bowling	Overs	Mdns	Runs	Wkts
Nye	19	1	104	1
JH Parks	33	3	120	3
Wood	10	1	30	0
J Langridge	20.4	5	84	4
Cox	10	2	34	1
Holmes	3	0	15	1

Sussex 2nd innings

JG Langridge	c Sellers	b Robinson	3
JH Parks	lbw	b Verity	0
HW Parks	c Hutton	b Verity	9
G Cox	c Wood	b Verity	9
J Langridge	c Mitchell	b Verity	0
HT Bartlett	b Verity		3
*AJ Holmes	b Verity		4
+SC Griffith	b Verity		1
JK Nye	not out		3
DJ Wood	run out		0
RG Stainton	absent hurt		
Extras	(b 1)		1
Total	(all out, 11.3 overs)		33

FoW: 1-0, 2-12, 3-12, 4-13, 5-19, 6-23, 7-30, 8-30, 9-33.

Bowling	Overs	Mdns	Runs	Wkts
Verity	6	1	9	7
Robinson	5.3	0	23	1

Yorkshire 2nd innings (target: 29 runs)

L Hutton	c Griffith	b J Langridge	1
W Barber	not out		18

A Mitchell	not out	11
Extras		0
Total	(1 wicket, 12.6 overs)	30

DNB: M Leyland, NWD Yardley, *AB Sellers, TF Smailes, +A Wood, EP Robinson, H Verity, WE Bowes.

FoW: 1-4.

Bowling	Overs	Mdns	Runs	Wkts
JH Parks	6.6	1	21	0
J Langridge	6	0	9	1

BIBLIOGRAPHY

Arlott J. 1981. Jack Hobbs: Profile of the Master. London: John Murray

Beckles H McD. & Stoddart B (eds). 1995. Liberation Cricket: West Indies cricket culture. Manchester & New York: Manchester University Press

Birley D. 1999. A Social History of English Cricket. London: Aurum Press

Bowes W E. 1950. Express Deliveries. London: Stanley Paul

Brodribb G. 1974. The Croucher: A biography of Gilbert Jessop. Guildford & London: Billing & Son

Brodribb G. 1976. Maurice Tate. London: London Magazine Editions

Britton C J. 1935. G. L. Jessop. Birmingham: Cornish Brothers Limited

Brookes C. 1978. English Cricket: The Game and its Players through the Ages. Newton Abbot: Readers' Union

Cannadine D. 1999. The Rise & Fall of Class in Britain. New York: Columbia University Press

Cardus N. 1984. Autobiography. London: Hamish Hamilton (original work published 1947)

Constantine L N. 1933. Cricket and I. London: Philip Allan

Constantine L N. 1946. Cricket in the Sun. London: Stanley Paul and Co. Ltd.

Constantine L N. 1954. Colour Bar. London: Stanley Paul and Co. Ltd.

Denman J & McDonald P. 1996. "Unemployment statistics from 1881 to the present day" in Labour Market Trends, Central Statistics Office

Frith D. 2002. Bodyline Autopsy: The full story of the most sensational Test cricket series: Australia v England 1932-3. London: Aurum Press

Gilligan A E R. 1933. Sussex Cricket. London: Chapman & Hall

Hendren E H. 1934. Big Cricket. London: Hodder & Stoughton

Hill A. 1986. Hedley Verity: A Portrait of a Cricketer. Kingswood: Kingswood Press

Hobbs J B. 1981. My Life Story. London: The Hambledon Press (original work published 1935)

Holt R. 1989. Sport and the British: A Modern History. Oxford: Clarendon Press

Horn, P. 2013. Country House Society: The Private Lives of England's Upper-class After the First World War. Stroud: Amberley Publishing

Hutton L. 1949. Cricket is My Life. London: Hutchinson & Co.

James C L R. 2005. Beyond a Boundary. London: Yellow Jersey Press (original work published 1963)

Jessop G L. 1922. A Cricketer's Log. London: Hodder & Stoughton

Jiggens, C. 1997. Sammy: The Sporting Life of S.M.J. Woods. Bristol: Sansom & Company

Kynaston, D. 1983. Bobby Abel: Professional Batsman. London: Seckler & Warburg

Lee H W. 1948. Forty Years of English Cricket. London: Clerke & Cockeran

Lewis G K. 1968. The Growth of the Modern West Indies. London: MacGibbon & Kee

Lewis P. 2014. For Kent and Country: Kent Cricketers in the Great War 1914-1918. Brighton: Reveille Press

Lilley A A. 1912. Twenty-Four Years of Cricket. London: Mills & Boon

Lyttelton R H, Ford W J, Fry C B & Giffen G. 1974. Giants of the Game. Newton Abbot: Readers Union (original work published c.1900)

Maclaren A C. 1924. Cricket Old and New: Straight Talk to Young Players
London: Longmans, Green & Co

Malcolm D. 2001. "'It's not Cricket': Colonial Legacies and Contemporary Inequalities" Journal of Historical Sociology Vol. 14 No. 3

Malcolm D. 2013. Globalizing Cricket: Englishness, Empire and Identity. London & New York: Bloomsbury Academic

McKibbin R. 1998. Classes and Cultures: England 1918-1951. Oxford: Oxford University Press

Mulligan W. 2010. The Origins of the First World War. Cambridge: Cambridge University PRess

Mulvaney J & Harcourt R. 1988. Cricket Walkabout: The Australian Aboriginal Cricketers on tour 1867-68. 2nd edition. London: Macmillan

Neale S. 2017. Over and Out: Albert Trott: The Man Who Cleared the Lord's Pavilion Kindle Edition. Durrington: Pitch Publishing

O'Day A (ed.). 1979. The Edwardian Age: Conflict and Stability 1900-1914. London & Basingstoke: MacMillan

Parkin C H. 1936. Cricket Triumphs and Troubles. Manchester, London & Reading: C. Nicholls & co.

Pugh M. 2009. We Danced All Night: A Social History of Britain between the Wars. London: Vintage Books

Robb G. 2002. British Culture and The First World War. Basingstoke: Palgrave

Rogerson S. 1960. Wilfred Rhodes: Professional and Gentleman. London: Hollis & Carter

Sale C. 1986. Korty: the Legend Explained. Hornchurch: Ian Henry Publications

Sandford C. 2014. The Final Over: The Cricketers of Summer 1914. Stroud: Spellmount

Sandiford, K.A.P. 1994. Cricket and the Victorians. Aldershot: Scolar Press

Smart J B. 2009. The Real Colin Blythe. Kingsbridge: Blythe Smart Publications

Stockwell S. (ed.) 2008. The British Empire: Themes and Perspectives. Oxford: Blackwell Publishing

Stoddart B. 1988. "Sport, Cultural Imperialism, and Colonial Response in the British Empire" Comparative Studies in Society and History 30 (04) 649-673

Stollmeyer J. 1983. Everything Under the Sun: My Life in West Indies Cricket. London: Stanley Paul

Streeton R. 1987. P.G.H. Fender: A Biography. London: Pavilion Books (original work published 1981)

Sutcliffe H. 1935. For England and Yorkshire. London: Edward Arnold & Co.

Sweetman S. 2015. Dimming of The Day: The Cricket Season of 1914. Cardiff: ACS Publications

Tate M. 1935. My Cricketing Reminiscences, London: Stanley Paul & Co.

Todman D. 2017. Britain's War: Into Battle 1937-1941. London: Penguin Books

Tomlinson R. 2015. Amazing Grace: The Man who was W.G.. London: Little, Brown

Warner P. 1950. Gentlemen v. Players 1806-1949. London: George G. Harrap & Co.

Warner P. 1946. Cricket between Two Wars. London: Sporting Handbooks

Wilde S. 2005. Ranji: The Strange Genius of Ranjitsinhji. London: Kingswood Press (original work published 1999)

Williams C. 2012. Gentlemen & Players. The death of amateurism in cricket. London: Weidenfeld & Nicolson

Williams J. 1999. Cricket and England: A Cultural and Social History of the Inter-war Years. London: Frank Cass

Williams J. 2001. Cricket and Race. Oxford & New York: Berg

Wilton, I. 1999. C.B. Fry: King of Sport. London: John Blake

Woods S.M.J. 1925. My Reminiscences. London: Chapman & Hall.

Woolley F. 1936. King of Games. London: Stanley Paul & Co.

INDEX

A

Abel. Bobby 8-12, 18-20, 24, 31, 32, 199, 236
Aboriginal Australians 135, 237
Achong, Puss 152, 155
Afghanistan 129
Alverstone, Lord 41
Ames, Les 63, 143, 154-156, 159, 162, 165, 167-169, 171, 172, 176-179, 189-191
Anthony, Merrill 160
Anti-Corn Law League 1
Arlott, John 89
Ashes 17, 22, 57, 83, 87, 91, 92, 94, 98, 108, 113, 123, 141, 142, 157, 215
Astill, Ewart 143, 147, 152, 155, 162-165, 169, 171-174, 180, 189-191, 201
Astor, Lady 198
Athenia (ship) 205
Australia 8, 10, 11, 15, 17, 22, 47, 50, 51, 57, 58, 62, 69, 86-88, 91, 93, 94, 97, 120, 122, 135, 139-142, 151, 156, 158, 187, 202, 213, 226, 235, 237
Austro-Hungary 37

B

Barbados 128, 130, 132, 137, 138, 144, 147, 148, 151, 153, 154, 160, 161, 174, 180
Barber, Wilf 203, 211, 214, 217, 227, 231, 232
Barlow, Umpire 75
Barnes, Billy 99
Barnett, Charlie 215

Barratt, Fred 143, 156

Belgium 37, 73, 74

Bencraft, Russell 42

Betancourt, Nelson 154

Birmingham 95, 97, 101, 108, 116, 123, 234

Blackheath 55

Blackout 204, 228

Blackpool 228

Blanckenberg, Jimmy 95, 100, 101, 103, 104, 116, 117, 124, 125

Blythe, Colin 35, 46, 48, 50, 51, 53-58, 60-62, 64-66, 74-77, 193

Bodyline 151, 156-158, 226

Bolshevism 85

Bombay 131

Bouncer 4, 98, 128, 148, 150, 151, 154, 157, 158, 161, 175, 179

Bourda 159-161, 169, 170, 181, 184-186, 189

Bournemouth 69

Bowes, Bill 203, 204, 206, 208-210, 212-214, 223, 225, 226, 228-231, 233, 234

Bowley, Ted 143

Boxing 10, 40, 71

Boycott, Geoffrey 90

Bradford 81, 95, 200, 229

Bradman, Donald 6, 17, 158, 166, 226

Brearley, Walter 208, 209

Bridgetown 128, 144

Brighton 11, 205, 206, 219, 236

Bristol 236

British Empire 1, 42, 127, 129-131, 134, 135, 138, 139, 142, 166, 237, 238

Bromley-Davenport, Hugh 137

Brown, Jack 19, 23-25, 27, 30-32

Browne, Cyril "Snuffie" 149, 154, 167, 168, 174, 176, 178-181, 184, 189-192

Burton, Tommie 138, 139

C

Calthorpe, Freddie 127-129, 143, 144, 147, 149-153, 155, 159, 161-165, 170-173, 177, 180, 181, 185-188, 190, 191
Cambridge 11, 14, 27, 88, 94, 106, 107, 115, 132, 133
Cameron, John Joseph 139
Canada 127, 137, 205, 229
Cannadine, David 3
Canterbury 207
Cape Town 93, 95, 116
Captaincy 86, 106, 107, 122, 154, 160, 166, 167, 201, 202
Carare (ship) 144
Cardus, Neville 17, 85, 99, 101, 102
Carpenter, Herbert 19, 25, 31, 32
Carr, Arthur 86, 201
Carter, Claude 95, 100
Caserta 229
Catania 229
Catterall, Bob 103, 116-119, 124, 125
Chamberlain, Neville 203
Chapman, Percy 96, 101, 117, 122, 124, 125
Chartists 1
Clarke, Michael 15
Class 1-5, 18, 29, 39, 42, 79, 81, 84, 85, 88, 106, 129, 130, 132, 133, 135, 136, 194, 196-201, 216, 221, 234, 235, 237
Clifton School 73
Commaille, Mick 104, 111, 115, 125
Constantine, Learie 128, 129, 133, 134, 138, 143, 148-152, 154, 155, 165-170, 173, 175-181, 184, 186, 189-192, 204
Constantine, Lebrun 138, 139
Cooch-Behar, Maharaja of 70
Cook, Alistair 90
Copson, Bill 204
Cornwallis, Stanley 201
Coventry City Football Club 146
Cox, George 208, 210-214, 220, 221, 227, 230-232
Cox, George Rubens 211
Cox, Percy 138
Cragg Wood 224

Cumberbatch, Archie 139
Cuttell, Willis 54
Czechoslovakia 203

D

Daily Chronicle of Georgetown 185
Daily Express 40, 105, 188
Daily Mail 35, 36, 41
Daily Mirror 38, 40, 41, 188
Daily News 20, 28
Danzig 218, 221
Dawson Eddie 143
Deane, Hubert "Nummy" 104, 117, 125
Delaney, Jerry 71
Dempster, Stewie 201
Deptford 55
Derbyshire 112, 138, 204, 222
Dixon, Cec 95, 100
Drake, Lady (ship) 127, 128, 159
Duleepsinhji 133, 143
Durban 93
Durham 112

E

Eastbourne 109
Eccleshill 95
Edgbaston 79, 96, 97, 99, 102, 103, 111, 114, 115, 118, 121, 123
enlist 37, 39-41, 44, 45, 69, 70, 74
Essex 16, 20, 63, 71, 140, 156
Eton 38, 39, 67, 82, 132
Europeans (team) 70
Evacuation 219, 227
Everton Football Club 45

F

Felix, Nicholas 7
Felixstowe 70
Fenner's 89
Fernandes, Maurice 160, 164, 165, 168, 170, 172, 174-182, 184, 189, 190
football 10, 12, 14, 40, 45, 83, 146
Foster, Reginald "Tip" 8, 14-16, 18, 19, 21, 27, 30-32
France 37, 72, 218
Freeman, Alfred "Tich" 46, 51-53, 55, 60-66, 68, 70, 75-77, 114
Fry, Charles Burgess 4, 8, 9, 12-16, 18, 20, 21, 27, 30, 31, 58, 193

G

Gatting, Mike 49
Gender Equality 1, 79, 80, 85, 198, 199
Gentlemen (team) 1, 5-8, 10, 12-14, 16, 18-21, 23-31, 89, 94, 108, 112
George, David Lloyd 194
George, Elizabeth 194
Georgetown 127, 137, 184, 185, 189
George V, King 45
George VI, King 199
Germany 37, 72-74, 193, 203, 205, 218, 219, 221, 222, 229
Gilligan, Arthur 94, 96, 97, 103-108, 110, 111, 114-126
Glamorgan 157, 202, 230
Glasgow 205
Gloucestershire 69, 74, 114, 156, 200, 215
Gooch, Graham 90
Gough-Calthorpe 129, 166
Grace, Edward Mills 7
Grace, William Gilbert 6-8, 10, 12, 13, 17, 18, 21, 42, 43, 84, 89, 145, 193, 199
Grant, Rolph 205
Gravenstafel 74
Green Howards 229
Greenock 205
Greenwich, Gordon 123

Grell, Mervyn 152
Griffith, Billy 214, 217, 227, 230-232
Griffith, Herman 128, 141, 148, 149, 154, 160
Griffiths, Reginald 73, 74
Guiana 127, 153, 159, 160, 164, 165, 168, 170, 175, 185-188
Guildford 234
Gunn, George 143, 147-149, 154, 155, 167, 168, 174, 176, 177, 190, 191
Gunn, John 16, 19, 21, 25-27, 30-32

H

Haig, Nigel 52, 60, 64, 65, 67, 68, 71, 75-78, 143, 147, 149, 162-164,
    170, 171, 174, 175, 179, 180, 189-191
Hammond, Wally 99, 142, 200, 204
Hampshire 42, 69, 82, 93, 114, 138
Hardstaff, Joe 159, 160, 162, 171, 183, 189
Harris, Lord 4, 5, 44, 81, 85, 131, 134, 138, 139, 201, 202
Harrow 39, 132
Havant 228
Hawke, Lord 54, 84, 87, 112, 113, 122, 136, 201, 202
Haynes, Desmond 123
Hayward, Tom 18, 23-27, 31, 32
Headingley 57, 211, 225
Headley, George 149, 150, 153, 154, 163-167, 171-174, 176, 184, 187,
    189, 190, 192, 204
Hearne, John Thomas 49, 55, 58-61, 65, 66, 68, 69, 75-77
Hearne, John William 48-53, 55, 62, 64, 68, 71, 75-78, 96
Hebden, George 35, 53, 65, 66, 72, 75, 76
Henderson, Neville 218
Hendren, Elias "Patsy" 17, 48, 49, 51, 52, 59, 62, 67, 71, 75-77, 101,
    124, 125, 131, 143-147, 149, 150, 152-156, 159, 167-169, 173, 176-183,
    188, 190, 191, 201
Hill, Ledger 82
Hill, Umpire 182, 189
Hills, Umpire 230
Hill's 176
Hinds, Delmont "Fitz" 138

Hirst, George 44, 224, 226
Hitler, Adolph 218
Hoad, Teddy 147, 149, 154
Hobbs, JAck 18, 42, 51, 53, 69, 86, 88-92, 94, 98-101, 111, 117-119, 122-125, 142, 146, 147, 166, 182, 201
Holmes, Errol 200
Holmes, Jack 205, 206, 213, 219, 220, 227, 228, 230-232
Holmes, Percy 96, 99
Horsforth Hall 224
House of Commons 1, 80, 198
House of Lords 1, 194
Hove 13, 44, 81, 107, 109, 110, 193, 205-207, 209, 213, 214, 217, 222, 228, 230
Huddersfield 225
Huish, Fred 48, 53, 60, 65, 67-69, 73, 75-77
Humphreys, Edward "Punter" 51, 58, 67, 69, 70, 75, 77
Hunte, Errol 155, 161-163, 168-171, 177, 178, 185, 189-191
Hutton, Leonard 15, 90, 99, 203, 204, 206, 207, 214-217, 220, 227, 228, 231, 232, 235

I

India 48, 69, 70, 72, 73, 131, 134, 135, 140, 187, 202, 228, 229
Ireland 129, 145
Isherwood, Lionel 82
Italy 229

J

Jamaica 142, 149, 153, 160, 163, 164, 167, 174, 185-187
Jardine, Douglas 156-158, 226
Jennings, David 74
Jennings, Thomas 74
Jephson, Digby 14, 16, 29-33
Jessop, Gilbert 16, 18-21, 23, 24, 28-33, 42
Jesus College, Cambridge 89
Johannesburg 92, 100

John, George 161
Jones, Arthur 12, 20, 23, 29-33
Jones, Charles 167, 176-178, 182, 189, 191, 192
Jones. Ernest 19
Jupp, Vallance 91

K

Kennedy, Alex 93, 114
Kensington Oval 129, 144
Kent 4, 5, 34-36, 40, 44, 46, 51-71, 73-75, 77, 91, 101, 110, 114, 118, 135,
    200, 201, 204
Kilburn, Jim 220
Kitchener, Lord 37-40, 44, 47
Kortright, Charles 16, 19, 20, 26, 27, 29-33

L

Laker, Jim 53
Lancashire 18, 45, 48, 54, 65, 81, 83, 84, 87, 94, 106, 110, 112, 113, 121,
    122, 133, 134, 197, 200, 204, 222, 224
Lancashire League 45, 81, 84, 112, 113, 133, 224
Langridge, James 211, 212, 220, 221, 223, 226, 227, 231-233
Langridge, John 206-208, 210, 211, 230, 232
Larwood, Harold 142, 156, 157, 209
Lauwe 73, 74
Lawrence, Walter (trophy) 213
Layne, Oliver 139
Leamington Spa 71
Lee, Harry 4, 5, 46-48, 62, 70-72, 75, 76
Leicestershire 138, 201, 204, 222, 228
Leveson-Gower, Henry 141
Leyland, Maurice 142, 203, 206, 215, 221, 222, 231, 233
Lilley, Dick 16, 19, 24, 25, 28, 30-32, 236
Lincolnshire 112
Lipski, Jozef 218
Liverpool 138

Lloyd, Richard 194
Locke, Tony 53
Londesborough, Lord 44
London 6, 15, 40, 45, 71, 72, 74, 137, 199, 219
Lord's Cricket Ground 1, 5-8, 10, 12-14, 18, 21, 22, 27, 30, 34-36, 40, 41, 46-49, 52, 57, 60, 64, 66, 68, 71-74, 80, 92, 107, 135, 140, 146, 160, 188, 203, 207, 208, 214
Lucas, Robert Slade 137

M

MacBryan, Jack 96
MacDonald, Ramsay 194
Maclaren, Archie 8, 13, 57, 84, 87, 97, 105, 236
Maidstone Journal 135
Makepeace, Harry 88
Malcolm, Dominic 130
Mallett, Harry 151, 156
Manchester City Football Club 146
Manchester Guardian 16, 21, 85, 87, 101, 114, 115
Mann, Frank 93, 107, 108
Maple Cricket Club 132
Martyn, Henry 16, 30-32
Marylebone Cricket Club 141, 189
Marylebone Cricket Club 4, 24, 27, 41, 44, 47, 64, 84-87, 92, 93, 107, 108, 112, 113, 121, 122, 127, 129, 131, 135, 136, 139-143, 146, 148-154, 156, 158, 159, 163, 164, 167-170, 172-174, 180, 185-187, 200, 202, 203
Mason, Jack 16, 18, 19, 21, 25, 29-33
McCanlis, Walter 55, 56
Mead, Phil 92, 93
Mead, Walter 15, 31-33
Melbourne 18, 22
Middlesex 4, 17, 22, 34-36, 39-41, 43, 45-52, 54, 55, 58, 59, 61, 62, 64-66, 69-76, 80, 115, 137, 143, 145, 146, 152, 155, 159, 178, 184, 203
Middleton 224
Millward, Arthur 109

Mitchell, Arthur 203, 210, 212, 214, 217, 220, 221, 230-233
Mitchell, Frank 56
Moberly, John 42
Montreal 205
Montrose (ship) 205
Morrison, William 142

N

Nauwab of Pataudi 133
Nawanagar 133
Nelson Cricket Club 133
Newbolt, Henry 34, 38
Newlands 93
New Zealand 15, 140, 142, 143, 187, 202, 203, 207, 214, 228
Norfolk 138
Northamptonshire 74, 83, 109, 110, 134, 139
Nottinghamshire 12, 41, 48, 56, 80, 156-158, 161, 167, 170, 200, 207, 225
Nourse, Arthur "Dave" 95, 103, 115, 124, 125
Nunes, Karl 141, 186
Nupen, Eiulf "Buster" 95, 100, 104, 117, 124, 125
Nye, John 217, 219, 220, 227, 231, 232

O

Ollivierre, Charles 138, 139
Oxford 12, 14, 95, 132, 228, 235, 237-239
O'Connor, Jack 147, 149, 150, 154, 155, 159

P

Palatia (cricket team) 70
Palmer, William 139
Panama 149
Paravicini, Lady Eva da 207
Pardon, Sidney 81, 84, 86, 92, 94

Parker, Charlie 114
Parker, George 95-97, 100-104, 118, 124, 125
Parker, John 139
Parker, Umpire 230
Parkin, Cecil 94, 97, 111-115, 118-122, 124, 126
Parks, Harry 210, 227, 230, 232
Parks, Jim 206, 207, 210, 212, 213, 218, 220, 222, 223, 226, 228, 231-233
Parliament 37, 194, 198, 204
Pegler, Sid 95, 100, 102-104, 117, 118, 124, 125
Pembroke College, Cambridge 106
Persia 229
Peterloo Massacre 1
Phillips, Umpire 30
Players (team) 1, 2, 5-9, 15-21, 23-32, 94, 112, 113
Poland 203, 218, 219, 221
Ponsonby, Loelia 199
Preston, Henry 74
Priestley, Arthur 137
Prince of Wales 40, 42, 196
Pudsey 216

Q

Quaife, Willie 19, 20, 23, 31, 32, 85
Queensferry 70
Queen's Park 132, 137

R

Race 127, 129, 133-136, 188
Ranjitsinhji 8, 16, 133, 134, 239
Rawden 224
Reeves, Umpire 124
Rhodes, Wilfred 16-20, 25-27, 30-33, 57, 64, 84, 86, 143, 147-149, 152, 162-165, 171-174, 182-184, 189-191, 193, 201, 224-226
Ribbentrop, Joachim von 218

Roach, Clifford 141, 148-150, 152, 155, 160-164, 167, 170-172, 178, 181, 182, 184, 189-192
Robertson, William 47
Robinson, Ellis 212-214, 223, 226, 227, 230-233
Robinson, L G 91
Rochdale 113
Rotherhithe 9
Rugby Football 10, 38, 44, 45
Russell, Charles "Jack" 88, 92, 93
Russia 37, 85, 193
Rutherford, Robert 141

S

Sandham, Andrew 71, 143, 147-152, 154, 155, 159, 167, 168, 174, 175, 186, 190, 191
Sandiford, Keith 39
Saville, Stanley 53, 55, 65, 71, 75, 76
Scarborough 6, 44, 221
Scotland 70, 94, 132, 197
Sealey, Ben 152
Sealy, Derek 147, 153, 154, 160, 165, 173, 175, 179, 189, 191
Sellers, Brian 203, 212, 222, 226, 230-233
Serbia 37
Seymour, James 58, 67, 70, 76, 77, 201, 202
Shamateurism 5
Shamrock Cricket Club 132
Shannon Cricket Club 132
Smailes, Frank 209, 210, 212, 214, 223, 230, 231, 233
Smart, John Blythe 57
Smith, Ernest 16, 25, 30, 32, 33
Smith, Sydney 134, 139
Sobers, Garfield 17, 188, 215
Somerset 8, 10, 11, 66, 80, 129, 140, 166, 200
Somme, Battle of 71, 72
South Africa 22, 37, 44, 57, 79, 92, 94-98, 100-105, 107, 108, 111, 114-120, 123-125, 140, 142, 158, 187, 202, 217

Southampton Football Club 12
Spartan Cricket Club 132, 133
Sporting Life 41, 52
Sri Lanka 90
St. Hill, Wilton 152, 154, 155
Staffordshire 138
Stanyforth, Ronald 159
Stevens, Greville 148, 150, 152-154, 159
St Hill, Edwin 149, 153, 154, 160, 167, 168, 172, 175, 176, 178, 183, 184, 189-192
Stingo Cricket Club 132
Stoddart, Brian 131, 136
Stollmeyer, Jeff 205
Streatham 63
Streeton, Richard 108
Sudan 37
Surrey 8, 9, 11-13, 16, 41, 44, 46, 69, 74, 80, 83, 89, 90, 107, 138, 140, 200, 203, 222
Sussex 4, 13, 16, 44, 106-109, 115, 121, 133, 140, 143, 193, 204-208, 210-212, 214, 217-221, 223, 225, 227, 228, 230, 232, 235
Susskind, Fred 103, 115, 125
Sutcliffe, Herbert 90, 98-101, 123, 124, 142, 201, 203, 216, 217, 220, 229

T

Tarilton, Percy 147
Tarrant, Frank 46-48, 50, 51, 55, 58-62, 67-70, 72, 73, 75-77
Tate, Maurice 94, 96, 97, 103-106, 108-111, 114-121, 123-126, 142
Taylor, Herbie 92, 97, 100, 102-105, 111, 115, 124, 125
Taylor, Ross 15
The Oval 6, 7, 9-11, 80, 108, 112, 135, 200, 215
The Sportsman 40-43, 52, 53
Tonbridge 54, 56
Townsend, Charlie 14, 20, 29-31, 33
Townsend, Leslie 144, 162-165, 169, 171, 174, 178, 179, 189-191

Trinidad 127-129, 131, 132, 134, 137, 143, 151-154, 156, 160, 162, 163, 169, 170, 175, 178
Trott, Albert 12, 16, 19, 21-23, 25-27, 30-32
Troughton, Lionel 46, 53, 59, 61, 62, 66, 68, 71, 72, 75-77
Trumper, Victor 17
Tufton, J S R 44
Tunbridge Wells 110
Tyldesley, Dick 94, 121
Tyldesley, Ernest 96

V

Verity, Hedley 203, 206, 211, 213, 214, 223-233
Victoria, Queen 1
Vine, Joe 4
Voce, Bill 143, 147-153, 155-158, 161-164, 167, 170, 171, 174, 182, 184, 189-191, 209

W

War 34, 36-45, 53, 56, 58, 63, 69-74, 79-81, 85, 86, 89, 92, 98, 106, 109, 110, 112, 133, 140, 146, 156-158, 193-199, 202-209, 214, 215, 218, 221, 222, 225, 226, 229
Ward, Albert 18, 21, 23, 30-32, 125
Ward, Tommy 104, 117, 124, 125
Warner, Pelham 28, 29, 39, 43, 45, 54, 56, 71, 86, 97, 105, 113, 122, 137, 141, 146
Warwickshire 140, 163, 175, 225
Washbrook, Cyril 216
Webbe, Alexander 4, 5
Weekly Dispatch 119, 122
Westermaas, Umpire 183
West Indies 127-130, 134-143, 147-149, 151, 153, 155-157, 160-162, 164, 166, 167, 171-174, 176, 179-190, 202-205, 238
Weston, Henry 53, 64, 65, 73, 75, 76
Wheeler, Umpire 30
Whitehead, George 51, 59, 67, 73-77

Wieltje 74
Wieluń 221
Wight, Vibart 165, 174, 177, 178, 189, 191, 192
Wilde, Simon 134
Wilson, Herbert 44
Wilson, Rockley 88
Winchester 39
Wisden 6, 10, 14, 15, 20, 27, 28, 47, 64, 81, 83, 84, 86, 88, 90, 92-94,
    98, 101, 108, 110, 114, 142, 157, 188, 212
Wood, Arthur 203, 210, 223, 233
Wood, George 102, 103, 106, 117, 124, 125
Wood, Jim 214, 220, 223, 227, 230-232
Woods, Joseph "Float" 138
Woods, Sammy 8, 10-12, 16, 19-22, 25-30, 32, 33
Woolley, Frank 42, 46, 48, 50, 53-55, 59, 61, 62, 64, 66-70, 74-77, 89,
    91, 96, 97, 101, 102, 118, 119, 124, 126, 143, 146
Worcestershire 14, 82, 204
Wyatt, Bob 145, 147, 162, 163, 167, 168, 172, 175, 176, 188-191

Y

Yardley, Norman 203, 219, 221-223, 231, 233
Yorkshire 16-18, 24, 44, 48, 54, 56, 66, 74, 83, 84, 86, 87, 98, 99, 112,
    113, 122, 138, 139, 174, 182, 184, 193, 197, 200, 201, 203, 204, 206-
    217, 219-225, 227, 230-232, 238
Ypres 74

Printed in Great Britain
by Amazon